POLITICAL CHOICE AND SOCIAL STRUCTURE

Political Choice and Social Structure

An Analysis of Actors,
Interests and Rationality

Barry Hindess

Edward Elgar

Published by
Edward Elgar Publishing Limited
Gower House
Croft Road
Aldershot
Hants GU11 3HR
England

Gower Publishing Company
Old Post Road
Brookfield
Vermont 05036
USA

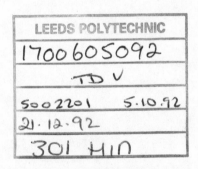
British Library Cataloguing in Publication Data
Hindess, Barry
  Political choice and social structure: an analysis
  of actors, interests and rationality.
  1. Social systems
  I. Title
  301

ISBN 1-85278-093-2 ✓

Printed in Great Britain by
Billing & Sons Ltd, Worcester

Contents

Acknowledgements

The Introduction makes use of material originally published in 'Actors and social relations' in M. Wardell and S. Turner (eds.), *Sociological Theory in Transition*, London, Allen & Unwin, 1986, and 'Taking choice seriously' to appear in the *International Political Science Review*.

Chapter 1 was originally published in *Sociology*, 16, April 1982; Chapter 2 originally appeared in *Economy & Society*, no. 13, 1984; and Chapter 3 was first published in J. Law (ed.), *Power, Action and Belief*, Sociological Review Monograph no. 32, London, Routledge & Kegan Paul, 1986. Chapters 1 and 2 are published here with only minor changes, but Chapter 3 has been revised in response to critical points raised by Behan McCullagh.

Chapters 4 and 5 are based on 'Classes, collectivities and corporate actors' to appear in S. C. Clegg (ed.), *Organization Theory and Class Analysis*, Berlin, de Gruyter and 'Class analysis as social theory' in P. Lassmann (ed.) *Politics and Social Theory*, London, BSA, and I am grateful to the editors and publishers for permission to publish this material here.

Chapter 6 is reproduced, with minor changes from S. Lash and S. Whimster (eds.), *Max Weber*, Rationality and Modernity, London, Unwin Hyman, 1987.

Versions of Chapter 7 have been given as seminar papers in a number of locations. Chapter 8 was presented at a conference on 'Ideas of Social Science' organized by the History of Ideas Unit at the Australian National University in March 1988. Chapter 9 is based on a paper given at the 1988 conference of the Australasian Political Science Association.

I have thanked many of those who have helped in the development of my arguments at the time of publication of the papers referred to above. My gratitude remains, but there are far too many names for me to list them all here. I must, however, thank the following for the assistance, criticism, disagreement, encouragement and support I received while revising the papers for publication in this book:

Geoffrey Brennan, Jill Deck, Helen Felton, Ann Jungmann, Behan McCullagh, Stephen Mugford, and Phillip Pettit.

Barry Hindess

Introduction

> . . . people of my generation were brought up on these two forms of analysis, one in terms of the constituent subject, the other in terms of the economic in the last instance, ideology and the play of superstructures and infrastructures. (Foucault, 1980: 116)

The picture presented here by Foucault's interviewers may be a little overdrawn. These were not the only forms of social analysis on offer, although they may have been the most distinctive and even, in some respects, the most rigorous. Nevertheless, there can be no doubt that modern social thought has been plagued by versions of methodological individualism and structuralism. This book explores some of the consequences of abandoning these positions and the debate between them. The first insists that social life is to be understood in terms of the constitutive actions of human individuals. In the contemporary social sciences, its most influential representatives are the forms of rational choice analysis widely used in economics and now proliferating in political science and sociology. The second analyses social life in terms of the functioning of social wholes in which effects are said to be produced by the action of the structure. The tensions between these positions appear in recurrent disputes about the relationship between individual and society, agency and structure. Each side, in the disputes between them, is able to trade off the obvious weaknesses of the other – namely, the difficulty of denying that individuals do indeed make choices and act upon them on the one hand, and the merely gestural character of attempts to account for structural features of social life as the products of those decisions on the other.

Now, for all their apparent opposition there is also a certain complicity between these positions. In one, each human individual is a creative subject, freely constituting actions and social relations with others. In the other, each human individual is literally the subject of (that is, subjected to) the system of social relations in which 'it' internalizes its part and subsequently acts it out. What is shared here is a conception of the human subject as characterized by essential attributes of will and subjectivity: as a condition of its creative activity in the one case and of its subjection to its position in the structure in the other. Briefly, this involves the portfolio model of the acting individual, outlined in Chapters 7 and 8. The actor in this model is usually identified with the human person. Its action is seen as resulting from the interaction of the situation of action and the actor's more or less stable 'portfolio' of beliefs and desires (or interests). In rational choice models, for example, what produces action in any given case is the actor's rational assessment of the situation in the light of the relevant beliefs and desires. We shall see that the individualism of this position is little more than a matter of insisting that actors do indeed make choices and act on them. 'Structuralist' alternatives adopt much the same model of the actor, and add that the content of the portfolio is a function of the actor's social location – as in Marx's treatment of capitalist as personification, or Althusser's (1971) account of the subject as literally the subject of (that is, subjected to) the system of social relations in which it is implicated.

Rather than contribute further to the sterile debate between these ageing partners, the papers in this book challenge the assumptions of the portfolio model. They develop an alternative approach to social theory, which treats social phenomena as dependent on definite and specifiable conditions of diverse kinds. These conditions may include decisions and actions, and also social conditions that are external to any one individual and not themselves reducible to any general principle of explanation. In contrast to any thorough-going structuralism, it is important to recongize that actors do indeed reach decisions and act on some of them, and that their actions are, in part, a consequence of their decisions. Decisions themselves are reached through processes that are internal to the actor in question – that is, they are not simply expressions of the actor's position within a system of social relations.

One of the best known formulations of this last proposition appears in the title of Dennis Wrong's 'The oversocialized conception of man in sociology' (1976). In one form or another it is widely accepted. However, I shall depart from the more familiar versions in two important respects. First, actors are normally identified with human individuals. In *The Consitution of Society*, to take a recent example, Giddens takes it for granted that actors are human individuals. He criticizes much of the discussion of action in philosophy and sociology on the grounds that it abstracts from features he regards as central to human activity. I argue on the contrary for an abstract and general concept of actor. Our view of what it is to be an actor should be clearly distinguished from our view of what it is to be human. Human individuals are certainly actors but there are other significant actors in the modern world. An approach to social theory that fails to acknowledge such actors must be regarded as seriously deficient. Second, considerations of what is involved in actors' decisions and actions indicates a variety of ways in which they depend on social conditions that are external to the actors concerned. It follows that social relations cannot be reduced to the constitutive actions of human individuals. The creative human individual is not the essential starting-point for social analysis.

After discussing concepts of actor and social structure this introductory chapter briefly considers some of the implications of these arguments, both for substantive political analysis and for attempts in political theory to ground political commitments in notions of the human individual or of structurally determined interests. For the most part, I direct my fire against the ramifications of the portfolio model as it appears in rational choice analysis, Marxism, and the recently developed hybrid of rational choice Marxism elaborated by Elster, Przeworski, and others.[1] However, versions of the portfolio model are widely used in social and political theory, and the consequences of challenging it are equally wide-ranging.

Human individuals and social actors
An actor is a locus of decision and action. Actors do things, some of which are a consequence of decisons, and we call these things actions. The decisions themselves may be formulated by the actor in advance of the action itself or at the moment of action, but not all decisions will be of that kind. Some will not be conscious at all and some will be made on the basis of a practical knowledge that is difficult to formulate at the moment of action. In all these cases actors' decisions and the reasons for them have an important part to play in the explanation of what they do. Actors may also do things that could not be described as resulting from their decisions, and those things must be explained in some other way.

Now there are influential traditions of work in sociology and social psychology that might suggest a rather different usage. The various forms of role theory analyse social behaviour in terms of the performance of roles. Goffman emphasizes the dramaturgical aspects of social behaviour: it is in part a matter of the presentation of self. These positions suggest a concept of actor as one who performs a part, whether this be a role defined by the expectations of others or a mask to hide behind. In contrast to that usage I use the term 'actor' in the limited sense of 'a doer of things', and not, or not primarily, of one who performs a part. An actor in this sense is simply a locus of decision and action, not a mask with a person hiding behind it.

The abstract character of this conception of the actor has the advantage of reducing to a minimum the assumptions that are built in to the basic concept of actor. In particular, it allows us to identify issues that may be obscured by the all too easy identification of actors with human individuals. First, actors have reasons for some of what they do. This means that they must be capable of employing means of assessing situations in which they find themselves and reaching decisions about them. They must also have means of acting on at least some of the decisions they reach. Reference to an actor therefore always involves reference, if only implicit, to some definite means of reaching decisions and formulating reasons for their action, definite means of action, and some links between their decisions and their actions.

In contrast, the portfolio model presents an extremely limited concept of an actor. Its treatment of actors as by and large rational and endowed with a given portfolio of beliefs and desires has the effect of foreclosing questions of the techniques and forms of thought employed by them in assessing the situation of action, and of the social conditions on which they depend. The effect of raising questions of the conditions which make it possible for actors to reach decisions and to act on them is to suggest ways in which their choices are not reducible either to the creative activity of individuals or to mere effects of their structural location. I return to this point below.

Second, human individuals are actors in this sense, but they are not the only entities that reach decisions and act on them. Political parties, trade unions, capitalist enterprises, and state agencies are examples of actors other than human individuals. They have means of reaching and formulating decisions, and they act on some of them. The actions of capitalist enterprises or trades unions always depend on those of other actors – executives, managerial and other employees, elected officials, legal representatives, and sometimes other organizations. They therefore depend not just on those other actors but also on the specific character of the relationships in which they are implicated with them. There are cases in which the actions of human individuals depend on the actions of others in this way, but they need not always do so. This is a significant difference between human individuals and other actors.

It does not follow that one kind of actor is reducible to the other or that these other actors are themselves all of a kind (except in this one respect). To use a term such as 'association', 'group' or 'corporate actor' as a general label for these actors would be to risk understating their diversity. Chapter 4, 'Two kinds of person' takes Coleman's *The Asymmetric Society* as a striking example of this kind of problem. Coleman insists that there are two kinds of person in the modern world – natural (that is, human) and corporate – and that there is a clear conflict of interest between the two. I agree that actors other than human individuals pose significant issues for social and political thought but it is misleading to discuss such actors as if they were equivalently placed in relation to human individuals. I call them social actors, then, for two rather different reasons. One is simply to have a more convenient designation than the cumbersome phrase 'actors other than human individuals'. The other is to avoid the temptations of identifying these actors with any one kind of organizational structure.

Now, the idea that there are actors other than human individuals appears to be widely accepted, but there are two influential respects in which it may be abused. One is the claim that the actions of social actors are themselves reducible to the actions of human individuals and the other is the extension of the concept of 'actor' to entities that are actors in only the most allegorical of senses. Weber's methodological prescriptions at the beginning of *Economy and Society* provide a well known version of the first. A rather different version is forcefully presented in Nozick's much quoted account of why individuals may not be violated for the social good:

> There is no social entity with a good that undergoes some sacrifice for its own good. There are only individual people, different individual people, with their own individual lives. Using one of these people for the benefit of others, uses him and benefits the others. Nothing more. What happens is that something is done to him for the sake of others. Talk of an overall social good covers this up. (Nozick, 1974: 32–3)

Where Weber's individualism is methodological, Nozick's is both methodological and normative. It tells us that there is an important sense in which social life is a matter only of individuals and relations between them, and it tells us that all those individuals have rights which should be respected. Much of the rhetorical force of Nozick's argument depends on the unmasking function of his methodological individualism. It turns the tables on his opponents by requiring them to justify what he can present as trampling on the rights of some to the advantage of others.

Whatever the merits of the reductionist claim in principle there remains the question of its usefulness. In practice, as I argue in Chapter 4, the reductionist claim is little more than a gesture towards a programme of work that remains to be followed through. It diverts attention from the complex and difficult problems of analysing social actors and their conditions of action by representing them as instruments of some other set of interests – as in managerialist accounts of the corporation or the treatment of government agencies in much of public choice theory as the irresponsible instruments of politicians and public servants. Even if we were to agree that there might be a sense in which the whole of social life could be reduced to the actions of human individuals we should still be concerned with the decisions and actions of social actors and the conditions on which they depend.

As to the second abuse, I have just given several examples of actors other than human individuals. Problems arise whenever the concept of actor is extended to include collectivities that have no identifiable means of reaching and formulating decisions, let alone of acting on them. In contrast to capitalist enterprises which do have definite means of reaching and formulating decisions and of acting on many of them, classes, societies or men as a collectivity subordinating women as another collectivity clearly do not. These last are all spurious actors, and they are frequently invoked in political and social scientific discourse. The problematic effects of treating classes as if they were actors appear most clearly in Marxist political analysis, but they can also be found in some Weberian class analysis. I argue in the first part of Chapter 5, 'Class analysis as social theory', that reference to classes is either allegorical or else, at best, a shorthand way of referring to a set of specific actors (human individuals, various groups and organizations) whose actions are thought to be in the interests of particular classes.

The treatment of societies as actors is, if anything, even more widespread. Sometimes the usage is merely colloquial, as when a government is treated as speaking for the 'nation' or 'society' it governs. Other cases are more serious. For example, Talcott Parsons treats social systems (and therefore societies) as if they were actors, allocating the decision-making role to the functional subsystems, primarily to the polity. This is not the place to discuss that aspect of Parsons' work in any detail;[2] for present purposes it is sufficient to note that his treatment of social systems as actors slides between allegory and shorthand in much the same way as many Marxist treatments of class. Insofar as 'societal' decisions can be identified at all, they are formulated by specific actors that can also be identified, by governments or state agencies.

If what are called society's decisions are not formulated by some identifiable agency it is misleading to speak of decisions being made. To see what is at issue here, consider an example of the contrary view with reference to the social distribution of income and wealth. In an otherwise powerful argument against the individualism of rational choice arguments Levi tells us:

> It is not incoherent to regard a society that allocates commodity bundles through a market mechanism as an agent. The market mechanism in operation provides a procedure whereby the society makes certain kinds of 'social choice . . .' (Levi, 1982: 236)

It may not be incoherent, but this allegorical reference to society as an actor certainly obscures important questions as to how the allocation of goods and services is determined. The allocation of goods in a market economy involves many decisions, but there is no point at which 'society' formulates a decision in favour of some particular allocation and no other.

I argue that the careful restriction of the concept of actor to things that are able to formulate decisions and act on some of them is important because the assignment of responsibility to spurious actors is politically misleading. Only those who take decisions and act on them can be held responsible for actions, and the assignment of responsibility is an essential part of the analysis of social conditions and the consideration of what might be done to change them. To treat social conditions and events as resulting from the actions of collectivities that have no identifiable means of formulating decisions, let alone of acting on them, is thoroughly to obscure the social processes that bring about those conditions and events.

Arguments that assign responsibility to fictitious actors are politically misleading. To blame 'society' or 'the ruling class' for some state of affairs may be a way of suggesting that changes are desirable but it tells us nothing about how they might be brought about.

Action and reasons for action
I have suggested that actors have reasons for much of what they do and that they make use of some definite means of action. Consideration of their reasons and their means of action suggests significant respects in which social life is clearly not reducible to the constitutive behaviour of actors. It is trivially true, for example, that the actions of social actors always involves the actions of others. Human individuals may not be the constitutive subjects of social life, but they are the only actors whose actions do not invariably depend on the actions of others. Nevertheless, many of the most significant kinds of action clearly depend on conditions that are not entirely within the control of the acting individual. For example, the actions of capitalist enterprises depend on legal rights over the disposition of the enterprise's property and over what employees may be required to do or not to do. They also depend on the use of various techniques of control involving hierarchical chains of command and supervision, the collection and processing of information, and so on. The means of action that crucially distinguish the position of the capitalist employer (whether human individual or joint-stock company) from that of an employee depend precisely on their differential location within several intersecting sets of social relations.

The means of action available to an actor frequently depend on conditions that are not within the control of the actor in question. The point may seem trivial but it has serious implications for the conceptualization of power, some of which I outline in Chapter 1. 'Power, interests and the outcomes of struggles'. Perhaps the most common usage involves some version of Weber's concept of power as 'the capacity of an agent to realize his will, even against the opposition of others' (Weber, 1978: 224). What these conceptions share is the idea of power as a capacity to secure outcomes that may be deployed by particular actors in pursuit of their objectives. On this view, more power prevails over less so that, once the power available to contending parties is known, the outcome of conflict between them is entirely predictable. There are, of course, many cases in which outcomes can be predicted in this way. However, to take such cases as the norm is to deny the most striking aspect of conflict, which is precisely that outcomes are produced in the course of conflict itself and are rarely simple products of initial conditions. The idea of power-as-capacity seriously oversimplifies the conditions in which conflicts take place and the character of the forces active in them.

Now, there is another broad approach to the concept of power in which it is held to be active not only as regards the outcomes of particular conflicts but also in the suppression of certain interests and their systematic exclusion from political debate. I argue that this approach depends upon an indefensible notion of 'real' or 'objective' interests. An influential American textbook maintains that: 'Every explanatory theory of politics includes somewhere in its structure assumptions about persons and their real interests' (Connolly, 1983:73).

Interests are supposed to be explanatory because they provide actors with reasons for action. Perhaps the most common approach to the analysis of interests is to anchor them in terms of some concept of social structure. Actors have interests as a consequence of the social conditions in which they find themselves, as members of a particular class, sex, ethnic group or community, or as victims of monopoly power or multinational companies, and so on. On some accounts, different features of the conditions in which actors find themselves may provide them with distinct and sometimes conflicting sets of interests. Their interests then provide actors with reasons for action involving cross-pressures of various kinds. In this way, interests function as a transmission mechanism connecting actors' social location and their behaviour. Functionalist sociology treats norms and values as transmission mechanisms of a similar kind.

Chapter 3, ' "Interests" in political analysis', argues that Connolly's claim is mistaken, that we have no need to make assumptions about real interests. Whatever plausibility the various explanatory usages of 'real interests' may have depends on a failure to acknowledge the implications of the ways in which actors' reasons for action depend on conceptual and other conditions. First, interests have consequences only insofar as they provide some actor with reasons for action, and they therefore depend on the availability of the conceptual means for the appropriate reasons to be formulated by that actor. In the complex societies of the modern world (and perhaps in all societies) the means of reaching decisions available to actors are not uniquely determined by their social location. What is available may not be used and some of the limitations on what is available may be changed – for example, through education or specialized training.

Second, the character of actors' reasons for action as formulations (and of the beliefs, desires and interests to which they relate) renders them open to challenge through discussion, persuasion and propaganda involving others and also, as the idea of cognitive dissonance has long suggested, through reconsideration by the actor in question. Such challenges may not always be effective, but the fact that they are effective in some cases implies that interests should not be regarded as fixed properties of individuals or groups and that they are not structurally determined. We shall see that there are certainly connections between actors' social location and the interests which they acknowledge and act upon, but there is no simple correspondence between the two.

This feature of reasons for action appears to be taken more seriously in rational choice analyses, discussed in Chapters 7 and 8, and in other versions of methodological individualism. One of the most attractive features of rational choice theory is its insistence that actors do indeed make choices, that they have reasons for their choices and that their choices have consequences. These points seem to me indisputable, but the rational choice model of the actor does not follow from them. In these models, actors are endowed with some more or less stable portfolio of desires and beliefs which they bring to bear in rational consideration of what to do. The claim here is not, of course, that actors are invariably rational, but rather that the assumption of a large degree of rationality is a precondition for the intentional analysis of action.

The assumption of the rationality of actors' behaviour plays several roles in rational choice models. First, it means that there is a certain consistency in each actor's behaviour, reflecting a well-ordered preference structure on that actor's desires. Second, it implies a transparent connection between actors' desires and beliefs on the one hand and their decisions on the other. The connection is assumed to be transparent because it appears to take the form of a rational deduction leading from premises (the set of beliefs and desires relating to the situation of action) to their conclusion (the choice of what to do in that situation).

This is a characteristically misleading assumption of the portfolio model of human behaviour. Davidson and others have argued that the presumption of a large degree of rationality on the part of the actor is a precondition for the intentional analysis of behaviour.[3] We make what sense we can of actors' behaviour, including their verbal behaviour, by working back to infer the beliefs and desires that have produced it. His claim, in effect, is that this process of interpretation requires us to presume a fair degree of rationality and consistency. A closely related position in sociology can be found in the ethnomethodological argument that we should interpret social life as the skilled accomplishment of knowledgeable agents. Giddens presents a version of this claim as follows:

> . . . if there is to be any continuity to social life at all, most actors must be right most of the time; that is to say they know what they are doing and they successfully communicate their knowledge to others. (Giddens, 1984:90)

Chapter 8, 'Rationality or styles of reasoning' adapts an argument originally advanced by Hacking[4] to show that Davidson is mistaken on this point. Intentional analysis certainly requires us to suppose that actors employ some definite means and procedures to assess situations and reach decisions about them. We do not have to suppose that those procedures are themselves particularly rational.

Finally, Davidson's presumption of a large degree of rationality is presented as a condition of our understanding the behaviour of others. It does not imply the rationality of every belief or action we might wish to explain. Rational choice analysis usually goes some-what further to suggest that it is only when explanation of action in rational terms has clearly failed that we should even consider other kinds of explanation. I discuss some of the particular problems of this paradigmatic assumption of rationality as an explanatory norm in Chapter 7, with particular reference to the work of Jon Elster.

As for the portfolio model's more general assumption of the rationality of actors' behaviour (and the related view that actors are 'right most of the time') there is a persistent slippage between two rather different senses in which 'reason' and 'rationality' might be attributed to human actors. On the one hand, these terms may be used to refer to what used to be called a faculty of reason – that is, a generalized capacity to develop (or to follow) a connected chain of reasoning or argumentation. The analysis of action in terms of its reasons clearly presupposes some capacity on the part of actors to develop and to act upon what they regard as good reasons. The presumption of a faculty of reason in that sense might well be a precondition of communication and understanding and of the interpretation of cultures (both our own and others).

On the other hand, 'rationality' may be used to refer more precisely to the coherence and consistency of chains of reasoning themselves, to styles of argument and techniques of analysis and the manner of their employment by actors – and, by extension, to particular courses of action or items of behaviour.[5] The assumption that actors are rational in the first sense, that they believe themselves to have good reasons for much of what they do, tells us nothing about the coherence or consistency (that is, the rationality) of the styles of argument and techniques of analysis available to them, of the particular chains of reasoning and conclusions they might construct, or what they do as a result of those conclusions. Instrumental rationality, where it appears at all, is a feature of the relationship between the actor's objectives and the course of action decided upon. It is therefore a function of the techniques and forms of thought employed by the actor in the process of reaching a decision rather than an essential feature of that actor *qua* actor.

Failure to distinguish the senses in which actors might be said to be rational obscures questions of the techniques, means of assessment, and other forms of thought deployed by actors in the course of reaching their decisions. If the rationality of the bulk of their decisions were to be regarded, in effect, as a property of actors simply because they are actors, there would be no reason to enquire further into the techniques and forms of thought involved in making those decisions. We could say that actors made those decisions simply because they were rational, and because of their particular beliefs and desires – and that that is all there is to it. To dispute the portfolio model is therefore to raise questions concerning the techniques and forms of thought employed by, or available to, actors and questions of the social conditions on which those techniques and forms of thought depend. I say 'employed by or available to' here to guard against the all-too-convenient assumption that actors have only one means of formulating objectives and assessing their situation. Actors are frequently in a position to formulate and find reasons for a variety of distinct objectives and assessments of the situations in which they find themselves. This is what provides the scope for persuasion, propaganda and other activities aimed at changing actors' assessments and therefore their behaviour.

A different, but closely related, conception of actors' rationality is the concern of Chapter 6, 'Rationality and the characterization of modern society'. After considering the model of the action in Weber's methodological writings in the first part of the chapter, I go on to argue against the manner in which he characterizes the modern West in terms of the secular growth of instrumental rationality. There are two rather different issues here. One concerns the sense in which *societies* and the institutions and relationships within them might usefully be characterized in terms of the supposed quality of *actors'* orientations. If social relationships could indeed be analysed as the more or less adequate expressions of the inner principle of formal rationality, then there might be some point in characterizing the societies of the modern West and institutions within them in such terms. Otherwise the secular growth of formal rationality represents merely one widespread feature of such societies amongst many others. No general conclusions or problems (for example, Weber's 'iron cage') follow from its presence. Its consequences must depend on the conditions in which that growth has taken place. Since those conditions cannot be derived from the principle of formal rationality itself, they cannot be expected to have uniform effects throughout the diverse societies, social relations and institutions of the modern West.

Second, there are problems with the treatment of the modern West in terms of the world-view of instrumental rationality. There are numerous discourses representing parts of the world (education, psychiatry, criminal law, child-rearing, sexual relationships, or whatever) as relatively discrete fields of instrumental action. What is involved in each case is, first, the operation of what Foucault calls a 'regime of truth' (that is, criteria, norms and procedures for distinguishing 'true' propositions) and, second, a variety of claims to positive knowledge. Taken together, these provide means of identifying or arguing about 'reasonable' behaviour in the area of activity in question. To treat these diverse discourses as just so many expressions of the one world-view is to suggest a consistency amongst the various 'regimes of truth' that should not be taken for granted.

Social structure
I began by noting that methodological individualism and structural

forms of social analysis have more in common than the opposition between them might seem to suggest. In particular, they both make use of what I have called a portfolio model of the actor in which action is seen as resulting from the interaction of the situation of action and the actor's more or less stable portfolio of beliefs and preferences or interests. Individualism lays stress on the reality of actors' choices, while the opposition stresses the role of interests, norms and values as effects of social structure. In both cases actors' supposed rationality operates as a transparent intermediary between the contents of the portfolio and the action that takes place.

There may well be cases where the assumptions of the portfolio model create little difficulty, but it is unsatisfactory both as a general model and as an heuristic. The presumption of the rationality of actors' decisions simply evades the problem of identifying the conceptual techniques and other means of assessment employed by actors in evaluating their situations and reaching decisions about them. Similarly, the effect of taking the beliefs, desires or interests of the actor as an unproblematic starting-point for analysis has the effect of obscuring questions of the conceptual and other conditions which make it possible for those beliefs (or whatever) to provide actors with what they might recognize as reasons for action. The portfolio model has the effect of obscuring important questions of the techniques and forms of thought employed by, or available to, actors, and therefore of the social conditions on which those forms of assessment themselves depend.

What are the implications of these arguments for the idea of social structure? We may begin by noting that there is no possibility of interests (or anything else) operating as a mere transmission between soical structure on the one hand and actors' decisions about what to do on the other. Actors normally have a variety of forms of assessment of their situation available to them. Further, the conclusions of their deliberations depend on complex internal processes involving particular techniques and forms of thought which may vary considerably from one kind of actor to another. To make these points is to say that actors are not mere creatures of their positions in some social structure, of their class or gender or whatever. It is to say, in other words, that there is no such thing as a social structure operating outside of and above actors which produces its effects through the manipulation of the actors ensnared within it. If actors do indeed act on the basis of decisions, and if those decisions involve complex internal processes, there can be no reason to expect actors' decisions to accord with the requirements of society as a functioning whole.

The term 'social', then, should not be understood by reference to the operations of society as a functioning whole. The well-worn sociological demonstration that there are social preconditions of contract implies that social life involves something more and something other than the agreement of its participants. It does not require us to conceive of *society* as an entity operating outside of and above its actors. 'Social' conditions and 'social' structure refer us to a variety of practices and conditions with no overall unifying principle or centre. Precisely what practices and conditions are at issue will vary with the object of inquiry. Consider, for example, the 'social' conditions governing the availability of abortions. What is involved here is the intersection of a variety of medical, legal and administrative practices, and policies of governments and other agencies concerning the regulation of moral practices, public health and nutrition, the specification of certain medical categories in law, the use of statistical population profiles, and so on. 'Social' conditions in this case refer not to the functional exigencies of society, but rather to the complex interconnections between a variety of specific practices, policies and actors.

We are concerned then with 'social' conditions as they refer to the decisions and actions of particular actors, and with the interconnections within those 'social' conditions themselves. Decision and action take place under definite conditions and they face definite obstacles, some of which involve the practices of other actors. We are concerned with conceptualizing the sites of decision and action (the conditions in which they take place and the obstacles they confront) and the relationships between different sites. Since there is no common essence to the 'social' and no overarching social totality, what is called for here is not so much a general theory of sites of action and decision but rather an exploration of the conditions affecting particular sites.

I have already suggested some of the ways in which decision and action depend on the use of particular conceptual techniques and means of action, and therefore on the availability of these things to the actors in question. Precisely what is available may vary not only from site to site but also according to ascribed or acquired characteristics of the various actors involved in them. Foucault's discussion of medical discourses in *The Birth of the Clinic* (1973) shows how their availability may be restricted to those who occupy particular positions within medical institutions. For another example, consider how the development of specialized managerial techniques has affected the differential availability of decision-making resources and means of acting on them within large organizations. At the other extreme, there are conceptual techniques and other resources so widely available across a variety of sites that they may be regarded as characteristic of particular societies or cultures. Consider the effects of near universal literacy and the availability of telephones, duplicating and photocopying facilities within the more advanced societies.

As for relations between sites, the most striking concern the ways in which decisions taken in one site can affect, and may be intended to affect, decisions and actions in others. Legislation and judicial decisions, for example, can affect the conditions of action for management and unions across a range of enterprises. A different set of examples would be generalized forms of social analysis and organizational techniques which are, or may be, employed by actors at a variety of distinct sites. Consider the various forms of class analysis and discourses of worker solidarity, in which particular conflicts may be represented as parts of a wider struggle, and also their associated techniques of picketing and other forms of collective action. Such general forms of analysis and means of action can provide important conditions for the mobilization of support in particular sites of conflict, and perhaps for extending conflicts into other arenas – for example, through sympathy strikes and secondary picketing. The prospects for these last may, of course, be considerably affected by legislation. General forms of social analysis provide ample scope for dispute and interpretation in their application to particular situations and they frequently cut across other widely used discourses. During the 1984–85 miners' strike in Britain, for example, appeals to internal union democracy cut across the appeal of worker solidarity, with some groups of miners insisting on a national ballot before they would agree to participate in strike action.

A word of warning is in order at this point. Some sites clearly embrace a more general scope than others. Decisions taken at a national level have a different scope and a different range of effects than those taken elsewhere, say, by local governments or employers. It might be tempting to suggest a hierarchical organization of sites of decision and action, with those at higher levels incorporating those lower down – for example, with a national struggle between capital and labour incorporating disputes in particular workplaces and localities. In fact that would be a serious mistake. It would amount to the reintroduction of society-as-totality through a small number of all-embracing sites. Of course, what goes on in particular localities will be affected by conditions determined elsewhere, some of them at a broader social level. We have seen that there are all kinds of ways in which the conditions of decision and action at particular sites may relate to broader social conditions. However, particular sites of decision and action do not thereby lose their separate existences. Conditions in some sites will be affected by what happens elsewhere, and some sites will affect and be affected by a wider range of social conditions than others. But there are no sites in which decision and action are entirely subsumed within sites that are more general. Decision and action at a national level have a different range of effects from decision and action in local communities and workplaces, but there is no sense in which the one is entirely determined by the other. What happens at each level may have implications for the other, but they nevertheless exist as distinct and separate objects of political concern. Local and limited political struggles, if they are important at all, are important in their own right, and not merely as components of something grander.

Some implications

Where do these arguments leave us? Let me begin with some general comments about the analysis of social life before moving on to their implications for political analysis. Some readers may be disturbed by my undermining of the apparent intellectual certainties provided in rather different ways by the varieties of methodological individualism and their structuralist alternatives. If we cast these aside, what have we left? I have argued that reference to our common humanity is not enough to provide an intellectually defensible foundation for the analysis of social life in terms of the constitutive actions of human individuals. What of the other pole? If society is not a functioning whole, how is a relatively stable and enduring social life possible? If we cannot posit self-sustaining social totalities, how can we hope to make sense of the incredible complexities of human social interaction? This last is one of Talcott Parsons' fundamental questions and the 'obviousness' of his answer is central to his treatment of the systems of action. Similar questions and answers underlie Marxist treatments of society-as-totality and most accounts of the assumption of human rationality.

My purpose in raising these questions is only to undermine them. They employ the common rhetorical device of suggesting that the only alternative to the 'obvious' answer is chaos, either in social life itself or in our attempts to make sense of it. If only things were that simple! Neither social life nor our attempts to analyse it ever start from nothing. To say that there are no essential structures of social life provided by the operations of society as a self-sustaining system or totality is not to say that there are no relatively pervasive or enduring social conditions. In some sites of action there are conditions that are relatively easy to change. The formally free character of employment relations and the relatively easy availability of divorce in most Western societies provide obvious examples. Other conditions are more enduring. The general forms of law and property relations characteristic of the modern West would prove less amenable to change. Nevertheless there is no need to suppose that they are sustained by some necessity inherent in capitalism as a mode of production, or by some other version of the functional prerequisites. Rather they are implicated in complex networks of interconnected practices and conditions. There are relatively enduring connections between political and legal practices and conditions and forms of economic organization in most societies, and there is no need to posit some underlying necessity in those conditions as a precondition for analysing them.

However, this rejection of the idea of society as a functioning whole is no reason to favour the other extreme account offered by the portfolio model which suggests that social life is reducible to the constitutive actions of human individuals. To say that actors make decisions and act on them and, further, that those decisions are not wholly determined by the social conditions in which they are made is not to say that the patterns of social interaction are essentially fragile and entirely unpredictable. Nor is it to say that actors have *carte blanche* to do what they will. Actors make decisions and act accordingly, but they do so on the basis of the techniques, forms of thought, and means of action available to them. What these are is a matter of choice only to a very limited extent. Actors can, and sometimes do, work to change how they (and others) think, but they cannot adopt new techniques or patterns of thought quickly or at will. Readers who doubt this last point are invited to try purging their thinking of the effects of literacy!

Class politics
To bring these arguments down to earth, consider their implications for the analysis of politics in terms of the struggle between competing classes. I discuss this style of political analysis in Chapter 5, 'Class analysis as social theory'. It usually involves some combination of two elements, both of which I dispute. One is a notion of classes as actors, and the other is a conception of class interests as objectively given in the structure of society. I have argued that there are indeed actors other than human individuals, but that classes are not among them. For that reason alone (there are many others), the analysis of politics in terms of struggle between classes must be regarded as highly problematic. I have suggested also that interests should not be regarded as given by or reflecting social structural location. Interests have consequences insofar as they provide some actor or actors with reasons for action. Their 'objectivity' has no bearing on that issue. Conceptions of interests that are real or objective but not recognized by those to whom they are ascribed may well have consequences – in the actions of political parties and others who claim to represent those interests – but they provide no explanatory link between the social location of those actors and their actions.

Nevertheless, in the modern world, there are groups in all societies who do analyse politics and act, at least in part, in those terms. The significance of these groups naturally varies from one society to another and over time. But forms of politics involving class analysis have some support in most societies and in some cases they have been extremely influential. These phenomena suggest two areas of investigation.

One of these areas concerns the implications of class analysis for political calculation and action. On the one hand it allows political calculation to bring together a wide range of particular conditions and struggles into a unified pattern. On the other, that unification is supposed to perform an explanatory function – for example, where social conditions are explained in terms of the actions of capital or the ruling class, or of men as a collectivity subordinating women. The invocation of spurious actors or objective interests in this way has a clear polemical function. Unfortunately, it thoroughly obscures investigation of the conditions in question and political decisions as to what can be done to change them.

The other area of investigation is taken up in Chapter 5. It concerns the social conditions which make it possible for class analysis to have an appeal and political significance. 'Interests in political analysis' outlines several respects in which actors' situations may be connected with their beliefs and the interests which they recognize. Two of these are particularly worth noting here. First, the formulation of interests involves actors in the assessment of the conditions they confront and in locating themselves and others in relation to those conditions and possible changes in them. In this respect much of the conceptual purchase of class analysis is a function of its reference to pervasive features of property and employment relations. By the same token, part of the continued weakness of class politics is a function of the difficulty of dealing with the growth, since the late nineteenth century, of impersonal forms of property and of the employment of those who do not fall readily into the categories of capitalist or exploited wage labourer. This suggests an important respect in which the potential appeal of class analysis may have declined throughout this century.

Second, of course, class analysis is far from being the only mode of political assessment available to actors in the modern world. Those who do conduct their politics in class terms have to both compete and work together with adherents of other versions of class analysis and with agencies who conduct their politics in terms of other modes of assessment – in terms of individualism, nationalism, religious and other sectional divisions, and so on. Support for different ways of conducting and analysing politics is one of the outcomes of competition between them. It is never simply a reflection of social structure. The relative strength or weakness of class-based forms of politics in, say, Britain, Sweden and different parts of North America, cannot be explained without reference to the outcomes of past struggles over the policies of particular organizations and more widespread attempts to win support.

The status of political commitments

These comments on class analysis bring us to a different kind of issue, for the political commitments of many social scientists depend on some form of class analysis. There are others whose commitments depend on individualistic versions of the portfolio model of the actor which I examine in the last four chapters. The general issue here is that some of the most common ways of conceptualizing political objectives, concerns and commitments are rendered problematic by the critique of the portfolio model and associated positions outlined above. I comment here first on those involving some notion of objective interests and, second, on those in which human individuals are supposed to provide the ultimate point of reference for social decisions and objectives.

Many, but not all, forms of socialist politics involve a notion of interests as objectively given in the structure of social relations. The same is true of many versions of feminism. On that view of interests, one can act in support of the interests identified in this way (of the working class or of women) or one can act against them – but what those interests are is not a matter of choice. Marxist socialism and some kinds of feminism go further to derive their conceptions of interests from a holistic conception of society as an overarching structure that ties together diverse practices and conditions into a functioning social whole. The implication is that there is a fundamental structure to society with which any serious politics must be concerned. In particular, it is possible to distinguish between reform and revolution, between changes in social conditions that are merely cosmetic and others that involve fundamental changes in the underlying structure. It is in such terms that Marxists have been able to believe that history is on their side – or at least that history has laid down what the sides are going to be.

I have argued that such a conception of social structure cannot be sustained and that interests should not be seen as objectively given. The structure of society does not guarantee a potential majority for socialism or for anything else, and it does not determine what the fundamental lines of political struggle have to be. Socialists may find these arguments disturbing since they undermine the assurance that the viability of socialist politics is somehow given in the structure of capitalist society. The standard revisionist response has been to shift the foundations of socialist politics from a conception of objective interests to a conception of socialist values. This manoeuvre opens up a different order of problems to which I refer briefly at the end of Chapter 5.

On the other side are positions that depend on a fundamental principle of liberal political philosophy – namely that human individuals can, and should be, the ultimate point of reference for decisions about social conditions and objectives. That principle has a considerable influence in contemporary social and political thought. It appears, with various qualifications, in most versions of democratic theory, in the diverse forms of liberalism inspired by Hayek, Rawls or Nozick, in public choice theory in economics and much of rational choice theory in political analysis, and now even within academic Marxism. An influential style of critique of liberal political thought involves the 'communitarian' argument variously advanced by MacIntyre, Sandel and Taylor[6] that human individuals are not the constitutive subjects of social life. The final chapter, 'Liberal individualism and corporate actors' begins by commenting on the weaknesses of that line of argument.

Influential versions of liberal political thought may involve a limited conception of human nature, but the serious weaknesses lie elsewhere. Many significant social decisions are the decisions of social actors – that is, of government agencies, large corporations, trades unions, or churches – and are not simply aggregations of the decisions of human individuals. Social actors may be subjected to various controls and restrictions but it is impossible to conceive of a complex modern society in which social actors of some kind did not play a major role. They have concerns and objectives that are not reducible to those of human individuals. For example, capitalist enterprises, unions, religious organizations and local governments all have an interest in the economic policies of national governments. The concerns and objectives of many social actors have a somewhat doubtful status in terms of influential forms of liberal political thought, they may nevertheless be effective members of the political community. If they are excluded from formal channels of political influence, many of them will nevertheless make themselves felt in other ways. There is little to be gained by treating their political activity as presumptively illegitimate. The problem we face here is not to dispense with the political activity of social actors but rather to bring it under some kind of control and to establish conditions of its legitimacy.

I have suggested, then, that some of the most common ways of conceptualizing the status of political commitments contain in their foundations some version of the portfolio model of the human individual and sometimes a corresponding model of society. The critique of the portfolio model undermines those elements of their foundations. This is not, of course, sufficient to undermine the substantive political commitments of liberals, socialists or democrats. But it does show that attempts to ground those commitments in particular notions of the autonomous individual or of structurally determined interests are unsatisfactory.

Finally, the chapters that follow are a collection of essays based on papers written for different audiences over the last few years. These essays develop a set of distinct, but interrelated, arguments each of which moves by way of a critique of some influential position or style of analysis. They do not add up to an alternative general theory of social life or of society and it is not my intention that they should do so. My aim rather has been to pursue what might seem to be a more limited objective. Accordingly, this book explores a small number of key concepts and intellectual tools and examines their implications for a range of significant and interconnected issues in contemporary social thought.

Any appearance of modesty in this respect would be misleading. Not only is it not my intention to elaborate a general social theory but, as some of my earlier remarks will have suggested, I would not regard that as a viable intellectual objective. In fact, many of the arguments in this book are directed against one or other of the two most common starting points for a general social theory. They undermine both the idea of society as a functioning whole on the one hand and the idea that social life is reducible to the constitutive actions of human individuals on the other. If these arguments hold, then the analysis of social life refers us to an irreducible variety of agencies, practices and conditions and there is no reason to suppose that their interrelations can or indeed should be brought together into a unified general theory.

The purpose of these essays, then, is not to pursue the unattainable but rather to probe and refine some of the more widely used tools of social enquiry. The materials in two chapters have been substantially reorganized in order to avoid excessive duplication. Otherwise I have made only minor stylistic changes to papers originally published elsewhere. A small degree of repitition inevitably remains, but this is mostly confined to the introductory sections of some chapters. With the exceptions just noted this preserves the integrity of the papers as originally published and it allows the arguments of the different chapters to be read independently.

Notes

1. Especially, Elster, 1985; Przeworski, 1985; Przeworski and Sprague, 1986; and Roemer (ed.), 1986.
2. There is a clear discussion of the issue in Savage, 1981.
3. Davidson, 1980, 1984; Macdonald and Pettit, 1981; Doval and Harris, 1986.
4. Hacking, 1982.
5. There is a useful short discussion of this tension in the use of notions of reason and rationality in Williams, 1976.
6. MacIntyre, 1981; Sandel, 1982; Taylor, 1979, 1985.

1 Power, interests and the outcomes of struggles

This chapter considers the use of 'power', 'interests' and related notions in the analysis of social relations, and particularly in discussion of the outcomes of struggles and the conditions in which they take place. I use the terms 'outcome' and 'struggle' very generally, the first to refer to what happens as a result of the practices of one or more agents, a defeat in battle, the break-up of a marriage, or whatever. Outcomes in this sense may or may not conform to the intentions or objectives of any of the agents concerned. They are produced in the course of practices which take place under definite conditions and which confront definite obstacles, including the practices of others. I use the term 'struggle' to refer to any situation in which the obstacles include the opposition of other agents. The problem is, how do we analyse outcomes and the conditions in which some outcomes are reached rather than others? Here, I argue that commonly used analyses in terms of 'power' and 'interests' are often misleading and unhelpful, and I suggest the posing of a rather different set of questions.

I
The simplest way in which reference to power takes place in the analysis of outcomes concerns what might be called 'capacity–outcome' conceptions, in which power is defined in terms of the capacity of an agent to secure something. For example, Weber refers to 'the capacity of an individual to realize his will, even against the opposition of other' (Weber, 1978: 224). Or again, Giddens offers both broader and narrower conceptions of power. In the first it 'represents the capability of the actor to intervene in a series of events so as to alter their course' while in the second it is 'the capability to secure outcomes where the realization of these outcomes depends on the agency of others' (Giddens, 1976: 111). Distinct but closely related conceptions can be found in the work of Dahl, as part of Lukes' three-dimensional view of power, and even

in the work of Parsons. These conceptions differ over whether that capacity is defined in terms of 'will', 'objectives' or 'interests', and over the conditions in which it may be said to exist. Dahl, for example, effectively regards power as existing only in its exercise, so that the analysis of power relations consists in the identification of winners and losers in battles over what are regarded as key political issues.[1] For Giddens, on the contrary, power is a potentiality: it does not come into being only when it is exercised. In that sense the analysis of power relations goes beyond merely keeping the score in overt struggles. Parsons' conception of power is different again, since he does not treat it as an attribute of individuals.[2] Where, for most authors, power is a capacity attributable to particular agents, for Parsons it is generalized, meaning that the capacity is an attribute of a societal medium rather than of the individual who employs it in a given case. Just as the purchasing power of money is not an attribute of the possessor of that money (it goes with the money, not with the individual) so, for Parsons, the performance-securing capacity of power is that of the medium rather than of its possessor.

Now, for all the often considerable differences between them,[3] these conceptions share the notion of power as a capacity to secure outcomes that may be deployed by particular agents in pursuit of their objectives. What this involves in case of conflicting objectives is clearly formulated in a recent paper by Benton:

> If A and B are assumed to utilize their capabilities and resources in whatever conflict develops between them, then the outcome is predictable and unvarying. Where the causal weight of A's combined resources and capabilities is greater than those mobilizable by B, then A achieves A's objectives. (Benton, 1981: 177, emphasis added)

More power prevails over less, and what determines the outcome in a particular situation is the resultant, the vector sum, of the several powers employed in that situation. Benton goes on to modify his analysis while retaining the core notion of power as capacity. It is this shared notion of power as capacity, rather than other aspects of these conceptions, that I shall question in the subsequent discussion.

However, there are also more general usages in which power may be said to relate to outcomes. Here, power is supposed to be effective not only as regards the outcomes of particular struggles, but also in the determination of the conditions of struggle themselves. Power in this sense may be said to work through one or both of two mechanisms. The first operates by excluding some interests from the arenas in which decisions are reached. Examples are what Lukes refers to as the two-dimensional view of power,[4] which emphasizes the role of 'non-decisions' in preventing issues from surfacing, and 'power-elite' analyses. Thus, in *The State in Capitalist Society*, Miliband is concerned to argue that the social composition and formation of the state élite have the effect of excluding those with all but a narrow range of interests, and, in particular, those with an interest in securing fundamental social transformation.

The second mechanism operates on the consciousness of its victims by preventing them from recognizing their own interests. Some such mechanism is central to Lukes' three-dimensional view, in which power may be said to act even in the absence of identifiable conflicts or grievances,[5] and to the Gramscian conception of bourgeois hegemony. For Gramsci, the bourgeoisie in advanced capitalist societies rules through a combination of coercion and consent, the latter meaning that the popular classes are not even mobilized around their own interests (the overthrow of capitalist domination) but in another way altogether. Something similar is involved in the arguments of those Marxists, from Anderson to Poulantzas, who represent the parliamentary democratic form of state as a mechanism of fundamental mystification. Anderson, for example, argues that 'the general form of the representative State – bourgeois democracy – is itself the principal ideological lynchpin of Western capitalism whose very existence deprives the working class of the idea of socialism as a different type of State'. (Anderson, 1976: 30) The claim is that the mechanisms of bourgeois rule act to prevent the working class from forming ideas that are necessary to the successful pursuit of its interests.

In this chapter I argue against both capacity–outcome conceptions of power and these latter positions which extend them by attempting to cover not only the securing of particular outcomes but also the conditions which govern what kinds of outcome are possible and what objectives can be fought for. I make no claims that these exhaust the ways in which power may be conceived or that there are no other positions worth discussing. Foucault, for example, advances a powerful critique of notions of power as possession, gestures towards an alternative conceptualization in terms of the organization of strategic fields, and develops a complex analysis of the intimate connections between power and knowledge.[6] His arguments merit serious attention, but they raise issues of a different order from those considered here.

I argue that the securing of outcomes should always be seen as problematic, and that it is subject to definite and specifiable conditions in at least two respects. First, agents' means of action frequently depend on conditions outside their control. Second, the deployment of these means of action invariably confronts obstacles, which often include the opposing practices of others. Success in overcoming those obstacles cannot in general be guaranteed. Power as capacity to secure therefore disappears, for outcomes are not 'predictable and unvarying' in the way that this conception requires. Agents do indeed confront differential means and conditions of action, but it can be seriously misleading to analyse those means and conditions in terms of conceptions of power outlined above. These are vitiated, first, by their reduction of differential means and conditions of action to the effects of a single general principle and, second, by a problematic notion of interests as actual or potential basis of mobilization. I argue that interests cannot provide a general model of the mobilization of agents in particular practices and struggles.

II

Here I return to the general issue of the analysis of conditions relating to outcomes of practices. I introduce a number of simple, loosely defined concepts and a commentary on them as a way of bringing out some of the kinds of questions to be asked in dealing with particular outcomes or struggles, and I then proceed to the implications of these points for conceptions of 'power' and 'interests'. Outcomes are produced in the course of the agents' practices which are always subject to definite conditions and obstacles and which often include the practices of other agents. We are concerned with conceptualizing the sites of practices (their conditions and obstacles), particularly those in which the obstacles include the opposition of other agents. These are arenas of struggle.

Arena refers to the conditions of a particular struggle or set of struggles, to the modes of action specific to it (voting, argument, withdrawal of labour, and so on), and to the limitations on possible outcomes (for example, in the case of parliamentary struggles possible outcomes are legislation, changes in government policy or the composition of government, and so on). Although I argue that the precise outcome is generally not determined by the conditions of struggle, there are always definite limitations on what the outcome may be.

Force refers to agents and to forms of combined action of agents engaged in particular arenas. I use the term 'agent' to refer quite generally to a locus of decision and action, a human individual, joint-stock company, local council, or whatever. I make no presumption that some of these agents are essentially reducible to others as Weber suggests in his methodological writings. For the purposes of the present argument it is not necessary to consider the constitution of agents and their operation in any detail, but it is important to recognize that agents are always subject to a variety of conditions and that their decisions and practices derive in part from complex internal processes.

There is a partial recognition of this point in Benton's treatment of power as involving 'the intrinsic capabilities of A in conjunction with A's relationship to extrinsic resources.' (Benton, 1981: 175) Intrinsic capabilities here include such things as 'knowledge, skills, competences'. But the counterposition of the intrinsic capabilities of agents to their extrinsic resources is itself highly problematic. If it is to function as a locus of decision and action, an agent must involve definite mechanisms of reaching decisions and of acting towards at least some of the decisions reached. What those mechanisms are, or may be, will depend on the particular constitution of the agent in question. The reaching of decisions by an agent is not simply a matter of 'intrinsic' elements such as knowledges, skills or competences, but also of their deployment in some more or less complex process of assessment of its conditions of action. It may also involve struggles between agents, voting, lobbying, debate, and so on. But, in all cases, the reaching of decisions involves the deployment of some means whereby objectives, arguments or analyses may be formulated and in which the agent may be situated in relation to those objectives and decisions. What these means are and how they are deployed or relate to the internal mechanisms of the agent may vary, but they are clearly not reducible to intrinsic properties of the agents themselves.

These points are extremely brief and schematic, and some are developed in later chapters, but they will suffice for the present argument. To say that all agents depend on conditions of diverse kinds and that they involve complex internal processes is to avoid the problems associated with doctrines of reducibility and human creativity. The doctrine of the reducibility of social conditions to the actions of individuals amounts to a doctrine in support of incomplete specification. In particular, it involves the incomplete specification of the conditions of action of such non-human agents such as joint-stock companies, state apparatuses, among others. Such reduction of the general question of specifying the conditions of constitution and action of agents to the more limited questions of the human individuals involved may be understandable on the presumption that the action of humans has an ontological status superior to that of all other conditions, so that specification of these other conditions does indeed seem to be of secondary importance.

That presumption brings us the vexed question of 'creativity'. The one great merit of doctrines of human creativity lies in their insistence that agents' actions and objectives are not determined simply as a function of the conditions in which they find themselves – of class position, education, age, sex, and so forth. The drawback is that they appear to regard human action as containing some element that is essentially unconditional and therefore inexplicable: it is the unmoved mover of society and history. One of the most difficult problems for the analysis of both human and non-human agents concerns the specification of the mechanisms of decision and action and of the conditions on which those mechanisms depend. Talk of human creativity, or for that matter of 'intrinsic capabilities', is at best a gesture towards, and at worst an evasion of, that problem.

As for forces other than agents, it is clear that they depend on means of mobilizing the combined actions of distinct agents – for example, through shared or overlapping ideologies which provide means of formulating common objectives in particular contexts. But it is doubtful whether there is much of value that can be said about forces in general – compare the parliamentary Labour Party and the Ford shop stewards combine. All forces require the mobilization of combined action of distinct agents but precisely what that involves will vary according to the agents and arena of struggle in question and, in particular, according to the type of action open to forces in that arena.

Articulation of arenas refers to the ways in which distinct arenas of struggle are related to each other. One obvious mode of articulation concerns the ways in which outcomes in one arena may affect the conditions of struggle or the forces engaged in other arenas.

Examples are the effects of electoral struggles on the forces engaged in parliamentary struggles, and the effects of legislation or judicial decisions on conditions of struggle in enterprises. But it is also necessary to consider means and conditions of action common to a variety of arenas that are not currently subject to struggle. For example, generalized discursive means of formulating objectives and analyses which are, or may be, employed in a variety of arenas, those forms of discourse in which particular conflicts are represented as part of a wider social struggle, say, between the Left and Right, or the working class (and its allies) and monopoly capitalism, racist and anti-racist discourses, and so on.

Such 'ideologies' may be significant in providing some of the conditions of mobilization in particular struggles and of generating outside support and in providing a means of generalizing these struggles into other arenas. They provide means of formulating objectives and means of organization that go beyond what can be achieved in any particular arena, means of arguing the priority of some arenas over others, and so on. They may also be objects of struggle. Such ideologies are generally less than fully coherent, thus providing ample scope for disputes and organizational differences over priorities or objectives in particular arenas. Other examples of conditions common to a variety of arenas would be organizational techniques, such as the availability of non-availability of telephones, duplicating and photocopying equipment, among other things.

These definitions are, to say the least, loose and general, and they abstract from the conditions of specific arenas of struggle. Nevertheless they are not without significance. All struggles occupy definite arenas with definite conditions which may have differential effects on the conditions of action of agents and forces engaged in those arenas. They may be articulated on to other arenas in the sense that conditions set in one arena may affect the conditions and strategies of agents in other arenas. The constitution of an arena of struggle involves definite conditions, modes of action and possible effects which are all subject to variation within certain specifiable limitations.

To take a particular example, consider capitalist enterprises as arenas of struggle. Each enterprise involves a plurality of agents, the capitalist (a human individual or a legal subject such as a joint-stock company), and a variety of employees with different wages, working conditions, security of employment, and so on. The capitalist has certain legal rights over the property of the enterprise and its disposal, and also over what employees may be required to do or prevented from doing. In addition, management will have at its disposal a variety of control techniques operating through inspection and collection of information, hierarchical chains of command and supervision, and so on.

On the basis of these legal rights and control techniques management attempts to control the actions of employees. But those attempts are subject to obstacles which may vary both from the one enterprise to another and within enterprises: deliberate and organized resistance, unorganized bloody-mindedness, conflicts between groups of employees, lack of concentration, and so on. The point here is that there is nothing in the notion of capitalist enterprise as such to determine what control techniques will be attempted or the obstacles they will meet. And there is nothing to guarantee that management attempts will prove successful. There are well known cases where workers have successfully taken over plants, forced major changes in management plans and resisted changes in work intensity.

Thus the operation of capitalist enterprises involves capitalists and managerial employees in attempts to control the actions of others in the face of a variety of obstacles. However, all these agents will also be involved in other relationships; groups of workers may be in conflict with each other, they may belong to different unions attempting to extract mutually incompatible agreements from management, some workers may be trying to keep out blacks or women, to set up a closed shop, to establish a creche . . . The analysis of enterprises in class terms – that is, in terms of relations between capitalists and workers – brings out only one aspect of the differential conditions of the action of agents in enterprises. An enterprise may also involve other axes of struggle which cut across each other. Analysis in class terms specifies one set of features of the conditions of action of agents involved in production but it does not determine what the other conditions will be, nor does it ensure that the agents concerned will regard it as the most important issue to fight about. In particular, the differential legal statuses of employer and employee entail no necessary constitution of conflicting forces. Such forces as may develop and their constitutions must therefore be analysed in other ways: in terms of specific discursive means of formulating objectives and the effects of struggles to mobilize support around those objectives; consequences of technical and organizational exigencies for the differential conditions of action of agents, and so on.

What differentiates the capitalist from employees is not so much that the one has the capacity to control the functioning of the enterprise, whilst the others are devoid of such control. Rather, we are dealing with an actual or potential arena of struggle in which agents have differential means and conditions of action, the possibility of employing different types of strategy and deploying different weapons. These differential conditions do not, and cannot, guarantee that the capitalist will succeed in imposing control over the enterprise. In other words, the differential positions of capitalists and workers should not be conceived on the model of legally defined rights and obligations. While these certainly define some of the differential conditions of action of economic agents, those differential conditions are far from being exhausted by the legal forms of property and contract.

It is important to be clear what kind of effect legal requirements may have. At the level of legal definition, the capitalist may well have an unequivocal capacity to control his means of production. Nevertheless that capacity, in legal definition, is insufficient to guarantee the capitalist his control and it does not ensure that workers cannot exercise control of aspects of the functioning of the enterprise. The law does not determine or reflect the conduct of agents but it does affect some of their conditions of action, say, by assigning actionable rights to property owners or employees, or by assigning legal powers to regulatory agencies. It goes without saying that the assignment of legal rights or powers does not suffice to ensure their realization. Law itself provides another set of arenas of possible struggle so that the assignment of rights merely defines a particular mode of access to such arenas. It does not guarantee the outcome of legal process.

Finally, the reference to differential legal statuses gives one example of how conditions of struggle in one arena can be affected by conditions and organizations elsewhere, through the content of company law, union and other legislation. Other examples are the strength of unions and their policies on particular issues, the extent to which outside support can be mobilized for disputes within the enterprise on the basis of union and other organizations or general ideological objectives concerning rights of pickets, anti-racialism, or whatever.

Returning now to the general argument, what applies to capitalists and workers applies quite generally to all cases in which agents are confronted with differential means and conditions of action. The problem with the notion that the capitalist has the capacity to control the operation of the enterprise arises also for all 'capacity–outcome' conceptions of power. The problem is that, on closer inspection, the capacity vanishes as soon as it is recognized that the exercise of control, the realization of one's will or objectives, the securing of interests, or whatever, always involves the deployment of definite means of action in particular situations, that these means of action themselves depend on definite conditions and that their deployment may confront obstacles including the practices of others.

There are several issues here. First, the means of action that may be deployed by an agent and are relevant to its objectives will depend on the nature of those objectives and on the specific situation of action. Of course, there are means of action that can be deployed in pursuit of numerous objectives and in a wide range of situations. Money is a case in point. But it would be absurd to imagine that all means of action available to agents were so flexible. The notion of power as capacity obscures the specificity and variability of the means of action available to agents. There is a partial recognition of this point too in Benton's observation that 'the power differential between A and B [may] be different with respect to different objectives' (Benton, 1981:178). Quite so; but if an agent's power can vary significantly from one objective to another then there seems little point in retaining a concept of power as generalized capacity to secure objectives. Or again, consider Dahl's well known argument for the importance of specifying the *scope* of an agent's power. If 'power' has a definite and delimited scope then it can hardly be regarded as a *capacity*. Reference to scope involves, at least implicitly, reference to conditions which limit that scope and many of these are clearly not in the hands of the agent concerned. Reference to its scope, in other words, transforms 'power' from a generalized capacity of an individual to a function of definite social conditions and relations.

This brings us to the second issue. The means of action available to agents all depend on definite conditions, many of which are not controlled by the agents in question. This is particularly the case with what Benton calls 'extrinsic resources' deriving from an agent's 'relationships to other human beings, collectivities and material

things' (Benton, 1981:175). The point here is simply that the deployment of such resources in a particular struggle may well depend on
the action, inaction or compliance of other agents not directly
engaged in that struggle. That is one aspect of the articulation of
arenas of struggle. It means that talk of power as capacity can easily
obscure the extent to which an agent's 'capacity' may be dependent
on conditions outside that agent's direct control.

Now, there are obviously cases where the means and conditions of
action so favour one side in a struggle that the outcome can scarcely
be in doubt. The trouble with 'capacity–outcome' conceptions of
power is that they effectively treat such cases as paradigm instances
of arenas of struggle, so that once the powers of contending parties
are known then 'the outcome is predictable and unvarying' (Benton,
1981:177). If the world were so simple there would be few problems
for social analysis. The idea that outcomes can be determined simply
by adding up the resources and capabilities available on each side
and then subtracting one from the other ignores the two points made
above. But, and this is my third point, it denies the extent to which
outcomes of struggle depend on the ways in which the contending
parties deploy various means and conditions of action often under
complex conditions of struggle and the ways in which they are able to
affect the behaviour of third parties. In effect, it denies the most
basic aspect of struggle – namely, that outcomes are produced in the
course of struggle itself and are rarely the simple products of initial
conditions. Consider, for example, the long drawn-out struggle
between the USA and North Vietnam. Any 'capacity–outcome'
analysis of the resources available to each side would leave no doubt
as to the inevitable outcome.

Once 'capacities' are seen as conditional and as subject to the
deployment of definite means of action, they cease to be capacities to
secure, to *realize* or to *control*, and become at best capacities to act in
pursuit of certain objectives. Referring, for example, to Weber's
conception of power, an individual's realization of 'his will, even
against the opposition of others' (Weber, 1978:224) is the outcome
of definite practices under definite conditions, and possibly of
struggles against particular opposing practices. It is an outcome, not
the expression of capacity, as it is, similarly, for other versions of the
'capacity–outcome' conception. By reducing outcomes to the realization of capacities, they manage to ignore one of the most basic and
pervasive features of social life namely, that struggles over divergent

objectives really are struggles; they are not the playing-out of some preordained script.

These points suggest that the significance attached to power as capacity as an object of investigation may well be exaggerated in many instances. We should stop trying to account for outcomes in terms of power-attributes or capacities belonging to particular agents. Rather we are left with the problems of the means of action available to agents in specific situations of action. Arenas of actual or potential struggle would then have to be analysed not in terms of differential possession of quantities of power but rather in terms of the differential conditions and means of action available to the contending forces, their strategies and objectives, and so on.

Finally, the example of capitalist enterprises illustrates the point that general characterizations of arenas as involving capitalist class relations, hierarchical structures of authority, or whatever cannot suffice to determine the conditions and forms of struggle which develop in any particular case. There is no inherent reason to expect that differences between capitalists and workers in general or between those in authority and those subject to it will predominate over other conditions of struggle. Such sweeping characterizations at most specify certain aspects of agents' differential conditions of action, but they cannot determine what the other conditions will be, the particular forms in which agents mobilize into contending forces or the strategies and objectives they adopt.

Now, it may be suggested that these last comments overlook the crucial role of interests in determining the line-up of contending forces. Some will no doubt wish to add that certain general characterizations are of value precisely because they do define fundamental cleavages of interests. It is to this supposed centrality of interests that we now turn.

III

Where interests are thought to be pertinent to the analysis of outcomes it is because they are supposed to constitute either an actual or a potential basis for the mobilization of agents in struggles. The first clearly relates to 'capacity–outcome' conceptions of power, and in this case reference to interests provides an explanation for why agents act as they do. In the second case, interests are regarded as *potential* means of mobilization of agents whose ineffectiveness in a given situation has to be explained away. This is usually attempted in one of two ways: either those interests are said to be excluded from the arenas in which decisions are taken; or they are thought not to be recognized as such by those whose interests they are. These three ways of situating interests in relation to agents' practices correspond to Lukes' one-, two- and three-dimensional views of power respectively. What is shared by all these different positions is a conception of interests as objectives that are presumed to attach to agents independently of the particular struggles in which they may be engaged. Only if they are seen in this way can 'interests' appear as the basic datum in power analysis; they are what agents are fighting about, or would be fighting about, if only things were different. What power analysis then sets out to explain is why some interests win out and others lose. I shall comment briefly on two cases: the first where interests are conceived as being what agents mobilize around or express concern over, and the second where they are regarded as a potential basis of mobilization that may, or may not, be realized.

First then, we have interests as the objectives or concerns acknowledged by agents engaged in particular struggles. I have suggested that agents are to be regarded as loci of decision and action, involving definite processes of reaching decisions and means of acting on them. The objectives or concerns that provide agents with reasons for action must then be regarded as the product of some more or less complex process involving, say, unconscious processes, deliberation, or attempts at persuasion by others. They will be subject to variation according to changes in those processes and the conditions in which they operate. 'Interests', in the sense of recognized objectives and concerns, can hardly be regarded as attaching to particular agents as a given to power analysis. It is unclear, therefore, why differences in 'interests' should be regarded as a fruitful starting-point for the analysis of 'power relations'.

I have no wish to deny that forces may sometimes be mobilized on the basis of objectives that are given in advance of the struggle in question, or that discourses on 'interests' – whether their own or those of others – may play an effective role in the constitution of particular forces. The point is rather that 'interests', in the sense of acknowledged objectives, cannot be regarded as providing a general model or explanation for the ways agents are mobilized in struggles. 'Interests' in this sense clearly depend on the use of particular discursive means of formulating objectives and situating the agent in relation to them. I return to this issue in Chapter 3, '"Interests" in political analysis'. For the moment, it suffices to note that the forms of discourse available to agents generally allow them to formulate a variety of distinct and often incompatible objectives. It follows that the objectives around which agents do mobilize in any given case cannot themselves suffice to account for that mobilization.

Racist and sexist forms of discourse, for example, are available to workers in many enterprises which would allow them to formulate objectives that are incompatible with those of worker or union solidarity against management: refusal to work with blacks, restriction of women to certain grades of work, failure to respect picketing by blacks or women, and so on. But it would be absurd to account for the formulation of one set of objectives rather than another in terms of those objectives themselves, as this argument would be completely circular. What objectives are formulated or adopted depends not only on the availability of suitable forms of discourse but also on other conditions including the work of unions, political parties and other organizations, and of individuals in support of some objectives and against others. That is to say not only that objectives are not always given independently of particular conditions of struggle but also that they may be changed or developed in the course of struggle.

These points dispose of the idea that 'interests' can function as a general explanation for the mobilization of agents in struggles. It follows that differences in acknowledged interests may not always be the best starting-point for analysing the struggles that take place in a society. But what of the view that power may operate through the exclusion of all but a narrow range of interests from the relevant decision-making arena? It is clear that a particular arena of struggle-say, the Labour Cabinet towards the end of Callaghan's administration - will be constituted in terms of particular agents and forces with, at any given time, particular sets of objectives and able to deploy particular means of action and strategies in support of those objectives. Since adoption of some objectives by the relevant agents obviously implies that the non-adoption of others, in that sense it could be said that certain objectives are indeed excluded. Nevertheless, it is not clear what is to be gained by taking 'interests', as acknowledged objectives, as the starting-point and analysing arenas in terms of mechanisms operating on 'interests', either to include some or to exclude others. The operation of the Labour Cabinet, or any other specific arena, has to be analysed in terms of the constitution of its particular conditions and forms of struggle and the forces engaged in it, and of its specific articulations on to other arenas – in this case, the PLP, other parliamentary forces, the Labour Party NEC, the TUC and individual unions, various state apparatuses, and so on. Of course, 'interests' are sometimes excluded and – who can deny it? – there may be cases where that is the most significant feature of the way an arena is constituted. But, in general, to take acknowledged 'interests', whether included or excluded, as the starting-point is to seriously restrict analysis of the constitution of arenas of struggle.

Now consider the conception of interests as a set of objectives that agents may be prevented from recognizing through the operation of power. This conception has at least the merit of recognizing that the objectives agents recognize are not inherent in the agents themselves but are rather subject to a variety of conditions, including the practices of political parties, unions and other organizations. But that recognition is unfortunately combined with the view that agents (or at least human individuals and possibly some collectivities) do have real interests of which they may or may not be aware. On this view, different interests may be acknowledged in different situations, but some are more real than others. It is this conception of 'real' interests that underlies Lukes' three-dimensional view of power and the Gramscian notions of hegemony and of rule by consent.

There are several difficulties here. First, the attribution of 'real', but unrecognized, interests to agents is generally by virtue of their sharing some particular conditions with other members of a category: class, sex, being victims of monopoly power or of multinational companies, or whatever. Here interests are thought to inhere in agents as a direct result of their membership of a category which specifies certain of the conditions in which they find themselves. The problem is that some further explanation is required of why the conditions shared by agents in that category should be considered effective in determining real interests, while other conditions which are not shared by all agents in that category are considered ineffective. Why, for example, should conditions that are supposed to be common to those of the same gender or same class entail equally common interests that are 'real', unlike 'interests' pertaining to conditions not shared within those categories?

Second, to talk of 'interests' that are real but unrecognized is to suggest, at least in principle, conditions in which they would indeed be truly recognized. Lukes, for example, refers to conditions of democratic participation as allowing individuals to recognize what their interests really are (Lukes, 1976: 33).[7] There is the obvious difficulty here that there seems no good reason why interests acknowledged in one situation should be considered any more real than those acknowledged in another. Different interests may indeed be acknowledged under conditions of democratic participation than under conditions of authoritarian populism, and there may be all kinds of good reasons for preferring one set of conditions to the other. But that hardly requires us to consider one lot of interests 'real' and the other not.

What is at issue in this singling-out of certain 'interests' as ontologically privileged is a problematic of domination and, at least implicitly, of emancipation under the guidance of the enlightened few.[8] The problem posed here is: why do the dominated put up with it? Why are the popular masses not mobilized around their real interest (the overthrow of capitalist domination); why are they mobilized in ways which fail to pose their interest as an object of struggle? What has to be explained here is an absence of recognition and, therefore, of action. What is missing is enlightenment, and it is said to be missing because of rule by consent, bourgeois hegemony, three-dimensional power, or whatever – an approach which reduces a complex variety of specific conditions, practices and struggles to yet another of the great simplicities.

Once again, this conception of interests and the related conceptions of power, domination and hegemony are at best misleading guides to analysis. If we are concerned with arenas of struggle and the relations between them, then the problem is not so much why certain objectives – the real 'interests' – are not pursued but rather the identification of the determinants of those that *are* pursued: what means of posing objectives are available to agents and forces in particular arenas and how are they deployed in the mobilization of agents; how are these forces constituted and what means of action are available to them; in what respect are these forces, possible strategies and means of mobilizing support, dependent on conditions set in other arenas; and so on. These questions concern the identification of the particular conditions involved in the constitution of existing arenas, forces and objectives. It is not a matter of using some non-existent state of affairs (in which agents do pursue their real interests) as a measure of the present and trying to explain away its non-existence, but is rather a matter of identifying conditions and what can be done to change them.

IV

The starting-point of this chapter was the need to take seriously the practices of agents and struggles between them. That means taking seriously the particular conditions in which these practices and struggles take place and in which their outcomes are produced: the constitution of agents and other forces; the conditions of formation of objectives and of the mobilization of agents around them; means of action and possible strategies; limitations on the kinds of outcome that are possible; and so on. It also means taking seriously the central feature of struggles between agents with different and conflicting objectives – namely, that outcomes are produced in the course of struggles, they are neither a reflection of the initial conditions of action nor a simple consequence of a power differential between the contending parties.

Of course, there are cases where the resources available to agents are such that the outcome of struggles can hardly be in doubt. But I have argued that 'capacity–outcome' conceptions of power are fundamentally mistaken in taking such cases where more 'power' invariably prevails over less as paradigms for analysis of struggles and their outcomes. Agents may be more or less successful in their attempts to exercise control or realize their will, but they are successful to the extent that they overcome various obstacles and resistances. In that sense, the attainment of such objectives presupposes no inbuilt *capacity* to do so but is rather a matter of the successful deployment of resources and means of action in the context of particular conditions of struggle, not all of which are in the hands of the agent in question. The conditionality of outcomes involved here is not a kind that can be subsumed within a probabilistic conception of power, as some of Weber's formulations might suggest. We are dealing not with a stochastic process, but with the practices and struggles of definite agents and forces employing particular means of action and strategies in pursuit of their objectives under conditions which are only partially subject to their actions, and with the production of outcomes in the interaction of their different practices.

The conceptions of power discussed in this chapter are vitiated by their conception of interests as somehow determined outside the conditions of particular practices and struggles. 'Interests' function in power analysis in one of two ways. On the one hand they are identified as sets of objectives that are acknowledged by the agents concerned. 'Power' is then brought in to explain why some interests prevail over others. In this case, power analysis depends on taking a given distribution of 'interests' as the starting-point for analysis. Since there are no good reasons for regarding acknowledged 'interests' as inherent properties of agents, the effect of such a starting-point is to foreclose investigation of major problems concerning the constitution of arenas of struggle and the forces active in them.

On the other hand, 'interests' are presented as something that agents may be prevented from even recognizing by the operation of a power in the hands of an opposing interest. This approach encounters all the problems involved in the ontological privileging of some set of supposed interests. The explanation of failure to acknowledge those 'interests' in terms of the operation of a power – say, bourgeois hegemony or Lukes' three-dimensional power – sweeps aside the serious problems of the constitution of forces and arenas of struggle in favour of one of the grand simplifications of modern social thought. Whatever advantages may be thought to accrue to this way of characterizing struggles, it has little to offer for the serious analysis of social conditions and how they might be changed.

In short, I have argued that some of the most important conceptions of 'power' and 'interests' operate to foreclose serious analysis of the constitution of arenas of struggle and the forces active in them by means of gross and indefensible simplifications of the conditions in which struggles take place. I have introduced loosely defined concepts of arenas, forces and articulation of arenas as a means of indicating the complexity that is obscured by analysis in terms of 'interests' and 'power as capacity'. However, although it is doubtful whether much can be said in general about the characteristics of such concepts (hence the recurrence of such adjectives as 'particular' throughout this chapter) this should not be interpreted as an atheoretical plea for empiricism. Much depends on the questions that are asked and therefore on the concepts those questions depend on. I have tried to show that the posing of questions in terms of 'power' and 'interests' involves, at best, gross oversimplification precisely because those conceptions do pretend to be a general characterization of how arenas of struggle are constituted.

Notes

1. Dahl, 1958, 1961.
2. Parsons, 1969, Parsons' argument is frequently misrepresented by critics. For careful discussion and critique see Savage, 1981.
3. For a thorough discussion of the variety of sociological conceptions of power see Wrong, 1979.
4. See Bachrach and Baratz, 1962, 1963.
5. Lukes, 1976.
6. Especially Foucault, 1977, 1979, 1980. Three useful but very different discussions can be found in Cousins and Hussain, 1984; Minson, 1985; Wickham, 1983.
7. See the discussion in Hindess, 1976.
8. Cf. Benton's comments on 'the paradox of emancipation' (1981: p.162)

2 Rational choice theory and the analysis of political action

The dominant approach in contemporary economic theory elaborates on abstract models of rational choice. Highly idealized economic agents act to maximize their utility functions (or some equivalent) in markets that operate with varying degrees of efficiency to coordinate their actions. Agents are assumed to be rational in a sense that involves first, the use of appropriate means to one's ends and, second, a mathematically well-balanced preference structure exhibiting a certain consistency of choice. An actor preferring both A to B and B to C will also prefer A to C. Since the publication of Downs' *An Economic Theory of Democracy* in 1957, a considerable amount of intellectual energy has been devoted to extending this approach to the analysis of political phenomena on the grounds that the individuals involved in political behaviour 'need not be less rational than the individuals treated by economic theory: in fact they are the same individuals' (Margolis, 1982: 7). On such grounds it must seem that there is no area of human activity in which the rational choice approach could not be fruitfully applied.[1]

What is at stake here is the view that the abstract model of rational choice applies to economic agents essentially 'because they are agents. In short, they are human, and the realities of human nature must be accounted for in any economic analysis. *Ipso facto*, the same type of reasoning must be applied to every institution run by men' (Downs, 1957: 283). In this respect, the rational choice approach to political behaviour is merely another example of the attempt to extend a style of analysis that has proved influential in economic theory to other areas of social life. It is widely recognized, of course, that political behaviour may sometimes depart from the canons of strict rationality, but such departures are not thought to pose a serious problem for the rational choice approach. Downs refers us to Friedman's 'The methodology of positive economics' in support of his view that his models 'should be tested primarily by the accuracy of their predictions rather than by the reality of their assumptions' (ibid.: 21). This methodological view is widely shared by writers in the rational choice tradition.

From the standpoint of its protagonists, the rational choice approach shows every sign of being a progressive and expanding research programme. Starting from the rather simplistic arguments of Downs and Olson, it has developed a growing technical sophistication and can claim to have established a number of significant results. Here are just a few examples. First, early studies of voting behaviour had found that a high proportion of voters were extremely ill-informed about politics, recognizing the names of few senior politicians, ignorant of the policy positions of the party they supported, and so on. Downs shows that, given the costs of obtaining information and the low return on any one person's vote, such 'ignorance' on the part of the voters may well be 'rational'. Rational voters will rely on easily recognized cues, slogans, party labels, as the basis of their decisions (Downs, 1957: III).

Second, pluralist political theory has tended to assume that any interest shared by a significant proportion of the electorate would be represented by some organization, and therefore that significant interests would be organized. Olson shows that there is no reason to expect such an outcome unless other conditions are also satisfied. The costs to an individual of working to establish or support an organized interest are likely to be greater than the benefits perceived by the individual from the organized representation of that interest. It may therefore be possible for an interest that is widely shared amongst a population of rational individuals not to be politically organized. Olson argues that organization in such cases requires selective incentives, over and above the presumably shared interest, to account for the work of activists and officials. More generally, rational choice theorists can point to the impressive development of the theory of public goods to deal with problems of public choice and market failures from the standpoint of individual preferences. The theory of public goods also provides a neo-Hobbesian argument for the necessity of government – namely, that rational agents recognize that it would be irrational for any one of them to provide for the supply of certain public goods in the absence of coercion.

The use of rational choice models in the context of public goods is not without its problems. Some of the empirical applications of this approach – for example, on the politics of public expenditure and public finance – have been remarkably crude and ill-informed.[2]

Other difficulties, widely recognized in the rational choice tradition, are to do with the fact that the behaviour of hypothetical utility maximizers conflicts with everyday observation and with experimental results on behaviour in Prisoner's Dilemma games. The paradox of rational voting is perhaps the best known. In national or local elections, the chances of one person's vote affecting the outcome are minute. The effort of voting therefore outweighs any reasonable estimate of the return. Nevertheless, a remarkably high proportion of the electorate do vote, even when there is no legal compulsion or when the result is widely regarded as a foregone conclusion. Experiments with Prisoner's Dilemma games show that players do not even approximate the behaviour required by most models of rational choice. It is not difficult to deal with these and other problems by introducing suitable 'altruistic' motivations into the theory – for example, a 'duty' to vote. All that is required is to endow individuals with more than one set of preferences, and provide a non-trivial account of the conditions in which one or another set of preferences comes into play and of what governs the propensity to perform 'altruistic' acts. Much ingenuity has been expended on this issue.[3]

There can be no question here of attempting a general survey of the rational choice literature. Rather, the limited objective of this chapter is to raise some theoretical problems concerning the rational choice approach, concentrating on its conception of rationality and methodological individualism.

In effect, the rational choice approach takes as its starting-point the need to construct a model of the individual actor and its choices in order to study, in a deductive fashion, the interactions of a plurality of actors. I shall suggest that the conceptualization of actors, their decisions, and the conditions in which they are made raises important questions which cannot be posed within the rational choice approach. In particular, I reject the claim of some social scientists that the construction and elaboration of rational choice models 'offers more promise to the development of social theory than does any other [approach]' (Coleman, 1979: 76). Nevertheless, although no-one could seriously argue against the construction of rational choice models as such, there are problems with their heuristic use. Formal and informal models of rational action are often illuminating and may well suggest fruitful lines of further work, and assumptions that are not defensible in general may well have a use in certain limited contexts (a major concern of this chapter being to indicate just how limited those contexts are). Indeed, rational choice theory requires a number of specific postulates which may well have heuristic value in certain cases. But, if accepted in general they would foreclose serious investigation of issues of major theoretical and political importance.

I begin by identifying three postulates – those of rationality, homogeneity and individualism – as basic features of the rational choice approach and proceed to a commentary on each of them. My aim is to show that these postulates are unacceptable and that their heuristic use involves severe theoretical and political limitations, and to suggest a different starting-point with regard to the conceptualization of action. Finally, I indicate some of the problems with recent attempts to integrate elements of the rational choice approach into Marxism.

Preliminaries

It will be helpful to dispose of some preliminary points before proceeding. Consider the following remarks from Anthony Heath's *Rational Choice and Social Exchange*:

> It really does seem to me that an excellent way in which to begin any explanation of human action is to suppose that the actor is a rational agent with intelligible goals, an agent who chooses rationally between potential courses of action in the light of those goals. (This is not of course a view unique to the exchange theorists, nor is it one discovered for the first time by then. Weber certainly held this view, and so I suspect did Marx). If our rational choice explanation fails or is unilluminating, then we shall assuredly have to turn to other explanations in terms of unconscious drives, habitual action or other forms of non-rational action. But I think we do well, until firm evidence to the contrary is available to assume that our fellow men are as rational and intelligent agents as we usually suppose ourselves to be. (Heath, 1976: viii).

As a statement in support of the rational approach this passage suffers from several problems. First, it takes only a limited degree of self-knowledge to see that Heath's last sentence would be a reason for rejecting the rational choice approach out of hand. In fact, the rational choice approach does not normally depend on the presumption that, as a matter of fact, human behaviour is rational in the technical sense required by any particular theory. The argument rather is that models constructed in terms of rational choice and action have their value in predicting or illuminating significant features of social and political life. Indeed, the deliberate unrealism of the theory's simplifying assumptions is generally presented as a necessary condition for the construction of sophisticated formal models.

This brings me to a second problem. The 'rationality' of rational choice theory must always be understood in a strictly technical sense, which is obscured in much of Heath's account. There are problems with his contrast between the rational and non-rational, where 'habitual action' is cited as an example of the latter. It is not difficult, in view of the information and other costs of the alternatives, to find ways in which habitual action might be considered rational in the sense of rational choice theories – for example, by arguing along the lines of Downs' discussion of the rationality of voters' ignorance. More seriously, it is disingenuous of Heath, following a well established tradition in rational choice literature,[5] to assimilate this technical sense of rationality to the looser sense – in which an action is rational if it has a reason – or to the other senses characteristic of much sociological explanation. The view that action is rational in some loose sense does not entail support for rational choice theory.

Finally, what of the suggestion that it is desirable to start from a general presumption of rationality? The suggestion is that the assumption of rationality frees the enquirer from parochialism or ethnocentricity by attributing equal humanity to other people(s) – and there is a clear implication in Heath's remarks that failure to apply the rational choice approach in the first instance would be a moral lapse on the part of social scientist, a rationalistic intellectual arrogance. Similar accusations have been directed at functionalists and others by writers of the ethnomethodological and symbolic interactionist traditions. Becker goes even further, suggesting that too many social scientists are tempted to hide their own lack of understanding behind allegations of 'ignorance and irrationality, values and their frequent and unexplained shifts, custom and tradition, the compliance somehow induced by social norms, or the ego and the id' (Becker, 1976: 13). Here, many of those who use other than rational choice analyses are accused of a kind of intellectual deceit, hiding their own ignorance behind their references to the irrationality of their subjects. Moral failings are by no means uncommon amongst academics – who could deny it? But it is a poor argument to invoke moral superiority in support of one's own position or to allege moral failure against one's intellectual opponents.

The technical meaning of rationality

In attempting to specify the basic assumptions of the rational choice approach it is particularly important to distinguish between those which are in some sense necessary to the overall approach and those which may be modified without serious damage. Consider the useful characterization advanced by Hollis as the basis for his critical discussions. First, actors are rational and their rationality is seen in strictly utilitarian terms. Actors have a given set of ends, they choose between them in a consistent fashion and, of the means of action available to them, they select those most appropriate to the realization of their chosen ends. The ends themselves are neither rational nor irrational, they are simply there. Second, actors are social atoms. 'They could be picked at random from their groups, because it made no difference who they were' (Hollis, 1979: 6). They are human individuals but they are not seen as essentially located within a social structure of positions and roles. Hollis disputes all three, by raising the question of the rationality of ends, by a limited endorsement of *homo sociologicus*, who is neither consistently selfish nor an atom, and by questioning the Humean proposition that only desire can motivate.[6] He does not question the identification of actors with human individuals.

Hollis presents powerful objections to the rational choice approach but there remain several problems with his characterization and the critique organized around it. The most obvious concern the second and third elements. Many critics have pointed to the assumption of egoism as an obvious weakness of the rational choice approach. It generates numerous paradoxes and it does not accord with everyday observation or with experimental results on behaviour in Prisoner's Dilemma games. Barry therefore suggests that there are areas where the psychological assumptions of the economic approach are inappropriate. For example, voting and many other activities concerned with the provision of public goods seem to require that there are people for whom participation in these activities 'is not a cost' (Barry, 1978: 178).

Most work in the rational choice tradition does indeed equate rationality with the invariable pursuit of self-interest, but it is far from clear that the equation is necessary to rational choice analysis.

Sen, a not unsympathetic critic, argues that traditional economic theory endows the actor 'with too little structure' (Sen, 1977a: 235). His argument depends on an important distinction between 'sympathy' and 'commitment'. While both oppose the idea of egoism in certain respects, the former (in which the sufferings of others may be upsetting, directly affecting one's own welfare) can be readily integrated within rational choice theory. Commitment, on the other hand, is less easy to assimilate: it provides a motive for choices that may run counter to the welfare of the chooser. In this case the identification of rationality with egoism may be avoided by endowing the actor with (a) more than one preference order and (b) an internal device for deciding which order should come into play at any particular point. Where Sen suggests a ranking of preference rankings,[7] Margolis tries to integrate altruism into the rational choice framework by defining an allocation rule operating over an egoistic and an altruistic preference order to determine what proportion of an individual's resources will be devoted to self-interest or group-interested ends. The assumption of egoism may be a problem for most rational choice arguments but it is not an intrinsic feature of the rational choice approach. However, we shall see that such modifications pose a serious problem for it. For the moment, note that the issue of altruism is dealt with by modifications to the 'internal' structure of the actor – not by reference to the normative discourses within which the actor's calculation is embedded.

As for social atomism, there seems to be two distinct issues here. One concerns the character of public goods and the other concerns the significance of social relations or social structure. In this approach, public goods are defined by reference to individuals and valued by reference to their preferences. Their essential feature is that they are not private – that is, they cannot be provided for one individual without also being available to others (generally to all members of the society).[8] Clean air and national defence are often cited as examples. The problem of public choice with regard to the provision of public goods is then defined by reference to individual preferences, so that the value of a unit of a public good is the sum of what all citizens are willing to pay for that unit. If the individuals are assumed to be narrowly self-interested, as in most discussions of the issue, then they will evaluate public goods only in terms of what they are worth to themselves as individuals. But even without the assumption of egoism, public goods can be valued only by reference to the values placed on them by individuals. Social needs are either directly reducible to individual needs or they are defined indirectly by the 'altruistic' preferences of individuals. The characterization of public goods is individualistic in the sense that individuals, in the last resort, are their only relevant customers.

The other respect in which the rational choice approach is said to be atomistic concerns the very limited role it accords to the effects of social structure or social relations on actors. Action is a function of decisions made by human beings in pursuit of their needs. 'Structural' effects enter in to the explanation of action only to the extent that they affect the conditions in which action takes place – that is, the incentives, opportunities and costs that individuals have to confront:

> . . . in this view social relations are treated as structures of choices available to actors, not as sources of norms to be internalized and acted out. Social relations are the structures within which actors, individuals and collective, deliberate upon goals, perceive and evaluate alternatives, and select courses of action (Przeworski, 1982: 311)

There are two points to notice here. First, it is one thing to regard social relations as the conditions within which actors choose, and quite another to regard them as the available choice themselves. The difference lies in the forms of assessment and evaluation that actors bring to bear on the situations in which they find themselves. Przeworski, and much of the rational choice literature, persistently erases that difference. Second, it would not be difficult to develop accounts of socialization and of the emergence and perpetuation of norms within a rational choice framework.[9] This aspect of what Hollis describes as social atomism may be a feature of many models but it is not a necessary element of the rational choice approach.

However, there is another sense in which the rational choice approach imposes severe 'structural' constrains on individuals' choices. At one level, 'rationality' involves little more than a certain consistency of choice, each actor being characterized by a coherent decision rule that is always followed; but no rational choice analysis can operate with such a general notion of rationality. The construction of rational choice models requires not only that actors are rational in this sense, but also that all actors within certain categories are rational in essentially the same way – for example, that all entrepreneurs are profit maximizers in a sense that is similarly defined for all entrepreneurs, that political parties are vote maximizers, that individuals are characterized by preference sets with similar mathematical structures, and so on. What is at issue here is a kind of structural determination which supposes that membership of the appropriate social category predisposes actors to employ the stylized forms of calculation attributed to them by the model. For example, it is often argued by Marxist and neo-classical economists alike that a process of natural selection operates amongst satisficing firms. Their calculations are concerned with obtaining a certain threshold level of return rather than with optimizing in any strict sense, so that the survivors are profit maximizers.[10] Here 'rationality' is imposed on the actors by the logic of their situation.

In fact it is not difficult to show that there may be conditions in which maximizers may become extinct.[11] Again, there is considerable evidence to show that quite distinct modes of economic calculation may be employed by firms operating within a single national economy.[12] The coexistence of distinct modes of calculation may pose difficulties for the construction of equilibrium models of market coordination, but it need not imply that some models of calculation are less rational than others. The point here is that a uniquely defined mode of economic calculation (profit maximizing) cannot be deduced from the postulate of rationality, and neither is it necessarily imposed by the rigours of the marketplace. In effect, rational choice models require a general postulate of rationality on the part of actors and a further, usually surreptitious, postulate – namely, that what is to count as rationality is uniquely defined within each category of actor recognized by the model. That is a remarkably strong requirement. It cannot be derived from the assumption that all actors are rational, but it is necessary to the construction of the formal deductive models that are the distinctive characteristic of this approach. Thus, to question this 'structural' approach is to question the underlying theoretical strategy of the rational choice approach.

We therefore have the following postulates.

1. *Rationality.* Rationality is a property of actors who have given, well-ordered ends. Actors are rational insofar they choose between them in a consistent fashion, and they select the most appropriate of available means for the pursuit of their ends.

2. *Homogeneity*. Stylized forms of rational calculation are uniquely defined for all actors within each category of actors recognized in the model.

3. *Individualism*. Actors are human individuals. Social ends can be defined and evaluated only in terms of actors' preferences. The location of actors within sets of social relations affects their behaviour only through the incentives, opportunities and costs that actors confront.

These formulations are still rather loose, but they should be sufficiently precise for the present critical discussion.

Rationality

We can leave the assumption of given ends for later discussion and concentrate here on different elements of the postulate of rationality. Note first that rationality is supposed to be attributable not only to courses of action but also to actors themselves. Rationality in this sense is a property of actors which they carry around with them from one situation to another. It is exhibited not only in the actor's behaviour in pursuit of some particular objectives but also in the relations between the actor's objectives themselves. Rational actors are supposed to have well-ordered preference structures which lead them to exhibit a consistent pattern of choices across a range of situations. I begin by questioning the attribution of rationality to the actor, in the case of human actors. I argue below that there may be actors other than human individuals (for example, firms or states), but the strong commitment to the assumption of rationality in the rational choice literature appears to be tied to the notion of the actor as human individual. I have already suggested that some doubt must be cast on that assumption by even a limited degree of self-knowledge.

But there are more substantial objections. It is well known that actors frequently behave in ways that appear not to conform to the postulate of rationality. For example, there may be major changes in actors' preferences with the result that they fail to exhibit a consistent pattern of choices over time. In this case, lack of consistency is the consequence of two or more distinct preference sets coming into play at different times. It might seem that the coexistence of distinct preference rankings could be reconciled with the postulate of rationality in a more complex model of the rational actor, for example, by invoking higher-order preference rankings or by some other allocation device within the actor.[13] But, as Hirschman recognizes, something more is required to overcome the inconsistency between preferences; namely, 'a battle with oneself that is marked by all kinds of feints, ruses, and strategic devices' (Hirschman, 1982: 71). The choice of terms here is significant. The 'battle' determines which of the two competing rationalities comes into play. Actors have some leverage over their wants by means of complex internal processes whose outcome in any given case is not determined in advance of the battle itself.[14] Another example is the all too familiar problem of weakness of will (incontinence) in which individuals knowingly act against their considered judgement. Short of denying that there are genuine cases of incontinence there is no alternative but to accept the conclusion of Davidson's careful discussion: (What is special in incontinence is that the actor cannot understand himself: he recognises, in his own intentional behaviour, something essentially surd' (Davidson, 1980: 42).

So much for rationality as an intrinsic feature of the actor, a property exhibited across the whole range of the actor's behaviour. The argument here does not depend on the use of, say, psychoanalysis as providing an alternative model. All that is needed is to bring out the implications of acknowledging features of human behaviour that few, if any, rational choice theorists would wish to deny. It is not difficult to find analogues of these features for firms, states and other non-human actors. Incontinence and important cases of preference change are inexplicable if rationality is supposed to be a property of the actor, rather than of courses of action. I return to this point below.

Now, many rational choice theorists will readily admit that their models are not realistic. We have seen, for example, that Downs follows Friedman in the view that models should be judged 'primarily by the accuracy of their predictions rather than by the reality of their assumptions' (Downs, 1957: 21). This view need not detain us long. Friedman's position is that the reason 'unrealistic' assumptions can yield 'realistic' predictions is that the unrealism is aimed precisely at excluding what is inessential: 'A hypothesis is important . . . if it abstracts the common and crucial elements from the mass of complex and detailed circumstances surrounding the phenomena to be explained' (ibid.: 14). There are serious epistemological objections to such positivistic accounts of model-building, but these need not concern us here. The objection to rational choice theory at this point is not to the fact that it uses simplifying assumptions, but rather to the character of the ones that it uses. There is of course no objection to the exclusion of what is inessential. But in the event of dispute over what is or is not inessential to the behaviour in question then predictive accuracy in itself is not a sufficient vindication of any model. There are strong grounds for arguing that some of the features excluded from rational choice models (incontinence, major preference changes, commitment) do have an important impact on human behaviour. If the assumptions excluding those features are not relaxed and the theory still predicts accurately then, as Toye notes, there is a serious theoretical problem: 'to explain how it is that the discrepancy between the assumptions and the true state of affairs is inconsequential' (Toye, 1976: 443).

A second set of problems concerns the tacit identification of 'rationality' and 'intentionality' in rational choice models. I argue in later chapters that intentional analysis, dealing with actors' ends, their calculations and choices need not presuppose rationality except in the loosest possible sense. Explanation of an action in terms of reasons certainly involves consideration of what is to count as a good or at least an adequate reason for that action. In other words, it raises questions of what forms of reasoning, and what forms of assessment of reasons, are available to actors in particular social contexts. Such questions may well involve 'consideration of the nature of rationality, of coherence and consistency' (Davidson, 1980: 241), but we should be wary of presuming too much by way of coherence or consistency on the part of the actor. Actors make choices on the basis of calculations involving a set of ends and some assessment of the conditions of action, but there is no reason to suppose that these choices will be 'rational' – except perhaps in the colloquial sense that any action having a reason may be considered rational. What are we to make, for example, of decisions based on the use of straws and a manual such as *I Ching*, or of a political leader who consults his or her astrologer before taking major decisions? For an example somewhat closer to home for most readers, there is the problem of incontinence noted above – that is, of action that goes against the actor's own considered judgement. Or, again, there are cases where decisions have to be made in which there can be no one well defined rational decision. Games theory offers numerous examples, but it is not difficult to find other cases.

Evaluation of the risks associated with nuclear power plants involves assigning probabilities to various remote possibilities. The probabilities themselves must be guessed: they are unknown, but assumed to be small. Different sets of guesses give different overall evaluations and may 'justify' very different decisions. In this case there are several possible courses of action, and decisions are certainly made between them. These may be 'rational' in the sense that estimates are made and arguments considered, but there is no one process that is 'rational' on any strict definition which necessitates one decision rather than another.

Homogeneity

The postulate of homogeneity within each category of actor distinguished by a model is a technical requirement for the building of rational choice models. There is nothing in the notion of rationality as a property of the actor that requires rationality to be uniquely defined for all actors, or all actors within a given structural category (such as consumer, entrepreneur and so on). It may be inconvenient for the would-be model-builders if some actors have preference structures with cardinal ordering and others have lexicographical orderings, or if profit maximization has no uniquely defined meaning within an economy, but consideration of these possibilities and their consequences cannot be ruled out in the name of an assumed rationality. If the postulate of rationality is itself undermined along the lines of the previous section, it is difficult to see how the postulate of homogeneity can survive. Although actors generally have reasons for their actions there are no grounds for supposing that the form of reasoning involved should be the same for all voters, all parties, or all entrepreneurs.

This essentially negative point against the structural determinism implicit in the rational choice models nevertheless has important positive implications. If rationality is a property of the actor *qua* actor and if all actors within a structural category are rational in basically the same way, then there is no need to enquire further into the conditions necessary for their reasoning to take the form that it does. It takes that form because they are actors belonging to the category of voters, leaders, entrepreneurs, or whatever, and that is all there is to it. The effect of disputing these postulates is therefore to raise two kinds of questions that tend to be obscured in rational choice arguments. First, since the forms of reasoning employed by actors cannot be assumed to be given exclusively as inherent properties of the structural positions occupied by the actors themselves, there are the questions of what forms of reasoning, and of assessment of reasons, are available to actors. Second, there are the questions of the conditions necessary for an actor's reasoning to take the form that it does. Some of these conditions will relate to the actor's internal features (the psychic organization of a human individual or the managerial structure of a firm); others will be social or cultural, involving the availability of particular conceptual or discursive techniques, access to information, and so on.

Individualism

The individualism of the rational choice approach involves a number of distinct elements: that actors are human individuals; that social ends should be defined and evaluated solely by reference to the ends of actors; and that their location within sets of social relations affects actors only through the incentives, opportunities and costs presented to them. The first of these is clearly not necessary for the construction of models of rational choice. An actor is a locus of decision and action, where the action is in some sense a consequence of the actor's decisions. I develop this concept of actor in later chapters but it has two important implications for the present discussion. First, it requires that actors employ some means of assessment of situations and of reaching and formulating decisions. Action involves some form of calculation or assessment, but that is no reason for supposing that it involves rationality in the sense of rational choice theory. The calculation does not necessarily lead to a choice of means most appropriate to the actor's ends. Nor does it always result in the actor's choices exhibiting a well-ordered structure of preferences. I have suggested above that the point of treating rationality, where it appears, as a property of the course of action (in fact of the calculations and assessments involved) is precisely to raise questions concerning the forms of calculation and assessment available to actors. To the extent that these are dependent on social conditions they must be regarded as part of the actor's situation rather than properties of the actor *qua* actor.

Second, as we have seen, human individuals are by no means the only type of actor in the modern world – firms, political parties and national states are examples of other types of actor. They are entities that make decisions on the basis of some assessment of their situation and act accordingly. There are important questions to be asked about the kinds of reasoning employed by such actors and about how their decisions are transformed into action. But many rational choice theorists, and most of their critics, do seem to assume that these other types of 'actor' are ultimately reducible to human individuals. The methodological individualism of this position is frequently combined with a commitment to the principles of liberal political philosophy. I argue in Chapter 4, 'Two kinds of person', that there may be significant social actors other than, and irreducible to, human individuals. If the forms of reasoning employed by actors depend on conditions some of which are social in the sense of not being inherent features of the actors themselves, then social life is not reducible to the constitutive behaviour of actors. If that point can be admitted in the case of human actors then there should be no difficulty about admitting firms and other loci of decision and action to the status of actor.

The second element is that social ends should be defined and evaluated solely by reference to the ends of actors. This raises questions of political theory to which I return in the final chapter, 'Liberal individualism and corporate actors'. For the moment, one comment should be made. It seems clear that the individualism of liberal political philosophy need not depend on methodological individualism in social explanation, although the two positions are frequently linked. What happens if we separate them, if we admit (a) that there are actors other than human individuals; (b) that many social decisions are those of actors (governments or government departments, The National Trust, and so on) – and that they are not merely the more or less adequate aggregations of the decisions of a multitude of human individuals? Liberal political theory might well survive these points, but it would require considerable argument to establish what the theory of public goods seems to assume – namely, that the preferences of individual citizens should be the ultimate point of reference for the determination of social ends. A substantial literature has been devoted to problems of aggregating individual preferences into social decisions, following Arrow's argument that, under plausible assumptions, individual preferences may not aggregate into a well defined collective choice. Or, again, Rawls has made use of Prisoner's Dilemma arguments showing that the overall result of individual choices may depart substantially from the outcome most preferred by those same individuals.[15]

Such arguments establish problems in the theory of public goods but they still retain the basic assumption that social needs should be defined and evaluated solely by reference to the preferences of individuals. That assumption is problematic in at least two important respects. First, social ends are the product of some actual or hypothetical decision-making procedure – debates amongst elected representatives, delegate conferences, Cabinet and executive meetings, or whatever. There is no reason to assume either that decisions reached through generally agreed procedures should correspond to some aggregate of individual preferences, or that individual preferences will be independent of those procedures and the choices on offer. The distribution of seats in national elections rarely corresponds to the proportions of votes cast for competing parties. It does not follow that different electoral procedures should be adopted, or indeed that the distribution of votes would remain the same under changed electoral arrangements.[16] Second, it is far from clear that human individuals are the only actors to be considered in the process of defining social ends. Companies and trades unions, for example, are two kinds of actor that have legitimate interests in national economic policy objectives, and their concerns are not mere aggregates of the interests of their shareholders, employees or their members.

Finally, consider the claim that it is only through incentives, costs and opportunities that an actor's location within sets of social relationships has effects – in particular, that preference structures and basic forms of rational calculation are given properties of the actor. In the very short term, and for most actors, it may be entirely reasonable to regard their objectives and forms of thought as effectively given: in general people are not wildly unpredictable, and it is usually possible to reconstruct reasons for what they do. However, it does not follow that their ends and forms of thought must be accepted as given for the purposes of social theory or longer-term political analysis. We have seen that an unjustifiable and often surreptitious structural determinism is often slipped in at this point. It amounts to the view that only those structural social categories of interest to the model-builder are relevant to the ends of the actors and the forms of reasoning they employ, and that what is rational for the actors is uniquely determined by those categories. Rationality is making choices in circumstances which constitute rationality and therefore leave the actor no choice: rational choices are given in the logic of the actor's situation. That view may have an heuristic value in some cases, and if nothing more were claimed there would be little to dispute. But, as I have argued above, to assume that actors' ends and forms of thought are given is to proscribe questions of considerable theoretical and political importance. Other chapters advance a similar argument against taking a given distribution of interests as the starting-point for political analysis. Actors' ends and their forms of thought do change, partly as a function of what is available to choose from, and the point of several forms of political activity is to try to redirect them. The questions of the conditions of existence of certain ends and forms of thought, and of how those conditions might be changed have an obvious political importance.

Now, it might be objected at this point that changes can often be assimilated to the notion of given ends. Becker, for example, claims that changing preferences for market goods are themselves explicable in terms of stable underlying preferences (Becker, 1976: 5). That may be so in some cases, but the response misses the fundamental point. The objection here is not simply that the rational choice approach neglects important dynamic elements, but also that it treats actors, precisely because they are rational, as characterized by one form of assessment of their ends and conditions of action. There may well be contexts in which that is not an unreasonable assumption, but in many, perhaps most, political contexts actors have several forms of assessment available to them. Racist and sexist discourses are available to many British workers, which make it possible for them to formulate objectives that contradict those of worker solidarity against management leading, for example, to a failure to respect picketing by blacks or women. In this case, it would be entirely circular to account for the formulation of one set of objectives over another in terms of the objectives themselves. The objectives formulated will depend not only on 'internal' properties of the individuals concerned and the forms of assessment available to them, but also on other conditions, including the work of trades unions, political parties and individuals in support of some objectives and against others. The effect of insisting that the assumption of rationality and given ends, whether overt or underlying, should be the starting-point for all analysis is to foreclose serious investigation of major problems concerning the effects of social conditions and political forces on the formation of political interests and concerns and how they might be changed.

The Marxist hybrid

I have argued that what the rational choice approach has to offer political analysis is rather limited. But what of 'the new Marxism of collective action' (Lash and Urry, 1984), those combinations of rational choice theory and Marxism which display an overt concern with the political conditions necessary for radical social change? While it hardly merits the designation 'a new theoretical paradigm in sociology' (ibid.: 45), it clearly represents a large and growing body of work. I consider Elster's influential contribution to this literature in a later chapter. For the present, consider Adam Przeworski's work, one of the most ambitious and developed of these attempted combinations in the area of political analysis, as an illustration of the weaknesses of this 'new Marxism'. In *Capitalism and Social Democracy* (1985) and *Paper Stones* (1986), Przeworski offers two distinct but complementary accounts of the class compromise which he sees as characteristic of contemporary Western European capitalist societies. One argument examines the consequences, for a socialist movement, of choosing to enter the parliamentary and electoral arena, which has the effect of locking the movement into the logic of party competition. It therefore aims to win electoral majorities under conditions in which, at best, no more than a large minority is directly susceptible to a socialist class appeal. The result of engaging in the logic of party competition is to generate powerful reasons for the party to dilute its socialist principles and class appeal.

Przeworski's other argument considers whether workers' pursuit of their material interests will lead them to opt for socialism. Even on the assumption that socialism would be better than capitalism at satisfying material interests, there are conditions in which it would be rational for workers to prefer capitalism. These are, first, that the process of transition to socialism would involve some deterioration of material conditions and, second, that a class compromise can be established involving low levels of wage militancy in return for reliable levels of capitalist investment. Under conditions of corporatism in capitalist democracies, it would be irrational for workers to prefer socialism. These arguments share the conclusion that the pursuit of material interests within the conditions of capitalist democracy may be desirable, but that it should not be confused with the struggle for socialism.

Przeworski's hybrid combines the weaknesses of two strains of political analysis. The treatment of economic agents as bearers of functions defined by their structural position is indeed a weak point in much Marxist argument, and Przeworski is absolutely right to question it in his response to Roemer. Unfortunately, his alternative vision of social relations as 'structures of choices available to actors' (Przeworski, 1982: 311) merely reproduces the same problem in a slightly different form. If actors' choices are inscribed in the logic of their situations then the insistence on *choice* as an alternative to structural or 'sociological' accounts is merely gestural. With one significant exception, Przeworski's analysis of choices suffers in all the problems of rational choice models identified above. In particular, the choices and their consequences discussed by Przeworski are those of idealized rational actors endowed with a given set of ends. For all the references to the capitalist democracies of Western Europe there is no discussion of the specific forms of political calculation and evaluation employed by, or available to, parties or workers in those societies, and therefore no discussion of the political and other conditions on which they depend. In that sense he presents a speculative account of what politics in these societies would be like if parties and workers were indeed the 'rational' creatures he imagines.

His one significant departure from the standard rational choice approach merely compounds that problem, for there are crucial points in his argument that depend on classes being regarded as collective actors. The difficulty here does not lie in the notion of collective actors as such, but rather in the particular collective actors required for Przeworski's argument. To say that actors are loci of decision and action is to say there are specifiable mechanisms for reaching decisions and means of action. In that respect human individuals, national and local governments, capitalist entrepreneurs are all actors. Classes are not. Reference to classes as actors is either allegorical or, at best, a shorthand for a set of specific actors (human individuals and various organizations) that are thought to be identifiable with the interests of particular classes. Much Marxist analysis slides uneasily between these usages, and Przeworski's accounts are no exception. The effect of introducing rational choice formalism into the structure of his Marxist arguments is to preclude one of the strongest features of the best Marixst political analyses – namely, a hard-headed assessment of social and political conditions, the forces at work in them, and the room for manoeuvre for serious socialist politics.

Conclusions

I have suggested that rational choice theory involves postulates of rationality, homogeneity and individualism, none of which are acceptable. Against the postulate of rationality as a property of the actor, and therefore its actions, I have advanced two kinds of objection.

The first objection concerns the implications of acknowledging features of behaviour that few could deny. Weakness of will or incontinence and some kinds of major preference change cannot be reconciled with the rational choice notion of rationality as a property of the actor. I have suggested that an actor should be regarded as a locus of decision and action, where the action is a consequence of the actor's decisions. Action therefore depends, at least in part, on the actor's use of some form of reasoning, some means of reaching and formulating decisions. Rationality, where it appears, is a function of the forms of reasoning employed by actors, not a property inherent in the actors themselves.

The second objection concerns the identification of intentionality and rationality. Intentional analysis certainly presupposes that actions have reasons, but it does not presuppose rationality in any strong sense of the term. The postulate of homogeneity is a technical requirement for the construction of rational choice models that is often introduced surreptitiously. It implies a remarkably strong structural determination of the actor's forms of thought that must seriously undermine all but a merely gestural concept of choice: actors' choices are effectively determined by their structural location.

The point of disputing these two postulates is in no way to deny that actors have reasons for their actions, but it is to raise serious questions concerning those reasons which cannot be posed within the rational choice approach. These are, in particular, what forms of reasoning are employed by actors, what forms are available to them, and what conditions are necessary for an actor's reasoning to take the form that it does. To raise these questions is to undermine an important part of the individualism of rational choice models. The incentives, opportunities and costs presented to actors are certainly affected by their location in sets of social relations, but, except perhaps in the very short term, the consequences of actors' social location cannot be restricted to those effects alone.

A further element of the individualism of the rational choice approach is the assumption that actors are human individuals. That assumption is not a necessary feature of intentional analysis. I have argued that there are important actors other than human individuals – for example, government agencies and capitalist enterprises – but that classes are not amongst them. To say that actors are loci of decision and action is to say that they have identifiable mechanisms for reaching decisions and means of action. Reference to classes as collective actors is therefore either allegorical or else a shorthand reference to a variety of other actors. I return to the implications of this last point in Chapter 5.

Where do these arguments leave us? An initially attractive feature of rational choice theory is its insistence that actors choose between alternative courses of action, that they have reasons for their choices and that their choices have consequences. Although these points seem to me indisputable, there is no sense in which the rational choice model of the actor follows from them. Whatever the rational choice approach gains from that insistence is soon dissipated in its evacuation of many of the problems that actors' choices pose for social analysis. Rational choice theory evades these problems by taking as its starting-point a limited model of the individual actor, and by using that model as the foundation of its inquiries into the interaction of a plurality of actors. It is this that leads to its methodological individualism, its postulate of rationality and its peculiar version of the structural determination of actors' forms of thought. Rational choice models certainly endow the actor with 'too little structure' (Sen, 1977a: 235) but the problems go much further. Actors make choices that are rarely mere reflections of their social locations, and they frequently make them as the result of some reasoning process. These points raise questions which take us beyond the level of the individual actor: questions of the forms of calculation employed by, or available to, actors; questions of the social conditions on which they depend; and questions of how the forms of calculation available to actors themselves depend on the actors' location within particular sets of social relationships. To insist on the significance of choices is therefore to suggest something of the complexity that is unavoidably neglected in the formalism of rational choice analysis and, for that matter, in other forms of methodological individualism.

Notes

1. See Becker, 1976 for a forceful statement of this claim.
2. See the discussions in Tomlinson, 1981; Toye, 1976.
3. Hirschman, 1982; Margolis, 1982; Sen, 1977b.
4. The papers in Willer and Anderson, 1981 and Willer, 1987 are interesting examples.
5. Cf. the passage from Downs quoted in my opening paragraph.
6. Hollis, 1981, 1983.
7. See the Introduction to Sen, 1982.
8. Olson, 1965, 1982.
9. Taylor, 1982.
10. For example, Becker, 1976; Friedman, 1953.
11. Winter, 1964, 1971, and Nelson and Winter, 1982.
12. Cutler *et al.*, 1978, esp. part II; Williams *et al.*, 1983.
13. Sen, 1977a, 1982; Margolis, 1982; Hirschman, 1982.
14. There is an extensive discussion of these devices and stragems in Elster, 1979.
15. Arrow, 1963; Rawls, 1971; see also the excellent surveys in Barry and Hardin, 1982 and Sen, 1977b.
16. The general argument here is that electoral outcomes can hardly be analysed as more or less adequate reflections of the interests or preferences of the electorate. See Hindess, 1983, chs. 1 and 2.

3 'Interests' in political analysis

'Interests' is one of the most widely used and most disputed concepts in political discussion. To say that a policy, practice, or state of affairs is in the interests of an individual or group is to suggest that the individual or group would somehow benefit from it. That much, at least, is generally agreed. Interests in that sense may be regarded as providing explanations of action, and many commentators would agree with Connolly's assertion: 'Every explanatory theory of politics includes somewhere in its structure assumptions about persons and their real interests' (Connolly, 1983: 73). Interests are used to provide justification for actions said to be performed on behalf of others – for example, by politicians or social workers. Because they are thought to provide explanations they may also be employed in the course of attempts to estimate the likely actions of others.

Socialist political analysis in Britain, for example, is often conducted in terms of the actions of classes and of certain social categories (women, blacks, youth) and the scope for conflicts or alliances between them. What is at stake here is the idea that membership of a class or category defines an interest that exists independently of the practices of political parties and other organizations, and irrespective of whether the individuals concerned recognize it as their interest.

The interests of a class or social category are supposed to be a consequence of its position in relation to other classes and categories. Identified in this way, they can perform a number of functions in socialist political discussion. First, they may be used in explanation as, for example, in the argument that the Labour Party gains working class support insofar as it appeals to working-class interests, and loses support insofar as it betrays those interests or reduces that appeal.[1] Second, interests may be used to justify or evaluate some aspects of party, union or government policies, which may be supported or opposed in the name of the interests of the working class, pensioners, and other interest groups. Third, they may appear as features of the situation to be taken into account in assessing the potential support that may be won for some particular policy or programme.

Perhaps the best known theoretical foundations for such a concept of interests is provided by Marxism which regards class interests as, in some sense, given in the structure of class relations and proceeds to the analysis of political institutions and organizations as their more or less adequate embodiments or representations. Elsewhere I have argued that that approach has unacceptable political consequences.[2] Indeed there is an important sense in which it makes political analysis redundant: if politics is reducible to the representation of interests given by some underlying social reality, then the representations themselves – the practices of parties, unions, state agencies, and the like – are clearly of secondary importance. Rather than consider the social distribution of the interests that are effective in political life as given to politics from elsewhere, this chapter argues that we should consider instead the conditions in which political concerns and interests are formed and the ways in which their invocation may play a role in political life. For the moment, note that, if interests are regarded both as explaining political life and as given by a social reality which underlies political activity, then they are supposed to be 'objective' in two rather different ways.

The first is relatively unproblematic: interests are objective in that they do not depend on any subjective awareness on the part of those whose interests they are supposed to be. What is involved here is simply the idea that membership of some particular category of persons, considered in abstraction from other aspects of their lives, identifies an interest vis-à-vis members of other relevant categories. Considered only in their capacities as taxpayers, for example, those who pay the highest rate of income tax have an interest in the reduction of that rate. Or, again, individuals from different groups within a community will have different interests in proposals for its redevelopment. Reference to interests in this sense says nothing about the motivations of the individuals in question: it merely involves some plausible argument as to how the well-being of, say, higher-rate taxpayers would be affected by certain changes in the tax structure. There may be as many sets of differential interests of this kind as there are social differences and divisions.

Difficulties arise whenever interests of this kind are also said to be significant causal elements in social and political life. Marxist class analysis takes this further step when it claims that the interests of classes, and of individuals considered as members of classes, have significant political effects. They have an objective causal and explanatory character that socialist parties have to recognize as a precondition of effective political practice. I indicated some of the problems with this notion of 'objective' interests in Chapter 1. What should be noted here is that there is more to the notion of objective interests than the assumption that the content of those interests be given to politics from elsewhere. Indeed, in the concluding chapter of his general discussion of the forms of collective action, Tilly clearly recognizes that there may be a problem with treating collective interests as given. For example: 'Mobilization, collective action, and acquisition or loss of power, frequently alter a groups' interests' (Tilly, 1978: 228). Here, Tilly assigns a dynamic character to the distribution of collection interests, but continues to treat the division of the population into the groups or categories to which those interests are assigned as given in an extra-political structure of social relations. The interests of a group or category are determined by its positions in that structure, with the result that the contents of interests may change with the relative positions of the contending groups. Only if the basic structure of class relations is an extra-political given in this sense can politics be regarded as ultimately reducible to struggles between them.

That presumption of a given, politically significant, distribution of the population into distinct interest groups or categories may have a limited and short-term plausibility. At any particular moment many political interests and concerns must be regarded as effectively given – but only in the sense that they cannot be changed readily or in the short term by any of the forces currently engaged in political activity. But to say that many interests have to be accepted as given for the purposes of immediate practical policies is not to say that they have to be accepted as theoretically given in political analysis nor that they should be regarded as unchangeable in the longer term. The argument here is not that politics alone, still less political activity in the immediate term, is the source of all effective political interests and concerns. Rather it is that the activities of governments, parties and other movements have consequences that are too important to be ignored – not only for the forms of collective action and organization that may be adopted, but also for the formation and distribution of political interests within the population.

But such explanatory uses of interests are by no means restricted to the Marxist tradition. Weber, for example, treats values and 'material' interests as giving distinct and generally opposed reasons for action. Or, again, the pluralist tradition in American political science analyses political life in terms of the interactions of more or less organized interest groups, on the assumption 'that most people participate in those areas they care about the most' (Polsby, 1959: 235). The interests at stake in political life are therefore the ones that people organize around and campaign for. I suggested in Chapter 1 that the most influential critics of that tradition do not dispute the explanatory use of interests but argue instead that certain interests may be prevented from providing an effective basis for political action – either because they are excluded from the sites in which decisions are taken or because the agents whose interests they are fail to recognize them.

These examples are restricted to questions of political analysis, but they do illustrate widespread features of the explanatory uses of concepts of interests in social enquiry. First, interests are supposed to be relatively stable properties of actors, and their specification normally involves some reference to the possibility of intentional action. They serve to identify some of the objectives that actors set themselves, or would set themselves if only they were in a position to do so. Interests belong to that broad class of entities that have been supposed, by social scientists and others, to provide actors with ends, and therefore with reasons for action. Other members of that class include values, preferences, wants, fears, dislikes, needs, habits, and impulses.

How do interests relate to, and differ from, these other items that may provide actors with reasons for action? In *The Passions and the Interests* (1977), Hirschman has shown that there have been considerable changes in the way interests are conceptualized in relation to other possible sources of motivation. In modern times, interests are generally thought to differ from values in a relatively clear way: to promote actors' interests is supposed to be beneficial to them, while to promote their values need not benefit them at all. Many would follow Weber in suggesting that an actor's values are, or may be, freely chosen, but no-one would suggest that interests are a matter of choice in the same sense. Or, again, interests differ from impulses in being relatively stable. But what of needs, wants, and all the rest? The question is frequently addressed, and there is little sign of agreement on the answer.[3]

Second, interests appear to provide an explanatory link between action and social structure. On the one hand, actors have interests by virtue of the social conditions in which they find themselves, as members of a particular class, sex, age group, or community, as victims of monopoly power or multinational companies, and so on. On the other hand, those interests provide actors with reasons for action. The problem here, of course, is that different features of the conditions in which actors find themselves may be used to specify different, and sometimes conflicting, sets of interests. The identification of such cross-pressures and their effects has been an important theme in several traditions of political analysis, for example, in diiscussions of the affluent worker thesis, status inconsistency, contradictory class locations.[4]

Finally, the link between action and social structure raises the question of *real* interests. If interests are things that actors possess as a function of their membership of a class or social category or some other feature of their social situation, then the possibility must be considered that actors may be mistaken about the identification of their own interests. For example, children, the elderly and the insane may be regarded as having, at best, a limited capacity to identify their interests, thereby providing rationales for the intervention of relatives and professional agencies. In political analysis, the possibility of the misrecognition of interests has been elaborated in many different ways as, for example, in Marxist notions of false consciousness, in Lukes' three-dimensional view of power, and in Gramscian notions of hegemony and rule by consent. Some of the problems with these positions were considered in Chapter 1, but it should be noted here that this notion of interests takes us beyond the recognition that an actor's interests may be specified in different ways by both the actor concerned and various other actors – or by the same actor in different circumstances. It could further be suggested that some of those interests are more real than others. The notion that actors have real interests, and that they may act on a mistaken view of what they are, then poses the problem of how to distinguish those real interests from the pretenders. For liberal political thought, with its concern for liberty of the individual, this problem is more than merely academic: it poses the further problem of assesssing the conditions in which actors may reasonably be judged incapable of recognizing their own interests, so that others may be justified in acting on their behalf. The debate on these problems is interminable.[5]

I argue that many of these questions, and the debates around them, stem from a failure to recognize the specific place of interests and related concepts in the explanation of action. First, interests have consequences only insofar as they provide some actor or actor with reasons for action. Second, the specification of interests is always open to dispute: interests are not given properties of individuals or groups. In particular, they should not be regarded as structurally determined. Third, problems of the correct definition of interests in social analysis are frequently misconceived; but there are important questions to be asked about the conditions in which actors will acknowledge one set of interests rather than another, or in which the appeal to certain interests can be effective. Finally, I argue that the use of interests as a form of explanation of action is not necessarily wrong but is seriously incomplete.

Interests and actions
Reasons and decisions
An actor is a locus of decision and action, where the action is, in part, a consequence of the actor's decisions. Human individuals are actors in this sense, as are state agencies, capitalist enterprises, political parties, and various other bodies. Analysis of actors' actions, the struggles they engage in and the relations between them, therefore includes analysis of their decisions. The notion of interests that are real but fail to provide the actors whose interests they are with reasons for action has little to offer by way of explanation of their actions – although others may sometimes claim to act in their name. On the other hand, there is little point in insisting on the *reality* of certain interests if they are recognized by those whose interests they are said to be. It makes no difference to the effectiveness of those interests in providing actors with reasons for action that they might, on some account of real interests, be mistaken. What the appeal to interests that are real but not acted upon by those whose interests they are usually suggests is a problem of explanation. What has to be explained is not so much the decisions that actors take, and the reasons for them, but rather an absence: a non-existent state of affairs (in which actors do pursue their real interests) is posed as a measure of the present and the problem is to explain away its

non-existence. The problem is why certain objectives, identified in terms of actors' real interests, are not pursued, rather than the investigation of those that are.

Contrary to Connolly's claim, quoted above, explanatory accounts of politics need make no assumptions about actors' real interests. If the concept of interests is to play any part in the analysis of action it can only be because interests are thought to relate to particular actors' reasons for action and therefore also to their actions. Actors formulate decisions and act on some of them. They might also act on the basis of decisions that are not formulated, and some of those may involve reasons which the actor refuses to acknowledge. As an explanatory concept, 'interests' refers to some of the conscious or unconscious reasons for actors' decisions, to act or to do nothing, to support some policy or party, to oppose it or to abstain, and so on. Their decisions may relate to their own interests or to those of others, and they may relate to reasons of other kinds, to values, sudden impulses, or whatever. Whether or not the word 'interests' forms part of the reasons for a decision does not necessarily matter. Interests can also be said to provide reasons for a decision if those reasons relate to the benefit or well-being of some actor or actors. The interests of employees in a factory may be said to be involved in a decision to resist its closure, even if the word 'interests' is not used in their deliberations.

Interests that provide no actor with reasons for action can have no social consequences. They are effective, in the sense of having social consequences insofar as they provide reasons for actors' decisions – that is, by virtue of their conceptual and discursive character. They must be formulated if they are to be perceived, and if they are not themselves formulated then they must be reflected in reasons for action that might reasonably be attributed to the relevant actors. This point may seem trivial, but we shall see that it has important consequences for the ways in which interests may be said to have political repercussions.

To understand what is at stake here, consider a rather different approach to the discussion of interest – this time in terms of the visual imagery of perception. The problem with this approach is that it can divert attention from what is required for the actor or actors to formulate reasons for action. If interests are things that may or may not be *perceived*, then what has to be explained is actors' perceptions. The question is then: under what conditions will they see, or fail to see..? It is a problem of actors' subjectivity and the effects of social conditions on that subjectivity. To say that interests relate to actors' reasons is to insist on a further set of questions concerning the conceptual or discursive conditions which make it possible for certain reasons to be formulated at all.

Now, what is missing from this treatment of interests in terms of formulated reasons is an account of those cases in which actors may be unwilling or unable to acknowledge some of the reasons for their actions.[6] Consider an elected government which ignores popular feelings concerning schools, hospitals, and a variety of other issues until just before an election, and then professes a sincere concern for those issues and promises improvements after the election. There are grounds for doubting the genuineness of that concern and ascribing its appearance to an interest in re-election. The reasons are clear enough but they will not be directly acknowledged.

There are other kinds of cases in which some of the reasons for action are unconscious and therefore remain unacknowledged.[7] Nevertheless, even in those cases, the reasons we attribute to the actor must be within that actor's linguistic capacity: that is, the actor must possess the vocabulary and means of assessment in terms of which those reasons could be formulated. Thus, whether the reasons that are said to relate to actors' interests are conscious or unconscious, they still raise questions of the conceptual and linguistic conditions of their possibility.

Finally, interests not only provide reasons that enter in to some process of assessment, but they are also, at least in principle, products of assessment themselves. On some accounts of action there may be reasons for action that do not themselves depend on assessment. Two, possibly three, of Weber's four types of action involve reasons of this kind. There are certainly problems about the characterization of such reasons, but they need not concern us here. To say that a policy or state of affairs is in the interests of an actor is to say that the actor would benefit from its implementation. It follows that what the actor's interests are in any given case is always potentially open to dispute. Interests are reasons that may themselves require further justification: they depend on assessment or the possibility of assessment. To locate interests within the realm of reasons that are themselves open to assessment is to say that the range of possible interests depends on the forms of assessment available to the relevant actors. Interests depend on the forms of calculation and means of proposing objectives, and of locating themselves and others in relation to those objectives, that are available to actors.

Interests and forms of assessment

Interests depend on forms of assessment: if they are to provide actors with reasons for action it must be possible to present them as the outcome to some process of assessment ('this strike is in the miners' interests because . . .'). What is involved here is the construction of an account of the actors' situation and of how they might be affected by particular changes or actions. In many situations, a variety of distinct and competing ways of assessing the interests of specific actors or groups of actors will be available. Assessments may be produced using cost–benefit analysis, horoscopes, geomancy, or what seems to us some more rational process. The point is simply that they are the result of some definite process employing particular conceptual means of specifying the actors' situation and possible changes within it. Interests are the product of assessment. They do not appear arbitrarily out of nowhere, they are not structurally determined nor can they be regarded as fixed or given properties of actors. (I return below to the issue of structural determination.) Interests are always open to dispute, and the interests of particular actors may be differently identified by the actors concerned and other agencies, or by the same actors at different times. Does this matter? Does the assignment of conflicting sets of interests to the same actors pose problems for the use of interests in social analysis?

Consider the question of what interests are, or may be, effective in particular sites of action, social relations or struggles. The first point to notice is that this question has nothing to do with questions of the accuracy or 'validity' of the attribution of interests. Interests are effective, in the sense of having social consequences, not because their attribution is valid, but rather because of the part they play in the reaching of decisions by some actor or actors. In the 1984–85 miners' strike in Britain, for example, distinct and conflicting conceptions of the miners' interests were effective. The miners' interests were at issue in the decisions of miners who supported the strike and in the decisions of those miners who opposed it. Which account of the miners' interests was correct was itself a matter of dispute, and the conduct of that dispute had consequences in the changing pattern of support for the opposed positions – but it was not the 'validity' of one attribution of interests over another that determined its level of support.

Second, to say that interests are subject to assessment is to say that their specification is open to dispute. For example, there may be disagreement as to the consequences of the pursuit of a particular assessment of an interest. Political conclusions derived from some assessment of working-class interests (or those of the miners or owner-occupiers) are always in danger of being undermined by alternative assessments.

Third, to say that interests are effective insofar as they provide reasons for action is to say that they are reasons for the actions of particular agencies, for individuals or for organizations such as governments, trades union or political parties. The interests involved in those reasons may be their own or ones which they attribute to others. Trades unions may, for example, calculate both their own interests and those of their members, and they may also calculate the interests of various other constituencies – the labour movement, the working class, the unemployed and so on. Other agencies may also claim to identify the interests of those constituencies and to act in pursuit of them. However, there is no reason to suppose that the interests of the unions or their members as calculated by these various agencies will coincide, still less that they will necessarily correspond to union members own assessments of their interests. Indeed, there have been well known cases where a union's politics conflict with those of a majority of their members.

Interests that have social consequences are not always those acknowledged or acted upon by the actors to whom they are attributed, and it is not the validity of the attribution that secures their effectiveness. To investigate the political repercussions of interests it is necessary to begin with the assessments of interests (their own and others) by various agencies (unions, parties, faction, individuals) and with the decisions they make on the basis of those (and other) assessments. There are no grounds for supposing that the interests assigned by various agencies to particular actors – to unions, the working class owner-occupiers, or whatever – will coincide. Nor, of course, should we assume that actors' own assessments of their interests have any effective priority in determining the decisions of those who claim to represent them. Political parties and other organizations make their own assessments of the interests of those they may claim to represent, they do not merely aggregate them. They do more than merely aggregate by working to create or specify the content of the interests they claim to represent. They may also do much less, insofar as they fail to represent the concerns acknowledged by their members or supporters. In these respects, the interests represented by political parties cannot be seen simply as the more or less adequate reflection of the distribution of interests within the electorate.

To say that interests depend on forms of assessment is to say, finally, that their attribution is neither arbitrary nor a matter of entirely free choice. Interests are effective only insofar as they play a part in providing reasons for actors' decisions. Actors make decisions and try to act on them, but that does not mean that there are no limits to what they are able to decide or that they can always act on their decisions. The decisions they formulate and the reasons behind them depend on the discursive means available to them, and actors have very little choice over the nature of those means. Actors may work to change how they think, but they cannot adopt new discursive forms at will. Consider again the example of the 1984–85 miners' strike. The claims of those miners who supported the strike and the claims of those who opposed it involve assessments of miners' interests that were far from arbitrary. Both attributions of interests were products of definite modes of assessments of the miners' interests well established in British mining communities. Both attributions of interests could provide reasons for decisions within the decision-making procedures of the miners' union. Other conceptions of the miners' interests were certainly possible but, to be effective, they would have had to provide possible reasons within the current means of reaching decisions and of assessing what their interests are. For example, the claim that the miners' interests consisted of the sacrifice of one goat for every ten members of a pithead branch would have no purchase within current forms of assessment and decision-making!

Actors are clearly limited in the extent to which they can choose the forms of assessment employed by or available to them. But that is not to say that the forms of assessment they do employ are uniquely determined by their social location. Rational choice theories of political or economic behaviour tend to assume that actors' forms of thought are uniquely determined by their rationality and social location: political leaders and ordinary voters may calculate in different ways as a function of their different positions, but they are both essentially rational. These positions are discussed in other chapters. What should be noted here is that, if actors' forms of thought are given by their social location or if rationality is a property of the actor *qua* actor, then there is no difficulty about what interests they will identify or what conclusions they will draw from them. The problem with these positions is that, in many contexts, the forms of assessment available to actors allow the formulation of a variety of distinct and conflicting reasons, objectives and decisions. This possibility provides considerable scope for dispute and also for the persuasion, propaganda, and other forms of political work intended to change people's assessment's of their interests and how they might be served. What interests or reasons for action are acknowledged in any given case depends not only on the forms of assessment available to the actors, but also on other conditions, including the work of the individuals, political parties, unions, and other agencies in support of some assessment of interests and against others.

Validity
Finally, to distinguish questions of what interests are effective from questions of the validity of their attribution is not to say that questions of validity therefore have no place. The attribution of interests implies the claim that those whose interests they are said to be will benefit in some way from their successful pursuit. The validity of such claims is of obvious importance to political actors (including many social scientists). Nevertheless, they are open to question in at least two respects: there is, first, the question of whether the supposed benefits are really benefits at all; and, second, the question of whether they are likely to be realized by pursuit of the interests specified. In some cases there may be clear and unambiguous answers to such questions – there would be little dispute, for example, about the claim that the interests of the British people are served in the maintenance of elementary public health measures. But, in general, the attribution of interests is not so clear-cut, and an important part of political debate consists in disputes over what they are and how they might best be pursued. Such disputes can have significant effects on the balance of political forces around the issues in dispute – and sometimes more generally when the disputed issues are part of a wider ideological polarisation.

Interests and social relations

Perhaps the most common approach to the explanation of interests is to locate them in terms of some concept of social structure. Actors are said to have interests as a consequence of their position as members of a group or class in relation to members of other groups or classes. Most forms of Marxism analyse the distribution of interests in terms of a structure of class relations, which in turn is supposed to be largely a function of definite relations of production. Sociological critics of Marxism, such as Dahrendorf and Parkin, see the structure of class relations rather differently, but continue to account for interests in class terms. Others analyse the distribution of interests in terms of group, rather than class, membership. These positions share a view of interests as reflecting actors' location within a structure of social relations. The concept of interests then appears to provide an explanatory link between structural location and actors' behaviour.

What are the implications of the claim that actors do indeed make decisions and act on them for this 'structural' analysis of interests? I suggested in the Introduction that the concept of actor outlined above cannot be reconciled with any concept of society as a functioning whole governed by some unifying principle (central values, mode of production, or whatever) and producing necessary effects on actors as a consequence of their position in its structure. This section develops that general argument with specific reference to the concept of interests. I argue first that interests do not function as a mere transmission between actors' social location and their behaviour, and then move on the consider other ways in which actors' social location may have a bearing on their reasons for action and assessments of interests.

There are several reasons why the idea of interests as an explanatory link between action and social structural location is unsatisfactory. Consider first the notion of *real* interests – interests that are supposed to have an objective reality but are not necessarily recognized or acted upon by those whose interests they are thought to be. Interests attributed to an actor or actors that are said to be real, but nevertheless fail to provide those actors with reasons for action, provide reasons only for the action of other actors who may claim to recognize those interests without necessarily sharing them. In this case, real interests are ascribed to those for whom they do not provide reasons for action. Concepts of interests that are real but not recognized by those to whom they are ascribed may well have social effects – for example, in the actions of political parties and sects, the decisions of parents, teachers or social workers – but they provide no explanatory link between the social location of actors and their actions.

Such cases apart, we are concerned with interests insofar as they relate to the decisions, and therefore the actions, of particular actors. How far can interests that actors act upon or recognize as their own be explained as reflecting their social location? We have seen that, if interests are to provide reasons for action, it must be possible to present them as the outcome of some process of assessment. This raises two kinds of problem. First, I have argued above that the forms of assessment available to actors are not uniquely determined by their social location, and it follows that the interests actors recognize and act upon cannot be uniquely determined by social location either. There is a partial recognition of this point in those analyses that seek to identify 'cross-pressures' on actors as a function of distinct aspects of their social location – for example, in Olin Wright's notion of contradictory class locations.[8] What is at issue here is the idea that interests are determined by membership of particular social categories, and that the complexity of social life is such that these categories are not mutually exclusive. Unfortunately, such 'cross-pressures' approaches merely complicate a position that is fundamentally flawed – namely, the view that actors' forms of thought are determined by their social location.

Second, leaving aside the issue of competing forms of assessment, the outcome of actors' assessments of interests (their own and others') are not determined simply by the form of assessment they employ. First, the forms of assessment may leave considerable scope for interpretation. This is clear enough in the case of actors using geomancy or a manual such as *I Ching*. But indeterminacy, and therefore scope for interpretation, can also be found, for example, in non-trivial uses of cost–benefit analysis and in the forms of political calculation employed by even the most sophisticated left-wing groupings. Second, in considering actors' reasons for action, we are not generally concerned with the deliberations of perfectly rational actors. Unlike the idealized puppets of rational choice theory, actors' deliberations are rarely completely programmed by the form of assessment employed in any given case. Their conclusions are reached through complex internal processes which may vary from one actor to another and within the same actor over time.

These points undermine the idea of interests as an explanatory link between actors' social location and their actions. But to dispute that link is not to say that there are no connections between the interests that actors recognize and act upon and their location in sets of social relations. It is merely to say that those interests should not be seen as given by, or reflecting, actors' locations. Indeed, if actors act on the basis of their decisions, and if those decisions involve complex internal processes, then we should not expect the connections between actors' social location and the interests they acknowledge or act upon to conform to any one general model. Nevertheless, several possible kinds of connections can certainly be indicated. Some of these concern the availability to actors of means of assessment, and others are to do with means of action and its impact.

I have argued that interests depend on forms of assessment and that they must provide some actor or actors with reasons for action if they are to be effective in the sense of having social consequences. The possibility of acquiring particular interests and reasons for action depends on the availability of appropriate discourses to the actors in question. Foucault's discussion of medical discourses shows some of the ways in which the availability of specific discourses may be restricted to the occupants of particular positions within medical institutions and his later work has suggested a variety of connections between discourses and power relations.[9] The availability of the professional discourse does not of course guarantee that 'professional' interests will be formulated, let alone acted upon, in every case. The point is rather that the possibility of acquiring certain 'professional' interests is effectively restricted to those able to deploy the appropriate professional discourse. For a different, non-professional, example, consider how the development of specialist managerial techniques over the last century has affected the differential availability of sophisticated means of assessing the performance of large public and private organizations. Or, again, consider that the cultural and educational diversity of all but the smallest societies is enough to ensure that means of assessing their situation are not equally available to everyone.

These examples demonstrate that there are several ways in which individuals may differ with regard to the forms of assessment available to them at any given time. What is available may not be used, and limitations on what is available may be changed – for example, through education or specialized training. Nevertheless, what is available to an actor at any given time is not a matter of choice. The differential availability of discourses providing means of assessment gives one set of connections between the actor's social location and the interests and reasons for action.

A rather different set of connections concerns not so much the availability of discourses but rather their pertinence to particular actors. The formation of reasons for action involves actors in the assessment of conditions and in locating themselves and others in relation to those conditions and possible changes in them. For example, socialist discourses elaborating on the interests of the working class and other groups that might be regarded as its allies may well be available to actors who are not in any of these groups. Chartered accountants may have no difficulty in identifying the interests of the working class, women or blacks, in terms of the discourse of a Trotskyist paper such as *Militant*, without being able to locate their own interests in any clear way in terms of that same discourse. Many workers will confront similar problems in relation to the discourse of the Confederation of British Industry or Institute of Directors. Or again, part-time women workers may have some difficulty locating themselves in relation to trades union discourses conducted in terms of the 'family wage'. There is, of course, nothing about problems of this kind that is inescapable. The general point is that, if certain actors are unable to locate themselves in relation to the conditions they confront in terms of a particular discourse, then they will not be able to identify their interests in terms of that discourse. There is nothing to stop socialist parties say, from modifying their analyses to take account of such problems – as most socialist groups in Britain have tried to do in the case of women.

Two final sets of connections between actors' social location and the interests they recognize and act upon concern the means of action available to them and the differential impact of social conditions and changes in those conditions. If interests provide actors with reasons for action, then the interests and reasons they develop will depend on the possibilities for action that are (thought to be) open to them. What those possibilities are will depend not only on the forms of assessment employed by actors but also on the means of action available to them. All employees in a manufacturing enterprise may be affected by its strategies towards investment, product and marketing development – and in that sense they all have an 'interest' in what those strategies are – but, with the rare exceptions of some cooperative enterprises, they are not equally well placed to act on the determination of those strategies. The interests that are formulated with regard to those strategies by senior managers on the one hand and wage labourers on the other may well differ – both because they will be affected differentially and because they have radically different means of acting on them. The means of action available to workers, and therefore the interests or reasons they develop, will of course depend not only on their position within the organizational structure of the enterprise but also on the extent of unionization, the strength of shop steward organization within the enterprise, and so on.

As for the differential effects of social conditions, consider the example of the structures of the markets for various categories of housing in Britain. They have implications for the formation of political interests because conditions in those markets and changes in them have differential effects on the households and organizations that operate in them. Such patterns of differential effect provides the conditions in which parties and pressure groups attempt to identify interests and develop policies in relation to them.

Some words of warning may be in order at this point. First, to insist on differential impact here is not to say that effective political interests concerning housing can be read-off from the structures of housing markets and changes in them. The point is rather that the differential effects of social conditions have consequences for the pertinence of political appeals and campaigns for different sets of actors. Second, housing conditions should not be regarded as an extra-political given. The political significance of housing has been transformed several times in Britain since the Second World War, to a large extent as a result of government policies. Neither the character of the housing stock and the structures of the housing market, nor the pattern of political concerns and interests around housing issues, are readily amenable to change in the very short term through political action, but it would be absurd to regard them as given to political life by something entirely outside it – by economic growth, affluence, or whatever.[10] There is no original pre-political pattern of interests which politics could be said to represent or react to. I have used the example of government policies here in order to make the point. But it is clear that governments are by no means the only bodies whose actvities can transform the conditions to which actors relate in developing reasons for action and identifying their interests.

Conclusions

I have argued that interests have consequences only insofar as they provide some actor or actors with reasons for action, and that actors may find reasons for action in interests they ascribe to themselves and in interests they ascribe to others. The notion of interests that are real or objective (unlike other interests that actors may believe themselves to have) has no explanatory significance with regard to the actions of those whose interests they are thought to be. Interests either provide the actors to whom they are ascribed with reasons for action, or they do not. In the first case, the reality or objectivity of those interests has no bearing on their reasons for acting as they do. In the second case they play no part in the explanation of the action of those actors, although other actors may well claim to act in their name.

The interests that actors act upon are not given by their social location, but I have suggested several respects in why they may be connected with actors' locations in sets of social relations. These connections are to do with: differences in the availability of discourses providing means or assessment, and differences in their pertinence to different sets of actors; the differential access to means of action; and the differential impact of social conditions and changes in them. There are definite connections between actors' social locations and the interests they acknowledge or act upon, but there is no simple correspondence between the two. Actors are not mere creatures of their positions in sets of social relations, of their class or gender or whatever. The forms of assessment available to them are rarely so limited as to be given uniquely by their social location. The conclusions of their deliberations depend on complex internal and discursive processes: they are not determined solely by the forms of assessment employed.

It follows that there is no possibility of interests functioning as a mere transmission between social structure on the one hand and what actors do on the other. Interests cannot provide the means whereby the structure of society produces its effects. No doubt some readers will be disturbed by such blatant undermining of the notion of social structure as an entity operating outside of and above actors, and manipulating them to produce its necessary effects. In fact, there is nothing to regret in the loss of that conception of social structure. To say that there is no such thing as social structure which produces its effects through manipulation of the actors ensnared within it is not to say there are no relatively pervasive and enduring social conditions. Nor is it to say that social life is reducible to the constitutive actions of human individuals. This is so, first, because there exist actors other than human individuals and, second, because, while actors do indeed make decisions and act on them, neither their means of reaching decisions nor their means of acting on them are determined solely by the actors themselves. Their decisions and actions always depend on 'social' conditions, but those conditions will be of the most diverse kinds and there is no need to assume an essential 'structure' of society to which they all refer.

Interests are conceptions. If they are to have consequences it must be possible for them to be formulated by some actor or actors or otherwise to provide them with reasons for action. The interests and reasons for action that are developed by actors depend on the forms of assessment of conditions that they are in a position to employ. How do interests relate to, and differ from, other items (values, desires, aversions, and the like) that might also be said to provide actors with reasons for their actions? I have indicated how interests may be said to differ from impulses and from values in that interests relate to a calculation of benefit but the same cannot be said in general about either impulses or values. But it may be more useful ultimately to question the importance that is sometimes attached to the drawing of such distinctions. It is far from clear that distinctions drawn between, say, interests and values in certain kinds of moral discourse will be equally pertinent to all forms of assessment employed by actors. If we are concerned with actors' reasons for action and with the conceptual and linguistic conditions in which they are possible reasons for those actors, then it may be more important to concentrate on what is available to them by way of forms of assessment of conditions and of locating themselves and others in relation to those conditions. In this respect, the use of interests as a form of explanation of action is not necessarily mistaken, but it is certainly seriously incomplete.

Notes

1. For example, Cripps *et al.*, 1981, ch. 8; Panitch, 1976; see also the discussion in Hindess, 1983.
2. Cutler *et al.*, 1977, 1978; Hindess, 1983.
3. Barry. 1965: Connolly, 1983; Reeve and Ware, 1984.
4. Abrams *et al.*, 1960; Crosland, 1960; Goldthorpe *et al.*, 1968; Campbell *et al.*, 1960; Lipset, 1963; Wright, 1978.
5. See Reeve and Ware, 1984 and the references therein.
6. I am grateful to Behan McCullagh for bringing this issue to my attention.
7. Skinner has argued in 'Meaning and understanding in the history of ideas' 'that no agent can eventually be said to have meant or done something which he could never be brought to accept as a correct description of what he had meant or done'. (Skinner, 1969: p.28). This requirement takes no account of those cases in which action is motivated by unconscious reasons.
8. Wright, 1978, and the revised version in Wright, 1985. I have discussed these and related positions in Hindess, 1987.
9. Foucault, 1970, 1973, 1980.
10. Abrams *et al.*, 1960

4 Two kinds of person

Nobody would deny the importance in the modern world of actors other than human individuals – capitalist enterprises, churches, political parties, state agencies, trades unions, and so on. I call these social actors and I argue that, all too often, modern social thought has failed to take seriously their status as actors. One influential tendency has been to treat human individuals as the only real actors and another has been to extend the concept of actor to classes and other collectivities that have no identifiable means of making decisions and acting on them. Both approaches are seriously mistaken.

One of the most striking features of the modern period has been the development of corporations. There were corporate actors in the world well before the emergence of modern capitalism, but their numbers and significance have grown considerably since the middle of the nineteenth century.[1] Many, but by no means all, of these new coporate actors have been capitalist enterprises constituted on the basis of shareholding and limited liability. The joint-stock company is perhaps the most common example of a capitalist employer who is not a human individual. This development has sometimes been presented as a process of the separation of ownership (in the person of the stockholders) from control (in the person of the managers), most famously in the work of Berle and Means.

That presentation is misleading in several respects.[2] The joint-stock company is a legal person separate from its stockholders and employees. Stockholders own stock, which may give them certain voting rights over the appointment of directors and other matters affecting company policy, but they do not own the company's assets. In some cases, of course, a small minority of the stockholders do occupy a dominant position. They may then be regarded as effective owners of the company's assets. As for managers, they do indeed exercise control, but they do so in their capacities as agents of the corporation that employs them. The thesis of the separation of ownership from control effectively denies the status of joint-stock companies as actors. As a result, questions of the significance of corporate actors in the modern world are transposed on to a very different set of questions concerning the consequences of displacing one set of human individuals by another.

The growing importance of corporate actors throughout the modern period gives rise to two obvious sets of problems for the analysis of society in terms of classes and conflicts between them. One is that most forms of class analysis treat classes as collectivities consisting only of human individuals. How, if at all, do corporate capitalists fit into such classes? In the Weberian tradition, the answer is clear. First, class situation is defined in terms of a concept of life chances, which effectively restricts class membership to human actors. Second, of course, corporate actors are not real actors, since their actions are reducible in principle to those of human individuals. For Marxism, the question is more problematic. The dominant tendency has been to treat classes as consisting of human individuals, with shareholders and senior management as the capitalists involved in the case of joint-stock companies. But if classes are identified in terms of the occupation of positions in relations of production, then there are strong grounds for arguing that the capitalist class contains corporate actors as well as human individuals.[3] The effect of that argument is to undermine analysis of classes in terms of some subjective referent like consciousness or a shared perception of class interests.[4]

Another set of problems for class analysis follows from the fact that the very existence of social actors depends on their relationships with others. Corporations exist as actors by means of executives and other employees, some of whose decisions and actions are legally recognized as those of the corporation itself. Such agents are an important part of what has been called the new middle class, and debates over their class positions continue to generate a considerable literature. The significance of such questions has been much overrated. What makes class membership seem important to the participants in these debates is the prior assumption that it is the structural foundation of interests, consciousness and some potential for collective action. I argued in Chapter 3, '"Interests" in political analysis', that that assumption is false. It remains significant only as a consequence of the part it plays in certain forms of political and social scientific discourse, but it has no extra-discursive foundation in some 'objective' structure of society. What matters, then, is the question not so much the nature of the class position of some section of the new petty bourgeoisie (in some supposedly objective sense), but rather what role conceptions of its class position play in particular social or political analyses.

There is a loose sense in which the claim that there are important actors in the modern world other than human individuals would not be disputed. But that loose acceptance can obscure radical differences as to how precisely the notion of actor is to be understood. This chapter raises questions about the concept of actor, some of which have serious implications for many of the most influential forms of class analysis. What is required for something to be an actor, and in what sense can actors other than human individuals be said to make decisions, have objectives and so on? An actor is a locus of decision and action, and in that sense human individuals are far from being the only important actors in the world.

I contrast this abstract and general concept of actor with two very different approaches. One is the treatment of social actors as if they were themselves reducible to human individuals. Weber's explicit methodological individualism is the most obvious example, but there are many others. Coleman, on the other hand, has argued against such reductionist claims. In his view, there are two kinds of persons in the world, natural and corporate, and a clear conflict of interests between them. This chapter argues first that the question of reductionism is something of a red herring and, second, that Coleman's counterposition of the interests of natural and corporate persons is misleading. The following chapter, 'Class analysis as social theory', considers the extension of the concept of actor to collectivities (such as classes) that have no identifiable means of formulating decisions, still less of acting on them. Here, I begin with the concept of actor.

A minimal concept of the actor

An actor is a locus of decision and action, where the action is in some sense a consequence of the actor's decisions. Actors do things as a result of their decisions. We call those things actions, and the actor's decisions play a part in their explanation. Actors may also do things that do not result from their decisions, and the explanation of those things has a different form. This is a formal and abstract concept of the actor. Most accounts of action assume a more substantial concept of actor than is provided here. Actors are often said to be characterized by the possession of a more or less stable portfolio of beliefs and desires, they are frequently supposed to be rational and to possess a utilitarian structure of preferences, and more often than not they are assumed to be human beings. Giddens, for example, suggests that a serious problem with discussion of action in terms of intentions, reasons, and so on, is that it tends to abstract from features that are central to human activity:

> 'Action' is not a combination of 'acts': 'acts' are constructed only by a discursive moment of attention to the duree of lived-through experience. Nor can action be discussed in seperation from the body, its mediations with the surrounding world and the coherence of the acting self. (Giddens, 1984: 3)

Here, the minimal concept of actor is taken up and modified by the addition of several further assumptions. In particular, Giddens takes it for granted both that actors are human individuals and that their actions are coherent.

The minimal concept of actor incorporates none of the additional assumptions noted in the last paragraph. It says that a capacity to make decisions is an integral part of anything that might be called an actor, and it says that those decisions may have consequences. Other entities, like the moon or the river Thames, do things but they would not normally be described as making decisions and acting on them. This formal and abstract concept tells us nothing about the conditions that make it possible for something to be an actor, except that it must be capable of reaching decisions and of acting on some of them. By the same token it says nothing about other characteristics that actors might also possess. To say that actors' decisions play a part in their actions is not to deny that other conditions might also be involved in what they do – for example, that unconscious processes might play a part in human activities.

Human individuals are certainly actors in the sense outlined here, but there are many others. Capitalist enterprises, churches, criminal organizations, state agencies, political parties, community organizations and football clubs are all actors in the minimal sense that they have means of reaching decisions and of acting on some on them. I call these social actors, for reasons to be explained below. For the moment, a word of warning is in order. I have presented action as a function of the actor's decisions or intentions. Now, these intentions are themselves generally supposed to result from the actor's beliefs, desires and other states of mind.[5] The relevant states of mind here are propositional attitudes: that is, they

> . . . are identified most naturally by reference to prepositions that, in some sense, constitute their objects. Thus the belief that Paris is in France is a state of mind, conscious or unconscious, identified by reference to the proposition appearing in the that-clause, which tells us what in fact is believed: Paris is in France. A parallel story goes for desire. (Macdonald and Pettit, 1981: 59)

What is at stake here is the idea that actors' decisions follow from beliefs and desires by virtue of their meanings – that is, by virtue of what Winch calls 'logical' or 'internal' relations. We therefore have a notion of reaching decisions or forming intentions as a process of following the 'logical' order of meaningful relations between propositions, and it is in this sense that actors are normally supposed to be rational.

I return to the problems with this general approach to human action in later chapters. For present purposes we can suppose that discussion of action in terms of propositional attitudes is reasonable enough in the case of human actors. Many of their decisions involve propositions that are formulated and may (or may not) be spoken or written out. But the treatment of action as a function of such 'states of mind' pre-empts consideration both of what is to count as an actor and of the processes by which decisions are made. In particular, it involves a considerable refinement of the minimal concept of actor proposed here. There is no reason to attribute propositional attitudes, conscious or unconscious states of mind, or personalities to capitalist enterprises and other social actors. At best, it is an allegorical convenience, and it is certainly no substitute for analysis of the processes by which capitalist enterprises do make decisions. I prefer to say simply that some decisions involve propositions that are formulated, some involve states of mind such as beliefs and desires, and some involve both.

Reductionism

Now consider Weber's assertion that the actions of corporate actors

> . . . must be treated as solely the resultants and modes of organisation of the particular acts of individual persons, since these alone can be treated

as agents in a course of subjectively understandable action. (Weber, 1978: 13)

There are usually two aspects to the claim that the actions of social actors are reducible to those of human individuals, as if the latter were the only real actors. One concerns the attribution of a unitary subjectivity to humans but not to other actors. The decisions of corporate actors are frequently dispersed within the organization and they may well depend on complex data collection and monitoring systems.[6] Say that we are concerned with the pattern of investment displayed by a large corporation, and that we try to understand that behaviour as resulting from a mixture of standing policies and recent decisions. Intentional analysis in this case is hardly going to lead us in the direction of interpreting those policies as resulting from the consistent application of some more or less stable collection of beliefs and desires. Decisions are made and policies laid down at a variety of points within the organization, and we are more likely to interpret them in terms of the application of particular accounting practices, institutionalized techniques of information gathering and assessment, decision-making procedures, and their relationships to decisions and policies emanating from elsewhere.

The decisions of corporate actors, then, should not be seen as the products of a unitary consciousness. This point is entirely acceptable, but we should be wary of the presumption that human individuals are, in contrast, characterized by a unitary consciousness: that their decisions are not also the dispersed products of diverse and sometimes conflicting objectives, forms of calculation and means of action. The advantage of the abstract concept of actor proposed above is that it requires us to consider the processes by which decisions are produced, by humans as much as by social actors, rather than simply refer them to a supposed unitary subjectivity.

The other aspect of the reductionist claim concerns the fact that human individuals are the only actors whose actions do not always depend on the actions of others. The actions of capitalist enterprises or trade unions always depend on those of other actors – executives, managerial and other employees, elected officials, legal representatives, and sometimes other organizations. They therefore depend not just on those other actors but also on the specific character of the social relationships in which they are implicated with them. I call such actors 'social actors': each and every one of their actions involves social relations with other actors.

There are, of course, important respects in which human individuals are constituted as actors in and through their relationships with others – and in those respects human actors are necessarily also social actors. But they are nevertheless not social actors in the sense that I am using the term here. Some of the actions of human individuals depend on the actions of others in the way I have just noted, but not all of their actions do so. This is a significant difference between human individuals and other actors.

Does it follow from this dependence that social actors can be discounted as actors, that their actions are reducible to the actions of human individuals? In fact, such reductionist claims rarely amount to more than a gesture and they do nothing to reduce the importance of analysing social actors and their conditions of action. Even if we were to accept in principle that social actors were always reducible to human individuals, we should still be concerned with investigating their decisions and actions, and with their consequences.

There are indeed actors other than human individuals, some of whom have important consequences in the modern world. Considered in terms of their social impact, many of the most significant decisions are taken by actors other than human individuals – by governments, large corporations, unions, churches. If human individuals were the only real actors then these social actors would have to be regarded as the instruments of some other set of interests – as in Marxist accounts of the state, and managerialist and many Marxist accounts of the corporation. A different example is Friedman's (1980) account of the corporation as a mere intermediary for its stockholders, which enables him to treat legal restrictions on corporate behaviour as infringements of individual liberty, and government agencies as the irresponsible instruments of politicians and public servants. To say that human individuals are not the only real actors is to argue, on the contrary, that social actors should be regarded as actors with concerns and objectives of their own. It may be possible to subject these actors to controls and restrictions of various kinds. Some could even be dispensed with without any great loss to the rest of us. But it is impossible to conceive of a complex modern society in which such actors did not play a major role. Any approach to the analysis of modern societies that admits only human individuals as effective actors must be regarded as seriously incomplete.

Two kinds of persons?

In *Power and the Structure of Society*, and more recently in *The Asymmetric Society*, Coleman provides a striking contrast to reductionist treatments of social actors. He argues that there are two kinds of persons in the world today. There are 'persons like you and me [and] another kind of person as well: these intangible persons which the law once called "fictional persons" and I will call "corporate actors" to distinguish them from persons like you and me (whom the law calls "natural persons")' (Coleman, 1982: 6). In his view, the importance of corporate actors in the modern world indicates the emergence of a fundamentally new kind of society characterized precisely by what he calls asymmetric relationships. Relationships between natural and corporate persons are asymmetric partly because they are different in kind, but also because of differences in power, resources and interests. This new kind of society is asymmetric because relations between natural persons have been displaced, first, by relations between corporate and natural persons and, second, as a consequence of the first, by relations between natural persons in their capacities as occupants of roles within corporate persons.

In all societies there have been people who have acted together in pursuit of common goals. In that limited sense Coleman suggests that there have always been corporate actors. However, the distinctive modern form of corporate actor is a relatively recent development. Coleman begins his account of that development in thirteenth-century Europe, taking changes in law as a guide. 'If the law finds it unnecessary to conceive of persons other than natural persons, then this means that all actions can be traced back to natural persons' (1982: 7). In early medieval Europe social organization was primarily a matter of the organization of persons and, to the extent that there were corporate actors, they were 'with few exceptions, easily resolvable into the component persons of which they were composed, or easily identified with a particular natural person' (ibid.).

There are two crucial features of Coleman's distinction between modern and pre-modern corporate actors. One is that modern corporate actors, unlike those of the past, are organized around the pursuit of a single purpose. To ilustrate the point Coleman takes the university as a kind of 'living dinosaur' (1982: 16). Of course, universities have changed since the Middle Ages 'but they have not become modern purposive corporate actors. They do not have a single central purpose' (ibid.) I return below to this characterization of modern corporate actors. The other feature is that pre-modern corporate actors are essentially structures of persons. Where the modern corporate actor is a structure of roles or positions, corporate actors of the past were made up of persons. In this second respect, Coleman regards the family as 'the prototype of the corporate actor around which the old social structure was built' (ibid.: 123). Of course, there is also a sense in which the family can be seen as a structure of roles. The important point for Coleman's argument is that, in general the occupants of family roles are not readily interchangeable. A family is identified by its leading members and, in that respect, it is quite unlike, say, IBM and the majority of modern corporations.

In the old kind of society, then, the social structure was made up of persons who occupied fixed positions. The key change was the emergence and gradual development of a concept of corporate actor of a qualitatively new kind, a legal person distinct from its members. Towns were granted charters which constituted them as legal persons with interests, rights and resources distinct from those of any human individual; the Church was recognized as a person before the law; charters were granted to corporations as economic enterprises; trusts, requiring no charter from the state, were developed as devices for transferring property between generations and, especially in Britain, for enabling non-conformist churches to hold property distinct from their members; and finally, limited liability and co-operative forms of corporate entity were established.

The formation of such corporate actors and their growing importance had the consequence that natural persons were freed from the fixity of the old social structure. In effect:

> . . . the structural stability of society was provided by new, fixed functional units, the corporations. . . . It was the positions, as components of the new elements of society which provided the continuity and stability of structure. (Coleman, 1982: 15)

Notice that Coleman's argument here turns on the idea that alternative forms of social arrangements may perform equivalent social functions. The corporation appears as a 'functional element in social organization: a juristic person which could substitute functionally for a natural person' (1982: 14). We therefore have an implicit reference to the functional requirements of society. The change from structures of persons to structures of roles is presented as if it were a process of structural differentiation in which persons become separated from the roles they happen to occupy. In this account, corporations and roles and positions within them are the functional equivalent of persons in fixed positions. Natural persons have been freed from the fixity of their positions only because a new kind of fixity has emerged to take its place.

However, what matters for present purposes is that Coleman presents the modern corporation as a double-edged invention. On the one hand, it has encouraged the growth of individual freedom and of social mobility, both of which depend on the possibility of seeing a person simply as the occupant of a role or position. Authority is no longer absolute: it has ceased to be authority over persons as such but is limited in its application to persons as occupants of specific positions or roles. In Coleman's view, these are all positive developments, but they have their price. On the other hand, he finds several disturbing features of the new society. First, there has been a major structural change in society over the last 100 years or so with the result that 'corporate actors play an increasing role and natural persons play a decreasing role' (1982: 13). This gives rise to the following paradox. We have been freed

> . . . from a sometimes oppressive structure of the sort that existed in the Middle Ages. Yet the resulting situation is one in which most natural persons are *employed* by those impersonal corporate actors, and thus find themselves working for ends that are not their own. (Coleman, 1982: 37)

Thus the freedom of natural persons has been bought at the price of their subordination to the ends of (unnatural) persons.

Furthermore, the growing importance of asymmetric relationships produces changes in patterns of responsibility and dependency. The decline in (natural) interpersonal relations leads to a decline in personal responsibility amongst humans and to their increasing dependence on the state and other corporate actors. New personality types appear as the reduced importance of interpersonal relations leads to a reduction in personal concern for others. Where norms were once maintained through networks of personal relations, these are now breaking down and we find new modes of imposition and development of norms through the advertising and other activities of corporations. Finally, the rise of adult employment in corporations on the one hand and of schooling (in the hands of corporate actors) on the other involves new patterns of interaction between adults and children and a general reduction in the extent and intensity of adult involvement in child socialization.

Coleman finds many of these developments disturbing and he clearly regards the asymmetric society as raising matters of grave concern for natural persons. The problem we natural persons face is how to get 'the balance of rights and that balance of responsibilities among the different kinds of actors which will prove in the end most satisfactory to natural persons' (1982: 42). We have to evaluate our modern asymmetric societies, and we should do so in terms of the interests of natural persons. Of course Coleman recognizes that there are differences between natural persons. Nevertheless we should 'exclude the benefits to corporate actors per se as criteria for evaluation' (ibid.: 43). Corporate actors may be necessary, but their interests should be subordinated to those of natural persons. Coleman notes an obvious difficulty here – namely that the state, the most obvious candidate for the role of protector of the weak, is itself a corporate actor. We have to find ways of protecting the interests of natural persons that do not increase the power of the state.

What are we to make of these arguments? Coleman insists on the importance of social actors in the modern world and he maintains, correctly in my view, that social theory has paid them insufficient attention. His discussion of changes in patterns of responsibility and dependency which accompanied the growing importance of corporate actors is interesting and thought-provoking. Nevertheless, his account of these changes does raise problems in terms of the rise to prominence of a new kind of person. I have already noted a disturbing element of functionalism in the way that Coleman treats structures of natural persons and of corporate persons, and roles within them, as if they played equivalent parts in the maintenance of structural stability. There is a related problem with the explanatory ambitions of Coleman's discussion of the growing significance of corporate actors and the correlative decline of (natural) interpersonal relations. In effect, he presents us with an updated version of the old story of *Gemeinschaft* and *Gesellschaft*, loading an excessive weight of explanatory significance on to a single historical polarity and presenting altogether too simple a picture of societies at each end of the continuum.

More important for present purposes is his treatment of corporate and natural persons and their respective interests in which he raises the question of what can be done to protect the latter. There are several points to note here. First, there is a curious air of unreality in the suggestion that we (natural persons) should consider changes in the balance of rights and responsibilities 'among the different kinds of actors' (ibid.: 42) without taking the interests of corporate actors into account. The problem here is not that Coleman denies the reality of corporate actors nor that he effectively reduces them to human individuals. Quite to the contrary, he insists that they have concerns and objectives that are not reducible to those of human individuals, and it is precisely because of their importance and irreducibility that Coleman invites us to do something about them while we can. The problem lies rather in the implicit assumption that natural persons constitute an effective political community in the societies of the modern world.

Coleman is, of course, by no means alone in making that assumption. It also appears in a rather different form in much of contemporary democratic theory and again, for example, in those discussions of corporatism which present tripartite arrangements between government, business and organized labour as undermining our democratic institutions. The Social Contract between the Labour government and the British trades unions during the 1970s was sometimes attacked on the grounds that it gave private, sectional interests power to determine policies of an elected government. What is at stake here is the view that the interests of citizens, individually or in groups, are the only interests legitimately involved in the determination of the policies and personnel of government. We then have the assumption of a political community consisting exclusively of natural persons (citizens) in which the political activity of the majority of corporate actors is presumptively illegitimate. (There are left-wing and right-wing versions of this fantasy.)

On the one hand it is recognized that corporate actors are an important part of our society – and who could possibly deny this? On the other hand, they are not recognized as members of our political community. The problem is, of course, that many corporate actors are active members of our political community, whether we (natural persons) like it or not. Capitalist enterprises, trades unions, and other corporate actors all have an interest in, say, the economic policies of governments. If those interests are excluded from formal channels of political influence, many of them are well able to make themselves felt in other ways. It is impossible to imagine a parliamentary democracy in which both government and the electorate are not subject to the machinations of social actors.[7] The nature of those machinations may change, but there is no prospect of them being eliminated. It follows that we (as citizens or as natural persons) cannot expect to make collective decisions without the additional involvement of social actors. Thus, there is no sense in which we could seriously consider changes in the balance of rights and responsibilities between different kinds of persons, without corporate persons also being involved. Indeed, *The Asymmetric Society* is published by one of them.

The second point to note is that the idea of evaluating social systems in terms of the interests of natural persons as distinct from those of corporate actors assumes a unity of interest amongst natural persons as such. There are two rather different aspects of that assumption that should be questioned here. One concerns the character of the concept of interests involved in Coleman's discussion and the other concerns the counterposition of the interests of natural and corporate persons as if they were essentially opposed. On the first point Coleman recognizes that natural persons may have differing interests. The contrast between the interests of natural and corporate persons refers to something that members of each category are presumed to have in common simply by virtue of their membership. This means that what is at stake in his reference to the interests of natural persons is not necessarily a matter of what individual natural persons recognize as their interests at some particular point in time, but one of interests that are 'objective', in the sense that they pertain to persons simply by virtue of their status as natural persons.

Here Coleman provides us with yet another attempt to derive actors' interests from their social location. In that respect it suffers from many of the problems of Marxist and other accounts of objective interests considered in the previous chapter. Marxists frequently refer to distinct and opposed class interests while recognizing that there are differences within the working class and within the bourgeoisie. In much the same way, Coleman recognizes differences between natural persons, and between corporate persons, but nevertheless talks of the interests of natural persons as providing a criterion for the evaluation of social systems.

Once we question the presumption that natural persons share a unity of interests simply by virtue of their shared status, we can hardly evaluate societies in terms of those interests. Of course, there are social conflicts around opposed conceptions of interests, but it is erroneous to suppose either that these must reflect 'objective' or 'structural' differences in the social locations of the actors involved in those conflicts, or that different social statuses or locations must always give rise to such conflicts. In contemporary Britain many natural persons would see their interests as residing in the defence of some corporate actors (trades unions, hospitals, schools and universities) against others. Other natural persons have just voted in a government which perceives these matters rather differently.

This last point brings us to the second issue. Several features of Coleman's counterposition of natural and corporate persons suggest that there is an inescapable antagonism between them. First, there is a zero-sum relationship in which the increasing influence of one category of persons entails the decreasing influence of the other. At one point Coleman makes an analogy between corporate actors and 'man from Mars – a race of persons unknown in history. And this new race of persons has come to crowd out natural persons from various points in the social structure' (1982: 13). Second, there is the paradox that our freedom from medieval oppression has been bought at the price of our subordination to the ends of impersonal corporate actors:

> . . . both in the employment relation and in many of our other relations, as customers, clients, citizens, we natural persons find ourselves in a relation with an impersonal entity that is much larger and more powerful than we. (Coleman, 1982: 37)

The sense of antagonism will be heightened, for many readers, by his treatment of business corporations as prototypical corporate actors of the modern kind.

It is not inevitable that relations between natural and corporate persons should be presented in that way. First, we have seen that there is no necessary conflict of interests arising simply from the different legal statuses of natural and corporate persons. Second, although the joint-stock corporation may be a nineteenth-century invention (and in that sense it is comparatively modern), that is no reason to treat any other kind of social actor as an anachronism. The business corporation is not the only significant model of social actor in the modern world. Social actors share the fact that each and every one of their actions involves social relationships with other actors, but it does not follow that they should be treated as alike in other significant respects. There is no reason why natural persons should be expected to find other natural persons any less alien than they would find some corporate actors, and no reason why they should be expected to regard all corporate actors as equally alien.

A very different model of relations between human individuals and social actors is presented by English pluralism, especially the works of Maitland and Figgis and the early works of Cole and Laski.[8] Several features of this tradition are worth noting here. First, their discussion of social actors was centred not on business corporations but rather on groups and voluntary associations. Second, they regarded cooperative action through membership of associations as a central feature of human existence. Involvement in associations was to be seen as a means of defining and achieving human purposes rather than as a human subordination to the purposes of non-human actors. These points present a perspective on relations between human individuals and social actors that is utterly remote from Coleman's view. It suggests that groups and associations play an important part in the formation of the ends and purposes of human individuals and that they are essential means in the pursuit of some of the ends of their members. The pluralists therefore argued that protection of group rights was essential to the liberty of human individuals. Individuals should be free to form or to join associations to pursue some shared purposes and should likewise be free to withdraw from them if they wish. Finally, groups and associations had an existence independent of their individual members. Their existence did not necessarily depend on their status as legal persons. On the contrary, that legal status was often a matter of the legal recognition of an independent reality. It was no more (and no less) fictional than the recognition of human individuals as legal persons.

English pluralism provides a striking contrast to the Coleman's account of relations between human individuals and social actors. It is not without its difficulties – especially with regard to the personality of groups and the treatment of the state as no more than a specialized kind of group – but these need hardly concern us here. What is required for something to be an actor is simply a capacity to make decisions and to act on them, however that capacity itself is sustained. The minimal concept of actor introduced earlier allows us to treat social actors as actors without the need to invoke 'states of mind' or 'personalities' to account for their actions. For the rest, we can admit the importance of social actors for the ends and purposes of human individuals without taking the association as a general model for the analysis of social actors.

Social actors come in many different forms and they may relate to other actors in a variety of ways. The existence of some will depend on their possession of legal personality; however, the presence of effective illegal organizations in many parts of the world demonstrates that legal personality is not always a prerequisite for the capacity of social actors to take decisions and to act on them. Some social actors will be like Coleman's 'corporation' and others will be more like the pluralists' 'association' but there is no reason to take either as providing a general model. These points imply that there is no necessary cause for concern in the fact that we (human individuals) frequently 'find ourselves in a relation with an impersonal entity that is much larger and more powerful than we' (Coleman, 1982: 37). Such a relationship may be antagonistic but not inevitably so – it depends on the character of the 'impersonal entity' in question.

If there is cause for concern in the existence of relations between human individuals and social actors it does not arise from the fact that the latter are not themselves human individuals. To the extent that it arises at all, it does so for other reasons – for example, from the fact that all too many social actors are neither responsible to their members or employees nor more generally accountable for the wider social consequences of their activities or from the limitations of current mechanisms of legal regulation of their behaviour. Social actors should not be regarded as equivalently placed with regard to these issues. There are indeed important problems here but there is no general or universal problem of the balance of rights and responsibilities between natural and corporate persons of the kind that Coleman suggests.

Notes
1. Coleman, 1982, ch. 1.
2. Hadden, 1977, Thompson, 1986, Tomlinson, 1982.
3. Cutler *et al*, 1977, Scott, 1979.

4. See the discussion of the corporate ruling class in Clegg, Boreham and Dow, 1986.
5. This assumption is taken for granted in most forms of rational choice analysis and in analytical philosophy's treatment of intentional analysis. For the latter, see Macdonald and Pettit, 1891, and Doval and Harris, 1986.
6. See Thompson, 1986, esp. ch. 7.
7. I have discussed this issue in another context in Hindess, 1983, ch. 2.
8. The English pluralists are discussed briefly in Lustgarten, 1983, and at greater length in Nichols, 1975.

5   Class analysis as social theory

Classes and the relations between them have been regarded as significant objects in social theory for many reasons, some of the most prominent having to do with the supposed importance of classes in political life. That importance has been conceived in many different ways, but for present purposes we may distinguish two broad approaches.

The first treats classes as major social forces that are characteristic of certain types of society, and of modern capitalist societies in particular. On this view, class relations are not transitory or superficial phenomena. On the contrary, they arise out of basic structural features of society and they have significant social and political consequences. Marxism provides the most obvious instances of this approach, but there are influential non-Marxist versions. Giddens, for example, refers to class societies as ones 'in which class relationships are pre-eminent in the social structure as a whole' (Giddens, 1973: 132). Or, again, discussing the prospects for egalitarian social change in Britain, Goldthorpe refers to the working class as 'the social vehicle through whose action, electoral and otherwise, [it has] by far the best probability of being realised' (Goldthorpe, 1980: 28). I will return to these examples. It is clear that, within this broad approach, authors differ over their definitions of class and their accounts of how the relations between classes are to be understood. Nevertheless, they share a common insistence on the importance of classes and the relations between them for the analysis of capitalist societies.

At the other extreme is a usage of class which is more nearly classificatory. Class is used, along with concepts of sex, age, ethnicity, housing tenure, car ownership, union membership, and the like, for the purposes of distributional analysis – of income, health and illness, attitudes, voting behaviour, or whatever, Here, class may be relevant to politics to the extent that it relates to the distributions of political attitudes and voting behaviour within the population. The importance of class may vary from one society to another, and over time. It was once regarded as the most important social characteristic influencing behaviour in Britain, but now, according to Rose and McAllister (1986), it has been replaced by housing tenure.

Of course, the distinction between these broad approaches is not always as clear-cut as I have presented it here. If classes are competing social forces, then class differences may well have distributional implications. Nevertheless, classes may be regarded as social forces even if class differences do not show up in voting behaviour. In Marxist class analysis and in the work of the non-Marxist authors noted above, class position may be closely related to voting behaviour or it may not – but in either case class struggle is an important part of politics in capitalist society. In his commentaries on the Labour Party's 1983 electoral defeat, Hobsbawm (1983; 1984; 1985) can refer to 'the working class' as a social force while recognizing that there is no longer any clear correlation between class and voting behaviour in Britain.

On the other hand, the fact that class differences do have significant distributional implications in Britain and other capitalist societies does not establish that classes are themselves social forces. Regional differences also have significant distributional implications but it hardly follows that we should therefore regard, say, the South or the North-west as social forces. To argue, as I do, that classes are not social forces is not to deny the distributional significance of class divisions.

This chapter is principally concerned with those forms of social thought in which classes are regarded as social forces. Much of the appeal of class analysis rests on its promise that crucial features of political life in the modern world are to be understood in terms of relations between conflicting class forces. The first part of this chapter shows that that promise cannot be fulfilled. There are important actors other than human individuals, but I argue that classes are not amongst them.

This raises an obvious problem for the analysis of politics in terms of class conflict. The imagery of struggle is a central feature of the most important forms of class theory, and it suggests that classes are, in some sense, collective actors. What remains of that imagery if classes as such are not actors? Here again, I argue that the imagery is misleading, and that it remains important only as a consequence of the part it plays in a number of political and social scientific discourses.

The analysis in terms of class struggle is notoriously unsatisfactory, and yet it remains significant both in the academic social sciences and in the political discourses of sections of the Labour movement and of left-wing politics generally. The remainder of the chapter consists of reflections on this state of affairs. It raises questions, first, about the place of concepts and forms of argument as components of political life and, second, about the features of advanced capitalist societies which allow class analysis, despite its failures, to survive as a mode of political analysis.

However, before proceeding to my main arguments, it is worth making two general observations. The first is that class is by no means the only concept that is both theoretically problematic and politically significant. Serious problems can be raised about many of the concepts that play an important part in social and political life (and in academic discussion of it) – power, interests, rights, rationality, democracy – and some of them are discussed in other chapters. Forms of social analysis that are politically consequential, because they are employed by important political actors or movements, are all too easily undermined by theoretical work. In this respect, discussion of class analysis inevitably raises more general issues of the relation between social theory and politics.

This brings us to my second observation. There is no uniform way in which concepts, forms of argument and styles of political analysis operate as components of political life. Problems with analysis in terms of rights or democracy do not have the same ramifications as problems with class analysis. But the more serious point to notice here is that each of these concepts or forms of analysis will themselves be embedded in political life in a variety of different ways. We should be wary of seeing the relations between social theory and politics in terms of any simple dichotomy between theory and reality. This means, in particular, that the full extent of the political ramifications of problems with class analysis, or with notions of rights, democracy, or power, may be far from easy to establish. It would be a rationalistic illusion to imagine that the political significance of a form of social analysis is a function primarily of its validity or coherence. I will return to this point later.

I

I have suggested that the appeal of class analysis rests on a promise that cannot be fulfilled. To avoid possible misunderstandings of this claim it may be necessary to insist on the following points. First, the argument here is directed against class analysis as a general project, rather than against some particular Marxist or non-Marxist version of it. It is directed as much against Giddens' claim that, in capitalist societies, 'the class system continues to constitute the fundamental axis of the social structure' (1973: 294) and Goldthorpe's (1980) discussion of the concomitants of social mobility in terms of the conditions of concerted class action as it is against *The Communist Manifesto's* well known assertion that history is the history of class struggle.

Second, it is commonplace now to insist on the need to avoid reductionism. No serious exponent of class analysis, whether Marxist or non-Marxist, maintains that class analysis tells us all we want to know about the political forces at work in the modern world. Some go further to suggest that classes are becoming less relevant. Two of the classics of socialist revisionism, Bernstein's *Evolutionary Socialism* (1961) and Crosland's *The Future of Socialism* (1956), argued that economic development was displacing a politics of class, and that socialists must therefore base their support on the appeal of socialist values. Or again, the critical theory of Habermas does not so much reject class analysis as retain it as a residual element in a more complex theoretical edifice. Finally, the 'new' social movements literature suggests that class struggle has been displaced by other forms of politics in the more advanced societies of the modern world. In one way or another, these are different versions of the claim that class analysis is incomplete – and that it has become more so as the modern world has developed.

In contrast to the many forms of that position, I make the stronger claim that classes are not social forces at all, and that they never have been. Forms of political analysis depending on the notion of classes as social forces should not be supplemented by something else. They should be abandoned as an obstacle to clear political thinking. I have developed this argument at length elsewhere[1] and there is no space here for more than a brief resumé. The analysis of politics in terms of relations between competing classes usually involves one or both of two elements, both of which I dispute. One is a notion of classes as collective actors. The other is a conception of class interests as objectively given to individuals by virtue of their social location, and therefore as providing a basis for action in common. We shall consider these elements in turn.

The problem with the idea of classes as collective actors is that even the most limited concept of actor requires that the actor possess means of taking decisions and of acting on them. Capitalist enterprises, state agencies, political parties and trades unions are all examples of actors in at least this minimal sense – that is, they all possess means of taking decisions and of acting on at least some of them. There are other collectivities, such as classes and societies, that have no identifiable means of taking decisions, let alone of acting on them. Of course, there are those who claim to take decisions and to act on behalf of classes and other collectivities. But the very diversity of such claims should be sufficient reason to be sceptical about accepting any one of them.

The point of restricting the concept of actor to entities that take decisions and act on some of them is simply that actors' decisions are an important part of the explanation of their actions. To apply the concept of actor to classes or other collectivities that have no means of taking decisions and acting on them, and then to explain some state of affairs (say, the emergence of the welfare state or its current crisis) as resulting from their actions is to indulge in a kind of fantasy. Such fantastic explanations may well be thought to serve a polemical function, but they can only obscure both our understanding of the state of affairs in question and political decisions as to what can, or should, be done about them.

Now consider the suggestion that the idea of classes as social forces should be understood in terms of structurally determined class interests. These interests are supposed to be given in the structure of social relations, and the parties, unions and other agencies of political life are to be seen as their more or less adequate representations. There are many well known problems with this conception of interests, some of which have been considered in Chapter 3. For the moment, we should note that such a concept of interests may be used to perform several theoretical roles, of which two are particularly significant.

One is that it appears to provide an explanatory link between action and social structure. Interests provide us with reasons for action and they are derived from features of social structure. On this view, people have interests by virtue of the conditions in which they find themselves, as members of a class, gender or community, and different elements of those conditions may then be seen as giving rise to different, and sometimes conflicting, sets of interests. Functionalist sociology treats norms and values as if they provided an explanatory link of a similar kind.

Unfortunately for class analysis, the situation is rather more complicated. The majority of those to whom objective interests are attributed by class analysis rarely acknowledge those interests as their own. Przeworski (1986) has argued that class analysis has often been mistaken in the interests it has ascribed to the European working classes. But, in general, the idea that structurally determined class interests provide an explanatory link between social structure and action is a principle honoured more in the breach than in the observance. Far from providing an effective explanatory link, the idea of structurally determined class interests generates a host of explanatory problems. Why, to give just one example, do the British working class fail to acknowledge their objective interest in socialism? A large part of Miliband's *The State in Capitalist Society* is devoted to 'the process of legitimation' which is supposed to manufacture the 'consent' of the overwhelming majority whose real interests lie in the overthrow of capitalism. Here the idea of objective interests that are real but not recognized leads to the posing of an entirely imaginary problem: why do the working class, and others, not pursue their real interests? A non-existent state of affairs (in which real interests are pursued) is posed as a measure of the present, and the problem is to explain away its non-existence.

Conceptions of objectively determined class interests may well have consequences in other ways – for example, in the actions of parties or sects who claim to represent them, but in general they do not provide the explanatory link they appear to promise.

The other significant theoretical role of the concept of structurally determined interests is that it seems to allow us to bring a variety of relationships and struggles into a larger pattern. For example, the 1984–85 miners' strike, the 1986–87 dispute between the NGA, SOGAT and the Murdoch newspapers, and diverse other conflicts between groups of employees and their employers and other agencies (for example, the police) may be regarded as instances of a wider struggle between one class and another. Of course, the cases I have cited here do have features in common but that does not mean that they can be subsumed into such a wider struggle. What is at stake here is the idea that a variety of different relationships can be lumped together as so many instances of one more general relationship on the basis of characteristics ascribed to the participants – in this case, the class interests that are supposed to be represented on one side or the other. We have seen that something similar is involved in Coleman's treatment of the antagonistic interests of natural and corporate persons. This manoeuvre makes whatever sense it does only on the assumption that each class can be treated as a unified group because of those ascribed characteristics.

Since classes do not act collectively they cannot, as classes, enter into relations with each other. In effect, the use of class interests as a device for bringing together a collection of distinct relationships and struggles requires that we treat the participants in each one of those relationships (for example, those miners who supported the 1984–85 strike) as surrogates – that is, as standing in for the classes as such, the true players in an entirely mythical clash of the Titans. In this respect, it returns us to the fantasy of classes as collective actors.

Of course, no-one really believes in the clash of the Titans any more than they seriously maintain that politics is entirely reducible to classes and the struggles between them. Indeed, the fact that they are never required to appear in person is precisely what makes it possible for those mythical giants to play a crucial part in the action of class analysis. Their role is to provide the hidden foundations of all those attempts to analyse some particular state of affairs in terms of classes, or their surrogates, and relations between them – rather than in terms of the actions of parties, unions, capitalist enterprises, and other identifiable agencies.

For a clear non-Marxist example of what is involved here, consider the problem of class formation which plays an important organizing role in Goldthorpe's *Social Mobility and Class Structure in Modern Britain* (1980). Part of his concern is to correct misperceptions of the character of social mobility in post-war Britain, and in particular to register the extent of its departure from his ideal of an open society. More important for present purposes, however, is the attempt to investigate the consequences of the prevailing pattern of mobility for the prospects of collective action in pursuit of egalitarian social change.

Goldthorpe argues that the limited egalitarian reforms of the post-war Labour governments seriously underestimated 'the flexibility and effectiveness with which the more powerful and advantaged groupings in society can use the resources at their disposal to preserve their privileged position' (1980: 252). The only chance of real change would be through class struggle, and in particular through the collective action of the working class 'relying on their numbers and above all on solidarity and organisation' (ibid.: 29) to overwhelm the 'class-based opposition which it would inevitably meet' (ibid.: 256). Thus, the study of social mobility is important because of its consequences for the social conditions that are conducive or otherwise to the development of 'the shared beliefs, attitudes and sentiments that are required for concerted class action' (ibid.: 265). Accordingly, after presenting a mass of material on patterns of relative and absolute mobility, Goldthorpe proceeds to examine

> . . . the wider concomitants of such mobility, as these may be found in aspects of men's lives outside the sphere of work – for example, in the accompanying degree of discontinuity in their social relations with kin, leisure associates, etc. (Goldthorpe, 1980: 143)

His concluding chapter then considers the implications of those concomitants of mobility for class formation and the prospects of collective action.

Now, one of the striking features of this study is that Goldthorpe draws his conclusions with barely a reference to the organizations involved in British politics and their practices. Despite his declared concern for the prospects of egalitarian social change in Britain, he pays little attention to political parties, unions and employers, state agencies and other bodies – that is, to the principal agencies of political struggle in British society – or to the forms of political calculation in terms of which they conduct their struggles and attempt to mobilize support. Instead, like the Marxism he is so careful to reject, he proceeds as if 'classes' really were the main political actors in British society. The result is that the primary focus of political analysis in this study is on the conditions of formation and action of classes themselves – or rather of those smaller groups that stand in as their surrogates.

Goldthorpe's political argument in this study, then, effectively discounts the specific conditions of organization of parties, unions and the like, and the forms of organization and political calculation they employ, as if they were of secondary importance. It is only from this standpoint that it makes any sense to investigate the implications of mobility for the alleged conditions of 'concerted class action' as if they occurred quite independently of the activities of parties, the media, state agencies, and so on. What is at stake here is a failure to take seriously the consequences of organizations, movements and their actions, both for political forces and the conditions in which they operate, and for the formation of the political interests and concerns around which their struggles are conducted. Political attitudes, beliefs and practices may then be regarded as reflecting other social conditions – in this case the strength and self-consciousness of the various classes – the implication being that these other conditions are somehow more real than the political phenomena that reflect them. Here Goldthorpe effectively reduces political life to the struggles of entirely mythical agencies. In other contexts, of course, Goldthorpe adopts a rigorously anti-reductionist position.

This brings us to my final point in this section. No serious exponent of class analysis would be so foolish as to maintain that politics is entirely reducible to classes and the relations between them in the literal sense. When we examine political struggles we find state agencies, political parties and other organizations, demonstrations, riotous mobs, bodies of armed men, magazines and newspapers, but we do not find classes as such linked up against each other. Nor do we find that the issues at stake in political struggle take the form of direct conflicts between classes for political hegemony or over the specific character of the relations of production, capitalism versus socialism, feudalism versus capitalism, or whatever.

In their political analyses, Marxist political leaders have always insisted that political struggles are not immediately and directly reducible to classes and their interests.

> To imagine that social revolution is conceivable without revolts by small nations in the colonies and in Europe, without revolutionary outbursts by a section of the petty-bourgeoisie with all its prejudices, without a movement of the politically non-conscious proletarian or semi-proletarian masses against oppression by landowners, the church and the monarchy, against national oppression, etc., – to imagine all this is to repudiate social revolution. So one army lines up in one place and says 'We are for socialism' and another, somewhere else, and says 'We are for capitalism' and that will be a social revolution . . . whoever expects a 'pure' revolution will never live to see it. (Lenin, 1964, vol. 22: 335–6)

Marxism has combined this insistence on the specificity of political forces and issues with a theoretical insistence that political struggles should be conceptualized in class terms. The discrepancy between these positions is encapsulated in the idea of representation, in the difference between what is represented (classes, their interests and struggles) and its representation in specific political forces, issues and struggles. This idea of representation appears to allow specific political struggles to be treated as substituting for something that is not immediately present.

On that view, political forces are not directly reducible to classes; rather they represent them. Much of what passes as class analysis of, say, political conditions in contemporary Britain in fact consists of discussion of parties, unions, state agencies, and the media – together with an occasional gesture towards the class relations that are supposed to underly at least some of those conditions. Hobsbawm's commentaries on the state of the Labour movement following the defeats of 1979 and 1983 are an excellent case in point. At one level there is a more or less realistic assessment of political conditions – for example, Hobsbawm's comments on voting patterns and the gap between the concerns and aspirations of ordinary people and what the Labour Party appears to offer. Much of what he has to say at this level is sensible, if rather limited. At the second level are the references to mythical social forces, notably, 'the working class as a whole' and its potential allies, 'the women', 'the minority nations and ethnic minorities', 'the intellectuals'.

Of course, Hobsbawm's Marxist approach is rather different from Goldthorpe's non-Marxist one, but they both exhibit a general feature of attempts to treat classes as social forces. First, they operate at two distinct but supposedly related levels of analysis. At one level there are parties, movements, and the like and factions within them, as well as the doctrines and ideologies in terms of which they organize their conduct and attempt to mobilize support. Here we find more or less hard-headed accounts of the state of Labour's electoral support in the one case and of survey material in the other. At the other level is the clash of the Titans, the key to our understanding of the mundane. Second, there is a merely gestural connection between these two levels of analysis. Class analysis, in other words, pretends to combine an insistence on the irreducibility of politics with the explanatory promise of reductionism. How the trick is carried out, of course, remains obscure – and with good reason. If the mythical giants were called upon to perform a real explanatory role, no-one would be able to take them seriously.

II

Nevertheless, despite its many difficulties, class analysis remains significant both in the academic social sciences and in the political discourses of sections of the Labour movement and in left-wing politics generally. In most contemporary societies, there are groups which analyse politics and act, at least partially in class terms; in some cases such groups have been extremely influential. Surely, it might be argued, the persistence of movements acting at least in part in terms of class struggle, and the strength of some of them, shows that class analysis cannot be dismissed quite so easily as I have suggested?

In one rather obvious sense the answer can only be 'yes'. However, it is necessary to be cautious at this point and to ask not simply whether discussion of class is significant but also how discussion of classes, their interests and struggles, operates as components of various practices and social relations. In particular, we should avoid posing the issue in terms of a simplistic (or indeed sophisticated) opposition between discourse and reality, as if the question of the diverse ways that discursive elements function as components of social practices could be reduced to the epistemological issue of the adequacy of the one to the other. It is in such terms that the undeniable existence of movements organized around notions of class struggle, and their occasional successes, might be invoked as evidence in support of the 'realism' of the discourse of class analysis. In fact, there is a widespread tendency in Marxist thought to analyse classes in terms of the adequacy of ideas to an underlying reality: the distinctions between class and class-consciousness, class-in-itself and class-for-itself, and between objective and subjective conditions. These oppositions counterpose the objective reality of class to forms of ideology or consciousness so that the latter may be evaluated in terms of their success or failure in grasping that reality.

The mistake here is to confuse questions of the political significance of mode of political analysis with questions of its validity. Where conceptions of class interests are significant elements of political life there is certainly something to be explained, but it is not their validity that accounts for the significance of those conceptions. (Consider the example of Shiite Islam.) Support for movements and organizations operating in terms of class interests, or some other way of conducting and analysing politics is one of the outcomes of competition between movements for support – it is never a mere reflection of social structure. It is impossible to account for the relative strength or weakness of class-based politics in, say, Britain and Sweden without reference to the outcomes of past struggles over the policies and internal structure of particular organizations and conflicts within and between competing movements and organizations.

Conceptions of class interests may well be significant elements of political life, even though class interests as such (as distinct from conceptions of them) have no explanatory role. This point is frequently acknowledged in the literature of class analysis. Everyone now writes of the need to avoid reductionism and many authors insist that interests are not sociological givens. To take just one example, Clegg, Boreham and Dow argue in the final chapter of *Class, Politics and the Economy* (1986) that the development of social policy in the advanced capitalist economies can be understood in terms of a struggle between classes[2]. Classes have different interests in the institutional character of social policy and they can be expected to pursue distinct policy objectives. How social and economic policy develop in a particular society will therefore depend on the organizational and other resources at the disposal of the classes and on the success of the tactics they employ.

However, they also insist on the need to avoid reductionism: 'without organization there can be no "class interests". The notion of a class having a collective interest can only ever gain credence inas much as organizations are formed whose mandate entails the representation of "class interests"' (Clegg et al., 1986: 259–60). The implication here is that parties, unions and other organizations cannot be seen as mere instruments of some set of class interests given in advance of their articulation. However, they also write of the capitalist and working classes as if they were engaged in struggle for 'greater control over the capitalist system as a whole', and suggest that reference to classes and their real interests may perform 'an important heuristic function' (ibid.)

The heuristic function is, as I noted above, that talk of classes and their interests enables political analysis to bring together a wide range of discrete conditions and struggles into a unified pattern. It enables us to discuss the development of social and economic policy in terms of class relations without getting caught up in the details of policy discussion, the factions, parties and other organizations involved, and the confused and conflicting objectives that they pursue.

Unfortunately, that heuristic function involves a heavy theoretical and political cost. It would be difficult not to conclude that Britain's high level of unemployment and its deteriorating social services have come about largely because of the relative weakness of the working class and the strength of its opponents. The problem with that conclusion is not so much that it is wrong as that it is uninformative. If popular and organizational support for a politics conceived in terms of the interests of the working class is weak, we should not assume that there is a real working class collective actor just waiting to be revived. But without that assumption, reference to the weakness of the working class is merely allegorical. It suggests that something should be done, but offers precious little guidance as to what should be done to change the complex of parties, unions and employers associations at work in British society, the ideologies and forms of political calculation they utilize in the conduct of their activities, and the patterns of support they enjoy.

This last point returns us to the puzzle with which I began. The treatment of classes as social forces is manifestly inadequate and yet it remains significant in parts of the academic social sciences and in some areas of political life. In fact, I have already indicated one respect in which the structure of class analysis as a general project gives it a certain immunity from critical argument. The combination of elements of myth and fantasy with more or less hard-headed analysis offers several promising lines of defence. For one thing, it allows practitioners of class analysis to dismiss many others as reductionist or economistic. Non-Marxist class theorists habitually criticize Marxism, and Marxists frequently criticize each other, on precisely those grounds. Attacks on economism are an important part of Lenin's political analyses. Hobsbawm's (1984; 1985) rejoinders to his Marxist critics provide a more recent example. Those who are chastised in this way can, of course, accuse their critics of running away from class politics[3]. Indeed, the great advantage of the merely gestural character of the connection that class analysis provides between its two levels of analysis is that it always allows the defence that any particular critical argument has misunderstood how class analysis really works – and that what might seem to be its failures are really the results of faulty application.

In view of such defences, then, it would be wrong to imagine, even in academic life, that class analysis will give up the ghost merely on the strength of the arguments against it. It would also be a mistake to imagine that class analysis was uniquely situated in this respect.

Tales of rational economic man and his more or less close relations play a far more significant role than does class analysis in the academic social sciences. Systematic evidence and rigorous argument may play their part in some of these tales – just as they do in some forms of class analysis – but so too do powerful elements of myth and fantasy. It will take more than argument and evidence to dispose of these conceptions. The elements of myth and fantasy that sustain them in academic life can also be expected to operate in other contexts.

These comments relate to the character of class analysis as a mode of social thought, without reference to the ways in which it might function as a component in political life. We should be careful to distinguish questions of the political significance of class analysis (or of tales of rational economic man) from questions of its coherence or validity as a mode of analysis. In his essay, 'What is to be done?' Lenin insisted that '[w]ithout revolutionary theory there can be no revolutionary movement' (1961: 369). Now, although there is a sense in which the statement is correct, it is not the sense which Lenin intended. What he had in mind was Marxist theory, which he believed to be scientific. Unfortunately for Lenin's argument on this point, 'revolutionary theory' does not have to be scientific, or even particularly coherent, to play a significant part in politics.

All movements, parties and other organizations involve forms of political calculation, assessment and evaluation. They provide actors with means to identify the social conditions in which they operate, to set objectives and to recognize possible friends and supporters, enemies and other obstacles, and to find ways of dealing with them. In this sense there can indeed be no revolutionary movement without revolutionary theory. But it would be a rationalist illusion to imagine that its survival, or even success, requires the coherence, 'scientific' validity or objectivity of its forms of calculation, assessment and evaluation. There are numerous examples of more or less successful political movements making use of what will seem, to most readers of this chapter, bizarre and unsatisfactory modes of analysis. The very different successes of Thatcherism and German fascism are obvious examples. Another would be Shiite Islam. Although class analysis does not have the overt religious connotations as Shiism, the two are alike in at least the following respects. They have had a number of (somewhat equivocal) successes and have survived numerous failures. Both doctrines have means of accounting for their failures and of deriving a certain kind of comfort from them. They have also accumulated a fund of empirical examples to be invoked in support of their political generalizations. Few in the West, whatever their political persuasion, would claim that the political significance of Shiite Islam demonstrates its validity as a mode of political analysis. The same must also be said of class analysis.

Still, if validity or coherence is not a necessary condition for the political significance of a doctrine or 'theory', it must nevertheless provide those who employ it with some purchase on the world. That is, it must provide some means of assessing situations and of deciding on objectives to pursue within them, as well as means of identifying friends, enemies and obstacles and deciding what to do about them. Any reasonably elaborate body of contemporary social thought provides a variety of resources adequate to these purposes. What it must also do, of course, is provide means of coming to terms with conditions when things go wrong. The question of why the working class in the advanced capitalist societies have largely failed to recognize and act on their objective interests has generated a considerable literature of explanation within Western Marxism.

Two general features of class analysis are worth noting in these respects. First, the merely gestural character of its reductionism means that the two levels at which class analysis is conducted may operate with some degree of independence from each other. This, of course, provides class analysis with an invaluable device for coming to terms with its practical failures. I have already suggested, for example, that reference to classes and relations between them may, despite appearances, have little direct bearing on the practical political analyses and arguments conducted in its name. Hobsbawm's pieces on the British 1983 general election are good examples. A rather different point is that the invocation of classes, their interests and the relations between them, may have a different significance in the context of attempts to mobilize or maintain support, or in the conduct of internal disputes, than it does in a party's or organization's day-to-day decision-making.

This last comment brings us to the second feature. The mythical protagonists invoked by class analysis are not without a certain purchase of their own. The point here is simply that, in all versions of class analysis, the specification of the classes themselves invariably identifies property and employment relations as significant features of their account of the world. Part of the conceptual purchase of class analysis is a function of its reference to important aspects of work organization and of non-work social life. By the same token, part of the continued weakness of class politics is a function of the difficulty of dealing with the growth, since the late nineteenth century, of impersonal forms of property and of the employment of those who do not fall readily into the categories of capitalist or exploited wage-labourer. The point is not that class analysis lacks resources for dealing with these developments, but rather that it has far too many. Whatever else they may have achieved, the various contributions to the debates about the new middle classes have certainly undermined the clear-cut division between those who possess means of production and those who do not. This suggests an important respect in which the potential appeal of class analysis may have declined in the more advanced economies throughout this century.

There are, finally, two further complications to be introduced before I conclude this section. First, these general comments about the 'purchase' of class analysis take no account of the social situations of actors who may or may not be in a position to employ it. First, class analysis would have to coexist with actors' other concerns, objectives and modes of assessing situations. A political party concerned to pursue what it believes to be the interests of the working class as a whole is also likely to have a variety of more immediate concerns. In addition, due to the cultural and educational diversity of any complex society, actors will have differing modes of assessing and evaluating situations available to them. For example, the use of professional discourses generally requires specialist training and often the occupation of a particular professional position. Even if discourses are available to actors it does not follow that they will be employed. For example, accountants may find it difficult to locate themselves and their interests in terms of a class-based socialist discourse. Or, again, the modes of analysis employed by actors may well depend on the possibilities for action that seem to be available to them. While all employees in a manufacturing enterprise may be affected by its investment strategy, they are unlikely to be affected in the same way by that strategy or to be equally well placed to act on it. For these and other reasons, the kind of purchase on the world that class analysis has to offer can vary considerably according to different features of actors' circumstances.

Second, the degree of purchase on the world that class analysis offers at each of its levels of analysis provides no guarantee of mass support. Class analysis is very far from being the only mode of political assessment available to actors in the modern world. Those who do conduct their politics at least partially in terms of some form of class analysis have to work together and compete with adherents of other versions of class analysis and with agencies who have other ways of conducting their political activities – in terms of individualistic ideologies, nationalism, and religious and other sectional divisions. Political support for movements and organizations which conduct and analyse politics in differing ways is one of the outcomes of competition between them and is never simply a reflection of social structure. In this respect, the relative strength or weakness of class-based political movements in Britain, Sweden and the various regions of North America, cannot be explained without reference to the outcomes of past struggles over the policies and internal structure of particular organizations, conflicts between competing movements and organizations, and the outcomes of more widespread attempts to win support.

III

I have argued that class analysis is unsatisfactory as a mode of political analysis, and I have indicated some of the general features of class analysis that help it to continue as a significant element in the academic social sciences and in other political discourses. Let me conclude by returning to my comment on socialist revisionism. Class analysis operates in terms of some combination of two interrelated elements, a notion of classes as social forces and a conception of class interests as structurally determined. I have disputed both of them. Socialists who regard those elements as providing an insufficient foundation for socialist politics have traditionally stressed values in their place. Bernstein and Crosland, in rather different ways, both respond to what they perceive as the inadequacy of a politics organized around the pursuit of class interests by proposing that socialist politics be organized primarily around socialist values instead.

Now, there is no denying that appeals to values can be effective in some conditions, just as appeals to interests can be in others. But attempts to provide accounts of movements and the conditions of their support in terms of values are no more satisfactory than those conducted in terms of interests. If the revisionist analysis of the decline of interest-based politics as a function of capitalist economic development involves altogether too simple a view of the conditions in which interests are politically significant, then the value-based politics which it presents as the alternative is equally simplistic. In fact, there is an important sense in which the two belong together, with interests and values being seen as the two primary sources of motivation for rational action. If the appeal to one is unsatisfactory then the other must be brought in to take its place. In this respect, Marxism's materialist account of action in terms of interests, Bernstein's and Crosland's ethical idealisms, and Weber's combination of interests and values (ideal interests) are all variations on a common theme. Stories of rational economic man are constructed around a closely related theme. In this case, the perceived inadequacy of analyses conducted in terms of preference rankings provokes the remedy of introducing altruism as an alternative to self-interest as another source of motivation.

It would take too long to pursue the ramifications of this theme in any detail here. For present purposes, the problem with this theme – quite apart from all the difficulties associated with the notion of rationality – is the way it takes the motivation of action as the starting-point for its account of political life. Of course, motivations play a part in the actions of individuals, but it does not follow that a simple model of motivation (people pursue their interest, preferences, values, or whatever) is a suitable starting-point for social analysis. I argued in Chapter 3 that interests, values, or whatever are effective, in the sense of having social consequences, only insofar as they relate to the decisions and actions of some actor or actors. They depend on the possibility that they are able to be formulated by the relevant actors, and therefore on the modes of analysing and evaluating situations available to them. The interests, preferences and values pursued by actors are always dependent on the discursive and other conditions which allow them to be formulated.

The trouble with general accounts of socialist (or any other) politics in terms of the pursuit of either interests or values is that they bear little relation to either the range of modes of social analysis available to actors in complex societies or the complexity of the social conditions in which they may be employed. Movements, parties and other organizations obtain their support in different ways from a variety of differently situated groups and individuals.

Rather than attempt the construction of such general accounts we need to raise questions concerning modes of social analysis and the social conditions in which they may be employed and thereby have consequences for the decisions and actions of some actor or actors. Considerations of the validity and coherence of class analysis and other modes of social analysis may be important, but they cannot provide the answers to those questions.

NOTES
1. Cutler *et al.*, 1977, 1978, Hindess, 1983, 1987.
2. There are many versions of this argument. In addition to Clegg *et al.*, 1986, there is a good selection in Goldthorpe (ed.), 1984.
3. For recent examples see Fine *et al.*, 1984, and Wood, 1986.

6 Rationality and the characterization of modern society

In his review of Brentano's book, *The Development of Value Theory*, Weber argues that economic theory is concerned with working out the consequences of the assumption of economic rationality on the part of economic agents. Economic theory does this in purely analytic terms and independently of any psychological laws or assumptions. Weber goes on to suggest that the theory gives only an approximation to reality because, of course, the assumption that actors always act rationally does not hold. Nevertheless:

> . . . the historical peculiarity of the capitalistic epoch, and thereby also the significance of marginal utility theory (as of every economic theory of value) for the understanding of this epoch, rests on the circumstance that – while the economic history of some epochs in the past has not without reason been designated as 'history of non-economic conditions' – under today's conditions of existence the approximation of reality to the theoretical propositions of economics has been a *constantly increasing* one. It is an approximation to reality that has implicated the destiny of ever-wider layers of humanity. And it will hold more and more broadly, as far as our horizons allow us to see. (Weber, 1975: 33)

Here, as so often in his work, Weber characterizes the modern West as dominated by the secular growth of instrumental rationality. It is a theme that has been echoed by numerous subsequent writers. This chapter questions not so much the empirical adequacy of that characterization, but rather its conceptual foundations in a specific model of the actor. Weber's 'actor' is a human individual, analysed in terms of concepts of interests, values, a need for meaning, and a potential for rational calculation. The relations and oppositions between these concepts are central to Weber's typologies of action and of the forms of legitimate domination, and to his discussions of the tensions between formal and substantive rationality. Closely related models of the actor can be found in rational choice theories in economics, political science and sociology, and in much of the social science literature on 'rationality'.

Weber's model of the actor operates with a limited and inadequate account of the conditions of action, and especially of the discursive conditions necessary for actors to reach and formulate decisions. Similar problems arise in rational choice theories and other social scientific discussion of 'rationality'. Critical discussion of the relations between actors and the discursive and other conditions of action undermines both these models and Weber's methodological individualism. Social life is strictly irreducible to the actors' constitutive actions, and there are actors other than human individuals. Following a discussion of Weber's model of the actor in the first section, the remainder of this chapter considers problems, first, with his characterization of the modern West as dominated by the growth of instrumental rationality and, second, with his treatment of rationality as an intrinsic, if sometimes inhibited, feature of the human actor.

Weber's model of the actor

Some years ago I argued that Weber's definitions of sociology and social action represent a humanist version of the rationalist conception of action.[1] In this conception, action always involves, first, a realm of ideas (values, meanings, representations), second, a realm of nature and, third, a mechanism of the realization of ideas in the realm of nature – namely, human action. The mechanism may be defined at the level of the individual human subject, as in Weber's methodological writings, or at some supra-individual or social level, as in much of the work of Durkheim and Parsons. But, however such a mechanism may be thought to operate, the effect of its operations is to constitute some part of the world as the product of both natural and extra-natural, or ideal, determinations. Where the first is the proper object of natural scientific investigation, the second should be objects of understanding. Social or cultural phenomena, in other words, must be analysed in terms of the ideas (values, meanings, or whatever) which they express.

Weber's methodological protocols clearly present a rationalism in this sense. 'We shall speak of "action" in so far as the acting individual attaches a subjective meaning to his behaviour – be it overt or covert, omission or acquiescence' (Weber, 1978: 4). Action and behaviour are both events in nature, but action is also something more: it is the expression of a meaning, which is not itself part of nature. Weber's concept of action therefore postulates a realm of ideas (called meanings or ultimate values), a realm of nature, and the will and consciousness of the human individual as the mechanism of realization of ideas in nature. It is a theoretical humanism in the sense that the mechanism is supposed to operate solely at the level of the individual human subject. Weber insists that social relationships and social collectivities are always reducible in principle to the actions of individuals. They 'must be treated as solely the resultants and modes of organisation of the particular acts of individual persons, since these alone can be treated as agents in a course of subjectively understandable action' (ibid.: 13).

It is well known, of course, that Weber's attempts to conceptualize forms of social action are not always consistent with this methodological individualism. But, in his definitions of sociology and his explicit methodological protocols, the mechanism of realization of meanings and values is always the human individual: on the one hand, subject to physiological and psychological determinations and, on the other, a free agent, a subject of will and consciousness. Because action involves both natural and ideal determinations, the line between action and behaviour is often very difficult to draw. Indeed, Weber insists that a large and sociologically significant part of human behaviour is 'marginal between the two' (ibid.: 4]. This notion of action bordering on mere behaviour plays a central role in Weber's sociology. For example, in his preliminary outline of the fundamental concepts of sociology in *Economy and Society* (1978) he distinguishes four basic types of social action according to their mode of orientation. Two are rational: instrumentally rational (*zwechtrational*), defined in relation to a system of discrete individual ends and the rational estimation of means available for their attainment; and value-rational (*wertrational*), involving a conscious belief in an absolute value and its implementation independently of the prospects for its successful realization. The others, traditional and affectual orientations are explicitly conceived as on 'the borderline of what can justifiably be called meaningfully oriented action, and indeed often on the other side' (Weber, 1978: p.25). This suggests that 'action' should be seen as intrinsically rational – that is, it deviates from rationality to the extent that it is the product of merely natural determinations. While theoretical humanism must imply the possibility of borderline cases, it is clearly impossible to derive the specific categories of traditional and affectual action in this way.

Weber presents human behaviour as rational to the extent that it conforms to meanings and values, and non-rational to the extent that it does not. It is for this reason that he insists on the construction of *rational* ideal types. If we start from the presumption of rationality in our attempts to make sense of human actions, then the place of other, non-rational elements in behaviour may then be seen 'as accounting for the observed deviations from this hypothetical course' (ibid.: 6). A similar methodological presumption of rationality is one of the foundations of rational choice theories in the social sciences. It therefore follows from this starting-point that departures from rationality are to be understood as resulting from the interference of affectual, physiological or other elements at the level of the individual actor. We shall see shortly that a different kind of reason may also be advanced as to why action in some conditions may be more rational than action in others.

Action is the attempted realization of meanings or purposes. But what of the meanings or purposes themselves? In his final revision of the introduction to his studies of the economic ethics of the world religions, Weber added the following passage.

> Not ideas but material and ideal interests directly govern men's conduct. Yet very frequently the world images that have been created by 'ideas' have, like switchmen, determined the tracks along which action has been pushed by the dynamics of interest (Weber, 1946: 280).

I return below to the second sentence. For the moment, consider the distinction between material and ideal interests. The first is a matter of the distribution of material goods, and more generally of whatever concerns the health, happiness and well-being of human individuals. The second concerns their search for 'meaning'. Meanings are not a function of physiological or psychological needs alone, they also refer to something beyond the material realm, to ultimate values. In Weber's model of the actor these values must be conceived as ultimate givens: they are not derived from a knowledge of material conditions and they are not determined by material interests (although Weber does not deny that there may be an important 'elective affinity' between world-views and material interests [Weber, 1949: 56]). The realm of values is a source of irreconcilable antagonism and conflict in human affairs:

> [We] must recognize that general views of life and the universe can never

be the products of increasing empirical knowledge, and that the highest
ideals, which move us most forcefully, are always formed only in the
struggle with other ideals which are just as sacred to others as ours are to
us. (Weber, 1949: 57)

In effect, then, we have a model of the actor as a human individual, a
biological and psychological organism endowed with a potential for
rational calculation and acting in terms of both material and ideal
interests. This actor and its orientations provide Weber with the
means of characterizing the modern world in terms of the spread of
instrumental rationality, bureaucracy and rational–legal domination.

The final section of this chapter shows that Weber's model of the
actor gives a limited and inadequate account of the conditions of
action in general, and of what he conceives as rational action in
particular. I argued in 'Two kinds of person' (Chapter 4) that actors
should be conceived simply as loci of decision and action. Actors do
things as a consequence of decisions. These are called actions, and
the actors' decisions play an important part in their explanation.
Actors may also do things that are not consequences of decisions,
and their explanation takes a rather different form. This approach
has the advantage of reducing to an absolute minimum the assumptions that are built into the basic concept of actor. Actors have
reasons for at least some of the things they do. Any further
significant attributes that actors may be thought to possess (for
example, the various cognitive interests that Habermas presents as
constitutive of knowledge) must therefore be seen as contingent,
posing issues for investigation rather than as constitutive of actors as
such. In particular, actors' reasons and decisions are dependent on
the discursive conditions which allow them to be formulated. Naturally, Weber recognizes that much human action is not rational, and
that rationality is therefore subject to conditions. But those conditions are conceived in terms of the absence of irrational interferences with the otherwise intrinsic rationality of the actor. In effect,
the assumptions built in to Weber's model of the actor leave no space
for questions concerning the discursive conditions required for
actors to reach and formulate decisions.

An important consequence of this argument is that a typology of
actors' orientations, of the kind that Weber offers, is not a satisfactory starting-point for the analysis of social conditions. Indeed,
there are points where Weber might seem to be on the verge of

recognizing this problem. Consider for example, the second sentence quoted in the extract above (p. 125) 'Yet very frequently the world images that have been created by "ideas" have, like switchmen, determined the tracks along which action has been pushed by the dynamics of interest' (Weber, 1946: 280). As Schlucter notes in his commentary on this passage, [2] it suggests the need for a level of analysis (of world-views and their institutionalization) that goes beyond that of actors and their orientations.

In Weber's methodological writings action is said to depart from rationality to the extent that it is subject to behavioural (psychological or physiological) determinations. But there is in Weber's works another kind of reason why action may be less than fully rational. Consider the case of modern capitalism. In the author's introduction, published in Parsons' translation of *The Protestant Ethic*, Weber tells us that rational capitalistic economic action involves calculations in terms of capital: 'an actual adaptation of economic action to a comparison of money income with money expenses takes place, no matter how primitive the form' (Weber, 1930: 19). Rational capitalistic economic action presupposes the existence of money – that is, it depends on conditions that cannot be defined solely at the level of the acting individual.[3]

In the case of specifically *modern* capitalism, a great deal more than this is required: the rational capitalist organization of formally free labour; the separation of the business from the household; rational book-keeping; and rational structures of law and administration. '[M]odern rational capitalism has need, not only of the technical means of production, but of a calculable legal system and of administration in terms of formal rules.' Otherwise, there can be 'no rational enterprise under individual initiative' (ibid: 25). In other words, the rationality of the individual modern capitalist is inconceivable without 'the specific and peculiar rationalism of modern culture' (ibid.: 26).

What Weber represents as the most rational form of economic action depends on the prior elaboration of specific discursive forms (for example, in law and accountancy) and, more generally, on the realization of a rationality in the institutional organization of society itself. Here the rationality of the individual actor is a function of a pre-existing rationality at the supra-individual level of society. By the same token, the absence of rationality at the level of society reduces the scope for rationality at the level of the individual. With the best (that is, most rational) will in the world, medieval capitalists could not hope to attain the level of economic rationality that is possible in the modern West. Here again, Weber's own account of the conditions of rational action necessarily takes us beyond the level of individual actors and their orientations.

This necessity for a level of analysis beyond that of actors and their orientations is, of course, widely recognized in the literature. For example, Parsons brings a rather Weberian analysis of the unit act into a tense and perpetually uneasy relationship with a further level of analysis in terms of systems of action.[4] Or, again, Schluchter (1981) attempts a systematic reconstruction of Weber's developmental history, making use of Habermas' notion of an infrastructure of action systems. In these terms the human ability to communicate and act is the subjective correlate of an objective infrastructure. The problem with these analyses can be seen if we consider Habermas' own commentary on the limitations of Weber's treatment of rationality. Habermas criticizes Weber for his elision of two levels of analysis of rationality – one at the level of the actor and the other at the level of systems of action. Weber, together with Marx, Horkheimer and Adorno, identifies:

> . . . societal rationalization with the growth of the instrumental and strategic rationality of action complexes: on the other hand they implicitly have in mind a more comprehensive societal rationality. (Habermas, 1979: 192)

So far, so good. Unfortunately, he proceeds to locate what is missing from Weber's analyses at the level of actors' orientations. In distinguishing degrees of rationality of action,

> . . . Weber does not take the social relationship as his point of departure. He considers only the ends–means relationship of a teleologically conceived, monological action to be capable of rationalization. (ibid.: 194)

Habermas offers the concept of '"communicative action" in order to bring out those aspects of the rationality of action that were neglected in Weber's actions theory' (ibid.).

The treatment of social relationships in terms of actors' orientations is undoubtedly a weak point in Weber's arguments. The trouble with Habermas' proposed remedy is that it merely takes as its starting-point a different aspect of actors' orientations, and in this respect it hardly advances beyond the terms of Weber's own position. For all their emphasis on the need for a further level of analysis – for example, in terms of systems and their exigencies – many of these attempts to transcend Weber's limits nevertheless take actors and their orientations as an essential starting-point for their constructions.

In what follows I argue that actors' orientations are not generally an appropriate starting-point for the analysis of those aspects of social life that go beyond the level of the individual actor. Weber's analysis of rationalization is therefore problematic not only because it involves a level of structural analysis that is inconsistent with his explicit methodological individualism, but also because it is a form of characterization of social conditions based on actors' orientations. This chapter is primarily concerned with the second of these issues. I consider first the 'structural' question of the characterization of social conditions in terms of rationality (or any other orientation) before proceeding to Weber's concept of rationality itself.

The institutionalization of purposive rationality in the modern West

A product of modern European civilisation, studying any problem of universal history, is bound to ask himself to what combination of circumstances the fact should be attributed that in Western civilisation, and in Western civilisation only, cultural phenomena have appeared which (as we like to think) lie in a line of development having universal significance and value. (Weber, 1930: 13)

It is always tempting to read Weber as proposing a conception of history as the progressive realization of the purposive rationality which he presents as characteristic of the modern West. The point is not that Weber proposes a necessary developmental tendency in history, since his reference above to 'combinations of circumstances' clearly suggests otherwise. Rather, he appears to operate with a hierarchical principle of ranking in terms of which other societies or cultures may be analysed according to the extent to which they realize, or depart from, the rationalization said to be characteristic of the modern West. Weber certainly insists that modern rational capitalism presupposes definite social conditions of existence, but these often seem little more than expressions of rationality in other spheres – the rational organization of formally free labour, rational book-keeping, rational systems of law and administration, and so on.

If modern Western civilization appears as the realization of an essential rationality, then other civilizations may be conceived in terms of their departure from it. It is no surprise, then, that the decisive obstacle to the development of modern capitalism in the great civilizations of India and China proves to be that the Eastern civilizations embody a spirit alien to that of modern rational capitalism. The difficulty with this position is simply that it combines two incompatible principles of analysis. On the one hand a society or culture is the expression of an inner principle and on the other it is subject to numerous and distinct conditions of existence.[5] A similar principle of ranking appears in Weber's discussion of the types of social action. Some pages after his insistence on the construction of rational ideal types he goes on to suggest that mechanical and instinctive factors are completely predominant 'in the early stages even of human development' (Weber, 1978: 17). Here, as in the review quoted at the beginning of this chapter, Weber suggests that the theoretical tools of the social scientist are more nearly applicable the closer we approach the societies of the modern West.

In response to this interpretation, it would not be difficult to cite numerous passages in which Weber explicitly rejects any teleological account of history (especially, but not only, in his comments on Marxism). But what is at issue here is teleology as an explanatory mechanism. The denial of teleology is part and parcel of Weber's rejection of single-factor explanations. For example, Weber's treatment of developmental processes within the major world religions appears to involve an inherent rationalizing tendency.[6] But he insists that this is not the only mechanism in operation, and its significance is always as strictly limited in relation to other factors.

Again, the interpretation of the modern world in terms of the realization of a purposive rationality seems to be incompatible both with Weber's methodological individualism (but then any supra-individual level of analysis is problematic in those terms) and with his understanding of social life as involving irreconcilable interests and value conflicts. On the second point, consider Weber's treatment of the formal and substantive aspects of rationality. The former refers to the calculability of means and procedures, whatever the end pursued, while the latter refers to the assessment of outcomes in terms of a particular value standpoint. The rationalization of the modern West involves the spread of formal rationality, which goes along with a considerable diversity of substantive ends. The demands of substantive rationality are invariably frustrated – if only by the actions of others (or oneself) towards alternative substantive ends. If the world is shaped by struggles around competing material interests and values then it can hardly be analysed in terms of the realization of an inner principle. As for the tensions between formal and substantive rationality, what makes this such an issue in Weber's account of the modern world is not the fact that the demands of substantive rationality are frustrated, since that must always be the case. Rather it is that the modern West is supposed to be dominated by the world-view of formal rationality, which insists on seeing the world primarily as the field of implementation of human purposes (unlike the world-views of magic and the great religions). It is in terms of that world-view that the frustration of the demands of any substantive rationality appears so problematic.

This point returns us yet again to the realization thesis. The tension between formal and substantive rationality appears to be peculiarly characteristic of the modern period precisely because this period is supposed to be dominated by the world-view of formal rationality. If the modern West is not to be understood in terms of such a realization thesis then it is difficult to see why Weber (and all too many others) should make such a fuss about the rationalization of the world and its alleged consequences. If modern Western societies involve other significant developments, not themselves reducible to effects of rationalization, then they cannot be characterized as essentially embodying the world-view of formal rationality. In other words, no general propositions (or problems) concerning the character of life in the modern West follow from the extension of formal rationality. Short of conceiving of the modern West in teleological mode as approximating towards the expression or realization of a world-view of formal rationality, the consequences of any extension of formal rationality will always depend on the conditions in which that extension takes place – and these cannot be expected to operate uniformly throughout the various social milieus of the modern West.

Thus, even if Western societies were to have experienced a massive extension of what might, for present purposes, be termed formal rationality, that would amount merely to one distinctive feature of those societies amongst others. Neither cultures nor societies are expressions of world-views, and the consequences of whatever world-views or other cultural features might be said to exist within them will always depend on an irreducible variety of other conditions. I have presented the argument against the analysis of societies or cultures as the expressions or realizations of some predominant world-view in a general and abstract form. It is reinforced if we consider how limited and uninformative such a characterization may be. In the context of the present argument, this point can be made most forcefully by returning to the concept of actor. First, actors' orientations do not suffice to define or constitute the relationships in which they are involved. Paul Hirst has given a particularly clear demonstration of this point in his discussion of Althusser's attempt to account for the reproduction of relations of production by means of the ideological constitution of subjects[7] – but we have seen that the argument applies generally to all attempts to reduce relations to actors' orientations. The rationality or otherwise of actors may tell us something about the relationships between them, but it cannot tell us very much.

Second, I have indicated above why Weber's model of the actor, as a human individual characterized by a potential for rational calculation and acting in terms of material and ideal interests, should be replaced by a more general model of the actor as locus of decision and action. This is important in the present context for two reasons. First, where formal rationality (or whatever) is thought to be a socially widespread feature of the way actors evaluate their situation and act within it, that raises problems of explanation which cannot be adequately posed on the basis of Weber's model. I return to this point below. Second, as I argued in Chapter 4, once the concept of actor is freed from Weber's indefensible theoretical humanism, it is possible to take note of actors other than human individuals.

An actor is a locus of decision and action where action is, at least in part, a consequence of that actor's decisions. Human individuals are certainly actors in this sense, but they are by no means the only entities that reach decisions and attempt to act on them. State agencies, capitalist enterprises, churches, trades unions, political parties are all examples of actors other than human individuals, and they all have means of reaching decisions and of acting on some of them. Serious problems arise, of course, if the concept of actor is extended to entities that have no identifiable means of formulating decisions, let alone of acting on them. Classes, societies, men as a collectivity subordinating women as another collectivity, are all spurious actors that are sometimes invoked in political or social scientific discourse. I have discussed some of the problems with the invocation of such spurious actors in earlier chapters. Here, it is sufficient to note that, if the concept of actor is restricted to entities capable of reaching and acting on decisions, then there are numerous significant actors in the modern world other than human individuals. In that respect, any approach to the analysis of modern societies that admits only human individuals as effective actors must be regarded as seriously incomplete.

It is often said, by Weber amongst many others, that all such actors are themselves reducible to human individuals. But that is to mistake the significance of one important difference between human individuals and other actors. Human individuals are the only actors whose actions do not invariably involve the actions of others. The actions of capitalist enterprises, for example, always depend on those of other actors (executives, managerial, supervisory and other employees, legal representatives) and therefore on the specific character of the relationships between the enterprise and these other actors. The actions of human individuals are not always so constrained. This shows that there may be important differences between the conditions of action of human individuals and those of other actors. Nevertheless, it does *not* show that all social actors are equivalent (except in this one important respect) or that one kind of actor is reducible to the other.

The actions of social actors are critically dependent on the modes of assessment of their situation which they deploy in reaching decisions and on the specific sets of social relations in which they are implicated. In both respects, the characterization of their conditions of action in terms of rationality is, to say the least, less than informative. To take the modes of assessment first, consider the case of capitalist enterprises. Even if we were to accept, for the sake of argument, that capitalist enterprises were rational in their assessments, that would tell us remarkably little about how they might be expected to act. Marxist and neo-classical economists alike often suggest that the rigours of the market impose a uniquely defined mode of assessment (profit maximization) on enterprises. In fact, as I suggested in Chapter 2, it is easy to show that there is no such uniquely defined mode of assessment given by the assumption of rationality or by such rigours as the marketplace may impose.[8] The assumption of rationality, in other words, gives a misleading impression of uniformity, and it tells us little about the particular modes of assessment employed by a firm in any given case.

Similar points could be made about the relationships between enterprises (or other social actors) and the actors involved in their decisions and actions. Bureaucracy, in something like Weber's ideal-typical form, is often supposed to characterize the distinctively modern pattern of such relationships. It is distinctively modern, first, as the embodiment of instrumental rationality as a principle of organization and, second, in its dependence on that wider rationalization of modern-day social life which allows for appointment on the basis of ability, the separation of home from office, payment in money rather than in kind, and so on. In fact, as Turner and Factor have noted, much of the literature on complex organizations 'has been devoted to the criticism of the rigidity and limited applicability of Weber's conception even to those organisations that aspire to maximal efficiency and rationality' (Turner and Factor, 1984: 52). In this case too, the notion of rationality at best gives a misleading impression of uniformity in the organizational structures of capitalist enterprises, state agencies, or other social actors. Although there may be a sense in which instrumental rationality is an index of certain gross differences between our own and distinctively other civilizations, it would nevertheless tell us remarkably little about the modes of assessment employed by actors in the modern world, the diverse ways in which their capacities for action may or may not depend on other actors, and still less about the sets of more or less stable relationships that may obtain between actors.

Rationality and the concept of actor
The argument so far has suggested that the massive extension of formal rationality into many areas of social life (such as might be supposed to have characterized the development of the modern West) merely indicates one distinctive feature of modern societies amongst others. Short of a teleological analysis of these societies as (approaching towards) the realization of an essential inner principle, it is difficult to draw any general conclusion from that feature alone. Its eventual consequences will depend on other features of the society or culture in question, and these cannot be derived from the extension of formal rationality itself. Discussion of the rationaliza-

tion of life in the modern world is therefore less informative than has often been supposed.

This section moves on to a different order of problems by reconsidering the links between rationality and the actor which it is often said to characterize. I have already suggested the need for a different and, in certain respects, more general model of the actor as locus of decision and action. This formulation might appear to suggest that Weber's model of the actor could be regarded as a special case, and therefore as perfectly legitimate within limits. Unfortunately, the problems with Weber's model are more serious than a simple limitation in the range of cases to which it may be applied. The effect of treating rationality and other attributes as intrinsic features of the human actor is to foreclose serious questions of the discursive conditions of action, to impose a restrictive and unnecessary psychic unity on to the conception of actor, and to misrepresent the location of what might be called rationalizing tendencies in the modern world. To establish these points we need to reconsider the ways in which rationality (or other attributes) might be considered relevant to the conceptualization of actors and their actions.

We may begin by noting that concepts of the person differ from one culture to another, and also over time within cultures or civilizations. The modern Western conception of the person is not a human universal, a natural and given datum of human experience. 'Forms of specification of individuals exist in all societies', as Hirst and Woolley (1983: 118) point out, 'but they are not necessarily specified as individual subjects, as unique entities coincident with a distinct consciousness and will'. Within the general Western conceptualization of the person, those variants which insist on the propensity of the actor to act in accordance with a rational assessment of material and ideal interests have long occupied a predominant place in the discourses of politics and economics amongst others.

Now, it is not difficult to show that the model of rational economic man is descriptively inadequate. Indeed, Weber himself makes that point. He insists that we start from the presumption of rationality in our attempts to analyse human behaviour so that the place of non-rational elements in behaviour might be seen 'as accounting for the observed deviations from this hypothetical course' (Weber, 1978: 6). In Chapter 7, 'Taking choice seriously', I argue that there are severe problems with such a starting-point. In particular, it forecloses serious problems concerning the forms of discourse available to actors and employed by them in assessing their situation and deciding on a course of action.

But it is necessary to go further to indicate how such inadequate conceptualizations of the actor can nevertheless play such an important part in the modern world. The first point to notice here is that the significance of the model of rational economic man and related conceptions of the person is not a matter of 'realism', in the sense of approximating to an accurate description of how people behave. These models do not have their origin in careful observation of human behaviour in developing Western capitalist societies. They will not disappear merely because they can be shown to be inadequate in the face of theoretical argument and evidence accumulated in anthropology, history, psychoanalysis, and numerous experimental and fieldwork studies in our societies. The test of falsifiability is not a significant element in the life of such doctrines. What is at stake here is not just a matter of economic or political theory, of the more or less elaborate constructions based on rational economic man and 'his' close relations. It is also a matter of concepts of the person that are 'implicated to a greater or lesser degree in our legal system, in our conceptions of contract and the wage labour relationship, in many of our assumptions about education, and so on' (Hirst and Woolley, 1983: 131).

If realism is not necessarily to be expected of these concepts of the person, they must nevertheless have a certain plausibility. It must be possible to represent the relevant aspects of human behaviour in terms of the actions of such persons, and to have some means of accounting for actions that fail to conform – for example, through categories of mental illness, affectual and other non-rational sources of motivation, and so on. For example, the doctrine of revealed preference in contemporary neo-classical economics allows much of consumer behaviour to be analysed in these terms. The proposals of Weber and many rational choice theorists that we construct models of rational action, introducing affectual and other non-rational elements only when strictly necessary to account for deviations, performs a similar function. So, at a rather different level, do the normalizing discourses of psychiatry, penology, and the like. In *Discipline and Punish* (1977), Foucault has shown how the discourse of the prison can find reinforcement in the very failures of the prison system.

What is required then for the discourses of rational economic man and his relations to be implicated in significant areas of social life is that there should not appear to be too many departures from the norm, and that any departures can be explained away. This generally means that actors must seem to incorporate something approaching the appropriate model in their own assessments and decisions. It must be possible, for example, to assimilate the decision-making process in most capitalist enterprises fairly closely to the model of rational economic actor. This requirement will, of course, be relaxed for the very young, the senile, and others judged to have departed considerably from the rational norm. For the rest, models of rational action are implicated in significant areas of social life to the extent that the majority of relevant actors incorporate such models into their own assessments and decisions.

Does this mean that Weber's model of the actor, or something very like it, can be saved after all – at least with regard to modern Western societies? Fortunately not. One reason is that the location of rationality as an intrinsic, if sometimes inhibited, property of the actor forecloses serious questions concerning the discursive conditions of decision and action – a point which I develop in the following two chapters. But two further reasons are also worth noting here. First, the presumption of rationality as a property of the actor implies a certain consistency or coherence across the range of the actor's behaviour – except in those cases where 'non-rational' elements intervene. If it is located instead in certain features of the discourses employed in the reaching and formulating of decisions, then there is no reason to assume consistency or coherence across the range of the actor's decisions. Second, to say that some model of rational action is incorporated in an actor's assessments is not to say that other significant elements might not also be involved. A case in point would be the self-conscious rationality displayed by actors caught up in paranoia or certain forms of compulsive behaviour. These points demonstrate that, even if rationality were to be displayed by some actor or actors in significant areas of their activity, we should still be wary of regarding it as an intrinsic feature of the actors themselves.

Finally, if models of rational action are indeed implicated in significant areas of social life, this requires that those areas can themselves be represented as fields of instrumental action. In other words, there must be discourses in which the economy, politics, the criminal population, or whatever, can be represented as a field of potential action and effects in order to allow a 'rational' calculation of objectives and how to achieve them. The various more or less sophisticated economic discourses employed by capitalist enterprises, financial institutions and government departments would be examples. Foucault has made a similar point in his discussions of the interdependence of power and knowledge in the modern period:

> . . . these relations of power cannot themselves be established, consolidated, or implemented without the production, accumulation, circulation and functioning of a discourse. There can be no possible exercise of power without a certain economy of discourses of truth which operates through and on the basis of this association. We are subjected to the production of truth through power and we cannot exercise power except through the production of truth. (Foucault, 1980: 93)

Here the operations of power depend on the possibility of representing its field of operation in terms of a calculation of effects.

Perhaps a further attempt at rehabilitation might be suggested at this point. There is certainly a sense in which Weber is absolutely right to insist that the modern period has seen a massive extension of instrumental rationality. But here too it is necessary to be wary of Weber's account. First, there is a significant element of positivism in Weber's distinction between objective and subjective rationality. In the case of the former, techniques for achieving given ends are determined in accordance with scientific knowledge. The discourses of rational action implicated in the fields of law, economic activity or education certainly involve what Foucault calls 'regimes of truth' – that is, the operation of criteria, norms and procedures for identifying or arguing about 'true' propositions in any given case. We can distinguish assessments made in terms of the appropriate regime of truth (Weber's 'objective rationality') from other assessments made by actors. Such distinctions may be important, for example, in the event that actors are required to account for their conduct, should it be regarded as responsible or irresponsible, careless or considered, that of a 'reasonable man' or something other, and so on. But we can register those distinctions and their ramifications without necessarily unifying the various regimes of truth in the name of science or objectivity.

Second, there is no reason to regard the discourses representing some part of the world as a field of instrumental action as if they were themselves unified as just so many expressions of the one world-view or orientation. We should certainly expect to find connections between these discourses; features of one may be incorporated in others, and some may share common features (for example, elements of the normalizing discourses of psychiatry or clinical medicine may be incorporated into criminal law). But it would be a mistake to assume an overall coherence. Examination of the connections between law and psychiatry, although certainly revealing areas of incorporation, also reveals considerable areas of dispute and acute tension. The trouble with Weber's position here is that the rationalization of different fields is seen in terms of an inherent unifying principle at the level of the rationality of the human individual, and of the removal of its inhibitions in the shape of spiritual and other obstacles.

Summary and conclusions

To conclude, I have argued against Weber's treatment of the modern West as dominated by the growth of formal rationality at two levels. First, actors' orientations are not generally an appropriate starting-point for the analysis of social relationships. In this respect, the attempts by Weber and all too many others to characterize the modern West in terms of the alleged growth of formal rationality are at best relatively uninformative – an index of gross differences between our own and other civilizations – and at worst seriously misleading. If modern Western societies could be regarded as just so many expressions of the one inner principle of formal rationality, then it would certainly be possible to draw general conclusions from the secular growth of that orientation. But, in the absence of that indefensible teleology, it is clear that the consequences of any extension of formal rationality must depend on the conditions in which that extension takes place.

Second, there are serious problems with Weber's model of the actor as a human individual with a, frequently inhibited, potential for rational calculation and action. Not only are there actors other than human individuals, some of whose decisions have important consequences, but Weber's model gives an inadequate account of the conditions of action in general and of rational action in particular. Of course, Weber recognizes that action is not always rational, and that the rationality of action is therefore dependent on definite conditions. But his methodological injunction that we should start from rational ideal types requires that those conditions be conceived as the absence of interferences to the rationality of the actor. Against that position I argue that actors' decisions and the reasons for them are dependent both on complex internal processes and on the discursive conditions which allow them to be formulated. In this sense, rationality is a matter both of the discourses employed in the reaching and formulating of decisions and of their deployment by the actor: it is not an intrinsic feature of the actor as such. It is therefore possible to pose questions of the discursive conditions of action that are foreclosed by Weber's treatment of rationality as an intrinsic, if frequently inhibited, feature of the actor.

Weber's account of rationality imposes a spurious unity at the levels both of the individual actor and of such rationalizing tendencies as may be found in the modern world. There are numerous practical discourses representing parts of the world as fields of instrumental action, but the effect of treating them as so many expressions of the one world-view of instrumental rationality is to give an erroneous impression of their overall coherence and to obscure the difficult questions of the social conditions on which they depend.

Notes
1. Hindess, 1978.
2. Schluchter, 1981, p.25f.
3. Cf, the definition of money in Weber, 1978, p.75f.
4. There is a good discussion of the implications of this point in Savage, 1981.
5. See Hindess, 1978 for an extended discussion of this point.
6. Cf. Roth and Schluchter, 1979, ch. 1.
7. Hirst, 1979.
8. Cf. the discussions in Cutler *et al.*, 1978, part 11; also Williams *et al.*, 1985.

7   Taking choice seriously

> A major task of contemporary social theory is to show how individually rational behaviour may bring about social change and collective action. (cover of Elster 1983a)

'Rationality' means many different things in the social sciences, but one of the most influential contemporary usages is in the application of game theory to the analysis of social life. The sentence quoted above, which is taken from the editorial blurb for a series of books 'Studies in Rationality and Social Change' of which Jon Elster is an editor, is to be understood in that sense. A major objective of this chapter is to show why that sentence must be regarded as deeply problematic. Rational choice theory insists on the importance of intentionality, and it is right to do so, but what it has to offer in the understanding of social life is extremely limited, and it obscures problems of great theoretical and political significance.

Elster's work is particularly important in this context because, unlike most practitioners of the 'rational choice' approach, he is not primarily concerned with constructing technical models to deal with this or that aspect of social and economic behaviour. Rather, his work is concerned with theoretical and methodological problems that arise when explanation in terms of rational optimizing behaviour is taken as paradigmatic. Elster presents these problems as arising in a variety of contexts: where behaviour departs from the optimizing paradigm because optimal outcomes are not well defined; where the pattern of interaction between intentional agents generates obstacles to the realization of optimal outcomes; where there is interaction between agents' preferences and the constraints within which they operate; and where causal processes interfere in intentional behaviour. These problems are sometimes interpreted as inviting technical solutions through the construction of more sophisticated models of rational action. Elster's discussion, however, goes beyond technicalities and, in so doing, it provides an account of some of the theoretical and methodological presumptions of the rational choice approach to the study of social behaviour. For a critic of the rational choice approach that is the very great merit of his work. Some of the difficulties which I shall note are peculiar to Elster's treatment of these issues, but most have a more general significance.

We begin with Elster's account of rational, optimizing behaviour as the paradigmatic case of intentional explanation and his discussion of some significant departures from that paradigm. Elster, like other advocates of the rational choice approach, is well aware that rational, optimizing behaviour is not a universal feature of human existence. The importance of the paradigm is that it defines the theoretical location of all other cases as specific departures from the norm. In other words, the model of rational, optimizing action provides a more general conceptual structure for the analysis of intentional action in other contexts. The remainder of this chapter develops arguments against that conceptual structure. Actors do indeed make choices, and they act on some of them. Their choices have an important part to play in the explanation of what they do. But to insist on that point is not to accept the conceptual structure Elster offers for the analysis of intentional action. I argue that important issues about actors' choices and the social conditions on which they depend are obscured by the paradigmatic use of the case of rational, optimizing action, and that methodological individualism does not follow from the intentional character of human action.

The paradigm of global maximization

In the first essay of *Ulysses and the Sirens*, Elster suggests that 'in creating man natural selection has transcended itself' (Elster, 1979: 16). Unlike other living creatures, man is characterized by a 'generalised capacity for global maximisation' (ibid.). The import of 'global' here is temporal rather than simply spatial in that it refers to a capacity to transcend the immediate situation of action. Far from being a matter of more or less complex responses to environmental stimuli human activity also involves the capacity to relate to possible future states of affairs in terms of deferred gratification, the adoption of indirect strategies, and so on. Global maximization is an activity of consciousness, and it is this that distinguishes man from even the higher animals.

Two immediate consequences of this starting-point should be noted here. First, if people are indeed characterized by a capacity for global maximization, then some explanation is clearly required for the widespread failure to maximize. Much of Elster's work is concerned with this issue, and we return to some of his explanation below. Second, the idea that natural selection has transcended itself must, if we take it seriously, generate a whole series of difficulties. People are natural objects, subject to natural determinations of various kinds, and they have this maximizing capacity which is no longer subject to those natural determinations. The identification of rationality with the capacity for global maximization results in a strict dichotomy between 'rational' and 'non-rational', in which the latter is relegated to the category of non-intentional, causal explanation. Working with a rather different notion of rationality, Elster here reproduces the Weberian view of action as intrinsically rational and as deviating from rationality to the extent that it is the product of merely natural determinations. The interaction between the 'natural' elements in human behaviour on one hand, and the 'rational' or 'intentional' elements on the other, is rendered incomprehensible by the manner of their separation. The difficulty here is one of Elster's own making and it is certainly not a necessary feature of the rational choice approach. The claim that the assumption of rationality is a valuable heuristic need hardly presuppose Elster's particular dichotomy between the 'natural' and the 'rational'.[1]

Elster specifies the rational choice approach as involving a two-stage model in which the actor selects a course of action to pursue. First there are structural constraints which limit the courses of action that are possible. Second, there is a mechanism which operates on that feasible set to select the actions to be realized.

> Rational choice theories assert that this mechanism is the deliberate and intentional choice for the purpose of maximising some objective function. . . . (Elster, 1979: 113).

This account of rational choice theory allows Elster to identify the following alternatives to that theory. First, there is the structuralist approach which denies the importance of rational choice by insisting on the primacy of structural constraints. Choice is an illusion, and what we do is effectively determined by our structural locations (ibid.: 113–15). The second alternative disputes the reality of rational choice by insisting on the importance of cases where rationality is not well defined and pointing to cases of non-rational behaviour. Given Elster's dichotomy between rational and causal processes, any questioning of rational choice models in such terms amounts to the claim that the mechanism of selection of actions to be realized is a causal rather than an intentional one (ibid.: 115–16). Third, it is possible to dispute the stability of rational choice by reference to the mechanisms of formation and transformation of preferences. On that view, actors' choices are merely stages in a developing process, not the starting-point in the explanation of their behaviour (ibid.: 116).

Elster regards the first of these alternatives as implausible, and with good reason. In fact, it is something of an imaginery opponent, an artefact of his two-stage model of rational choice. Nobody would deny the reality of structural constraints, but Marxists and structural functionalists have been equally far from denying the reality of choice, insisting instead that structural conditions operate on and through actors' consciousnesses thereby affecting the terms in which they make their choices. Elster's caricature of 'structuralism' allows him to ignore their arguments on this point.

He takes the second and third alternatives more seriously, recognizing that they raise genuine difficulties for rational choice theories. These difficulties are to be dealt with, not by denying their existence, but rather by insisting that the rational choice model 'is logically prior to the alternatives' (ibid.: 116). The difficulties are to be incorporated into the analysis as theoretically deviant cases. In *Explaining Technical Change*, he goes one step further.

> . . . although there are strong reasons in principle to insist on the distinctions between intentionality and rationality, and between rationality and optimality, explanation in terms of optimization remains the paradigm case of intentional explanation in the social sciences outside psychology. (Elster, 1983a: 75)

Elster does not so much explain why rational, optimizing behaviour should be accorded that paradigmatic status in the social sciences (still less why psychology should be an exception), as insist that the postulate of rationality should function as a regulative idea. The effect of adopting that position is to impose a definite conceptual structure on the analysis of intentionality. This is represented in the diagram at the beginning of 'Intentional explanation', Chapter 3 of *Explaining Technical Change*, shown here as Figure 7.1. In this figure, irrational behaviour and the various kinds of behaviour that are rational but not optimizing are given their place below the paradigmatic norm of rational optimizing behaviour in the concep-

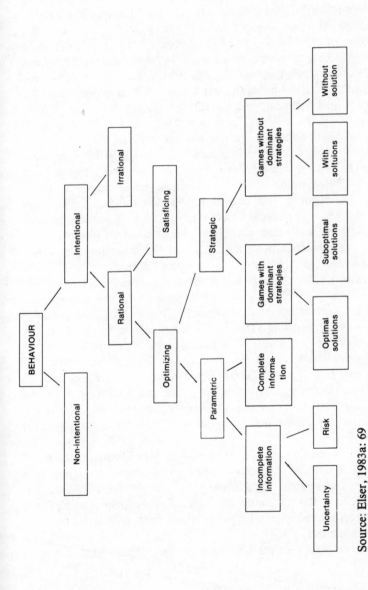

Source: Elser, 1983a: 69

Figure 7.1 The analysis of intentionality.

tual hierarchy. Different kinds of departure from rationality and optimality provide the most important principles of division.

There are several problems with this conceptual structure for the analysis of intentionality, but perhaps the most serious difficulty is that it tries to do too much with such limited theoretical equipment. In order to identify these problems, we must first consider Elster's treatment of departures from the paradigmatic case. For the purposes of exposition, these can be grouped into three categories: cases in which optimal outcomes are not defined or not realized; cases of interaction between constraints and actors' preferences; cases of interaction between causal and intentional processes. We shall consider these categories in turn.

Cases in which optimal outcomes are not realized

Although man is characterized by a capacity for global maximization, there may well be cases where optimal outcomes are not realized. The simplest of these are when an individual persists in the pursuit of incompatible objectives, so that rational deliberation provides no guide to action. Decisions must then be reached by non-rational processes – that is, in Elster's view, through the operation of some causal mechanism. Such cases raise the vexed question, which we consider later, of interaction between intentional and causal processes. Next, there is the question of social choice, usually understood as involving some aggregation procedure operating on individual preferences. We shall see in Chapter 9 that social choice need not be understood in such individualistic terms. It is not difficult to show that any defensible aggregation procedure defined over several individuals can generate an inconsistent pattern of aggregate preferences. There is a considerable literature devoted to the discussion of such issues[2] which, while raising dificulties for the rationality of social choice mechanisms defined in terms of aggregation over individuals, pose no problems for the notion of individual rationality.

More interesting for the rationality of individual behaviour are cases in which the obstacles to optimal outcomes derive not from problems of aggregating the preferences of several individuals but rather from the character of interaction between them. Elster distinguishes two general types of issue here: counterfinality and sub-optimality.

Sub-optimality refers to 'the deliberate realization of a noncooperative solution that is Pareto-inferior to some other payoff set obtainable by individual choices of strategy' (Elster, 1978: 122). It is the dominant solution in the Prisoner's Dilemma and other games where outcomes preferable to all actors can only be obtained by cooperation, which is prevented by the structure of the situation. An example is the game of competitive deflation played by advanced capitalist economies in which each deflates to protect itself, and all suffer in consequence.

The idea of counterfinality is more complex, and we shall see later that it raises very serious difficulties for Elster's position. In *Logic and Society* he defines it as:

> . . . the unintended consequences that arise when each individual in a group acts upon an assumption about his relations to others that, when generalised, yield the contradiction in the consequent of the fallacy of composition, the antecedent of the fallacy being true. (Elster, 1978: 107)

Consider two people walking towards each other in a narrow corridor. Each moves to one side to avoid the other, and they collide. More serious examples are not difficult to find. Elster gives the example of a capitalist economy in which each capitalist reduces wages in order to increase profits, the outcome being that both profits and wages fall overall. What distinguishes counterfinality from sub-optimality is not so much what actors do as their reasons for doing it. In the above examples, each acts on the assumption that others will continue as before, and it is that mistaken assumption about the actions of others that produces the unwelcome outcome. Elsewhere, Elster describes such behaviour as a matter of parametric rationality: rational behaviour within an environment (including other actors) that the actor assumes to be governed by fixed parameters.

Parametric rationality is significant for our purposes because it raises another set of questions concerning the relations between causal and intentional analysis. Elster suggests that causal interaction

> . . . takes place when each agent acts upon unjustified assumptions about the behaviour of others, e.g., when each agent believes that he is the only one who is adjusting to the environment, whereas all others merely follow habit or tradition. (Elster, 1983a: 84)

Interaction with others in terms of parametric rationality involves assumptions that are plainly false. In other words, 'people act rationally on irrational assumptions about the behaviour of others, i.e. on inexcusable false beliefs' (Elster, 1979; 157). If the beliefs are inexcusable it is not clear why Elster would wish to call the behaviour rational. I will return to this question.

Constraints and preferences

The second kind of departure from the paradigmatic case of rational optimizing behaviour involves interaction between individuals' preferences and the constraints on their actions: preferences may be shaped by constraints and constraints may be shaped by preferences. On the one hand, people may adjust their preferences to the options that seem to be available, and on the other they may, like Ulysses, bind themselves by imposing constraints in order to guard against their own anticipated irrationalities. The first of these is discussed in *Sour Grapes* (1983b) and the second in *Ulysses and the Sirens* (1979), especially in the title essay. Elster claims that these interactions between constraints and preferences together undermine what he calls 'the orthodox view' that 'choice embodies an element of freedom, the constraints one of necessity' (1983b: vii). He is particularly concerned with two sets of problems posed by such interactions.

First, there are problems to do with personal autonomy and responsibility for oneself. People may be capable of rational action, but they can also display weakness of will and they sometimes act 'rationally on irrational assumptions about the behaviour of others, i.e. on inexcusable false beliefs' (1979: 157). Responsibility for self requires that individuals take steps to guard such irrationalities. However, if their beliefs and desires are shaped by processes outside their control then there seems little point in talk about responsibility. In Elster's view, we therefore need a broader theory of rationality which involves 'a scrutiny of the substantive nature of the desires and beliefs involved in the action' (1983a: 15).

> If people are agents in a substantive sense, and not just the passive supports of their preference structures and belief systems, then we need to understand how judgement and autonomy are possible. This, in my view, is the outstanding unresolved problem both in philosophy and in the social sciences. (Elster, 1983b: 88)

Second, the dependence of preferences on constraints poses a problem for utilitarian analyses of social choice.

> Why should individual want satisfaction be the criterion of justice and social choice when individual wants themselves may be shaped by a process that preempts the choice? And in particular, why should the choice between feasible options only take account of individual preferences if people tend to adjust their possibilities? (ibid.: 109)

There are indeed reasons to be wary of taking human individuals and their preferences as the starting-point either for the analysis of justice and social choice or for social and political analysis generally. What should be noted here is that Elster does base himself on that starting-point, and then proceeds to examine various conditions of preference formation as giving rise to problems identified within that framework. Thus, interaction between preferences and constraints is important for Elster, first, because it exposes the formalism of much rational choice theory and suggests that it be supplemented by a theory of substantive rationality and, second, because he regards it as threatening to undermine the foundations of public choice analysis.

Intentionality and causation

Finally, there are departures from the paradigmatic case involving interaction between intentional and causal processes. Causality enters Elster's discussion at two levels.

> Sub-intentional causality is involved in the mental operations that are not governed by will or intention, but – metaphorically speaking – take place 'behind the back' of the individual concerned. Supra-intentional causality refers to causal interaction between intentional actors. (Elster, 1983a: 20)

Parenthetically, Elster notes that 'there is also intentional interaction between intentional actors which is studied by game theory' (ibid.).

We therefore have two distinct areas of problems concerning the interaction of causal and intentional analysis. Supra-intentional causality comes into play whenever rationality fails at the level of interaction. I return to this possibility below.

The case of sub-intentional causality is more complex. At first sight it seems to enter Elster's analysis whenever rationality does not determine action. Where optimal outcomes are not well defined, action cannot be the product of optimizing calculation. In such cases 'causal considerations must be invoked in addition to the assumption of rationality' (1983b: 2). The general case arises when 'the individual is traversed by causal process that escape him and which he does not understand' (1978: 158). For example, if an individual has contradictory goals 'there must be some mechanism that determines which of the contradictory desires will get the upper hand in a given situation' (ibid.).

Sub-intentional causality, then, comes into play when intentionality (that is, rationality) does not. Unfortunately, as Elster recognizes, there is a further complication here, for what he describes as sub-intentional *causality* must also play a considerable part in 'shaping the beliefs and desires in terms of which action can be explained *intentionally*' (1983a: 84–5). This is one of the places where Elster's dichotomy between the 'natural' (that is, causal) and the 'intentional' in human behaviour leads to trouble. If human action is subject to two distinct modes of determination, what happens when they conflict, when intentionality pushes one way and causality pushes another? Elster evades this apparent difficulty by attempting to define it out of existence. In effect, he claims to adopt the materialism of Donald Davidson[3] which insists that mental states just are brain states (Elster, 1983a: 20f). From Davidson's argument, it does not follow that we have any reason to expect an unambiguous correspondence between analyses conducted at one level (in terms of intentionality) and those conducted at the other (in terms of physiology). Thus, what would count as instances of the same intentional process need not be instances of the same physiological process.

On Davidson's argument, then, intentional and sub-intentional causal analyses operate in different conceptual registers and there is no general algorithm for shifting from one to the other. The two modes of analysis do not meet and there is no possibility, therefore, of any conflict between them. I have no quarrel with Davidson's treatment of this particular issue, but it does depend on maintaining a clear distinction between the two conceptual registers. Unfortunately we shall see that Elster's discussion of rationality and causality undermines that distinction by invoking interference from the one to explain departures from the other. He also tries to make use of Davidson's work in a more general sense, to which I return below.

Intentionality and individualism

I have argued throughout this book that actors do indeed make choices and act on the basis of many of them. To do that, of course, is to agree with Elster first that action involves a significant component of intentionality and, second, that what he describes as structural accounts of action are generally implausible. However, Elster's own discussion of what is involved in intentional explanation is misleading in several important respects. Intentional explanation does not entail a methodological individualism, and it does not have the structure outlined in Elster's account. Explanation in terms of optimization need not be taken as 'the paradigm case of intentional explanation in the social sciences outside psychology' (Elster, 1983: 75) and the awkward cases which Elster considers should not be identified primarily in terms of their departures from that paradigm. While his discussion of these cases does touch on important issues, I argue that it is severely impoverished, in part as a result of that paradigmatic mode of analysis. In particular, it neglects significant supra-individual features of the conditions in which action takes place, and it mistakenly relegates non-rational action to the categories of sub-intentional or supra-intentional causality. Before proceeding to the tangled relationships between intentionality and rationality, we must however, examine methodological individualism.

The presumption of methodological individualism is a pervasive feature of the literature of rational choice theory, although models sometimes admit actors other than human individuals, such as capitalist enterprises or political parties. In *Explaining Technical Change* Elster presents methodological individualism as if it were simply one instance of a generic feature of scientific investigation.

> Within a given scientific discipline there will usually be concepts defined at different levels of organisation and complexity. Within physics there are molecules, atoms, elementary particles, and so on in an apparently endlessly descending chain; within biology there are ecosystems, organisms, organs, cells and genomes; within the social sciences there are societies, organisations, industries, firms, families and individuals . . . .
> Generally speaking, the scientific practice is to seek an explanation at a lower level that the explanandum. . . . If we want to understand social revolutions, we seek an explanation in individual actions and motivations. The search for micro-foundations . . . .is in reality a pervasive and omnipresent feature of science. (Elster, 1983a: 23)

He goes on to suggest that lower-level concepts define the mechanisms that account for higher-level events. Explanation in terms of mechanisms has the great advantage of reducing time-lags 'between explanans and explanandum. A mechanism provides a continuous and contiguous chain of causal or intentional links. . .' (ibid.: 24).

This is a chinese box theory of scientific explanation: what big things do is to be explained in terms of the actions of little things inside them. It may be that this is a widespread feature of scientific explanation, but it hardly follows that it is a necessary one. Elster's argument that explanation always involves micro-foundations confuses the order of *concepts* in explanation with the order of *things* in terms of size. To justify methodological individualism on the grounds that concepts relating to the actions of human individuals are more basic than concepts relating to larger entities, such as societies or organizations, is simply to presuppose what has to be established.

Elsewhere, and in common with others in the rational choice traditions, Elster does not so much make a case in favour of methodological individualism as argue against what he imagines the theoretical alternatives to be. In *Ulysses and the Sirens* he maintains that the structuralist approach, which insists on 'the primacy of structural constraints' (1979: 113) in the determination of individual action, is implausible. We have noted that this account of the structural alternative is something of a caricature. Elsewhere, in *Logic and Society*, and again in *Explaining Technical Change*, he produces powerful and effective arguments against the functionalist variant of structural explanation in the social sciences.

The opposition is identified rather differently in Elster's book on Marx. This time it is methodological collectivism, which is based on the assumption 'that there are supra-individual entities that are prior to the individual in the explanatory order' (1985: 6). On that view, individual action would be derived from aggregate patterns. For example, there are passages in *Capital* where Marx treats the behaviour of capitalists as a consequence of their positions in the total social capital. Elster has no difficulty in showing that such an account of capitalists' behaviour is unsatisfactory. Or, again, there are numerous discussions which treat classes as if they were collective actors. Here too, Elster insists that the actions of collectivities are always in principle reducible to the actions of individuals.

The fundamental objection to what he describes as structuralism and methodological collectivism is that they are incompatible with intentional accounts of human action. Some of Elster's strictures on this point are entirely justified, but it does not follow that we must therefore resign ourselves to methodological individualism. It is one thing to insist that actions are not reducible to the positions of individuals in some overarching social structure or collectivity, and quite another to turn the argument around and say that all structural features of social life are strictly reducible to the actions of individuals. The slippage here from one position to the other turns on a simplistic opposition between structure and human agency of a kind that is all too common in modern social thought: either social life is to be understood in terms of the functioning of social wholes, or else it is a matter of the constitutive actions of human individuals. Each of these opposed positions derives its superficial plausibility from the obvious weaknesses of the other – from the gestural character of attempts to account for structural features of social life in terms of the actions of individuals on the one side, and the absurdity of denying that individuals do indeed make choices and act on them on the other.

Of course, actors reach decisions and act on many of them, so that their actions are in some part a consequence of their decisions. The decisions themselves are reached partly through processes that are internal to the actor in question and, in that respect, are clearly not reducible simply to the effects of the actor's position in some larger structure or system of social relations. Unfortunately, Elster's critique of structuralism and methodological collectivism depends on a very limited notion of the significance of social relations and of conditions that are external to the individual actor. In contrast to that methodological individualism I argue both that there are actors other than human individuals and that actors' decisions and actions depend on conditions that are external to the actor concerned. In particular, they depend on the discourses employed by, or available to, actors in evaluating their conditions of action, and they naturally depend on the means of action available to them. It follows that social relations cannot be reduced to the creative activity of those engaged in them.

Interaction between intentional actors

I suggested in Chapter 2 that rational choice models generally involve a postulate of homogeneity, to the effect that what is to count as rationality is uniquely defined for each category of actor recognized by the model in question. For example, if a model contains two categories of actor – capitalist entrepreneurs and consumers – then we have to assume that the former are profit maximizers in a sense that is similarly defined for all entrepreneurs (involving a single well defined notion of what is to count as capital and as profit, and the same set of decision procedures and time-scale of calculation in all cases), and that the latter are all characterized by preference sets with the same mathematical structure. At first sight this procedure may not seem too problematic. After all, if we notice that capitalists do not all employ the same mode of economic calculation then, of course, the model can be complicated to take account of the different modes of profit-seeking that can be identified.

There is no problem for rational choice theory, at least in principle, in taking account of differences in the forms of assessment employed by members of different social categories – although the practical difficulties of constructing workable mathematical models may be considerable. The theoretical problem lies elsewhere – namely in the assumption that the desires, interests and other criteria of assessment employed by actors, and therefore what are to count as rational decisions on the part of those actors, are determined by the social categories to which they belong. In effect, the construction of rational choice models presupposes a 'structural' determination of the forms of thought employed by actors, insofar as they are rational. We have seen that Elster rejects as implausible a structuralism in which the actor's choices are effectively pre-empted by structural constraints in the situation of action – and he is right to do so. Unfortunately, the rational choice approach, as he describes it, merely transposes the constraint from actors' situations, now assumed to be open, to their 'rationality', which is uniquely determined by their membership of the relevant social category. The 'structuralism' that Elster rejects and the rational choice theory that he favours use different theoretical means to produce the same overall result: what (rational) actors do is determined by their social location, either through the action of the structure in the one case or through their rationality in the other.

> At the limit, intentional interaction is the incarnation of collective freedom, the fully transparent rationality that incorporates into itself the expectations of other rational actors in order to converge upon some predictable course of action. (Elster, 1978: 159)

We may have doubts about this notion of collective freedom, but what makes it possible is the assumption that, given enough time, each rational actor can tell what is rational for others simply from a knowledge of their social location. In that case, all possible outcomes would be calculable in principle, and it would not be unreasonable to treat all actors as playing essentially the same game. Short of such perfection, Elster suggests that interaction will be governed by a combination of intentionality and super-intentional causality. As we saw with sub-intentional causality, causality at this level appears to refer simply to anything that involves less than rational outcomes.

In Elster's account there seem to be two main types of departure from collective freedom. The first arises when actors are caught up in games without solutions – in which case there is simply no telling what other rational actors might get up to. Outcomes will be determined by the (unpredictable) causal interaction between the actors generated by a-rational assumptions about the behaviour of others (ibid.: 158). But the more significant type involves a systematic departure from complete rationality which Elster describes in terms of parametric rationality and counterfinality. The purposive--parametric actor

> . . . assumes that he is free to adjust optimally in a constant or parametric environment. This assumption is in itself quite consistent . . . but if entertained simultaneously by all actors it generates counterfinality . . . .(ibid.: 159)

In making sense of Marx, Elster presents this as 'Marx's central contribution to the methodology of social science' (1985: 48). The general idea is that 'unintended consequences arise when agents entertain beliefs about each other that exemplify the fallacy of composition' (ibid.). Suppose, for example, that each capitalist reduces wages in order to increase profits. The result is that wages and profits in general fall. On Elster's account, what remains of value in Marx's analyses of the dynamics of capitalist production, once the effects of structuralism and methodological collectivism have been expunged, can all be translated into the idiom of methodological individualism and unintended consequences.

Lenin accused Kautsky of turning Marx into a common liberal. Now Elster proposes to turn him into a rational choice theorist, and a precursor of Robert Merton to boot. Note how the trick is performed. The counterfinality of capitalist production results from the fact that capitalists in general fail to engage in a fully strategic rationality. Instead they act rationally on the basis of irrational assumptions about the behaviour of other capitalists. Why are they all so stupid? The argument requires that capitalists are constrained to act in that way because of what seems rational to each of them by virtue of their social location. Marx's structural determinism is tossed out of the front door and quietly brought back in through the rear.

Those of us who have noticed that unintended consequences arise whatever beliefs actors entertain about themselves or each other will not be so impressed by Elster's account of Marx's 'central contribution'. The tale of the unintended consequence is one of the more banal commonplaces of the academic social sciences, and if that is all Marx has to offer one wonders why Elster has taken the trouble to write a book about him, let alone such a big one. Why make such a fuss about a few unintended consequences? The answer probably lies in the problems that methodological individualism always confronts in its attempts to deal with recurrent patterns of interaction and other structural features of social life. If social life is seen as resulting from the choices of individually rational actors, then some explanation is clearly required of the mess they make of things. For rational choice theory, with its surreptitious structural determinism, the unintended consequence operates as a more general and rather less benign version of the economists' hidden hand.

Intentionality and rationality

Intentional analysis of action presupposes that actors have reasons for what they do, and further that elucidation of their reasons goes a long way towards explaining the actions in question. Elster's elaboration of what is involved here makes considerable use of Davidson's arguments. We have seen that Elster makes inconsistent use of Davidson's argument that mental states just are brain states. He also uses Davidson in a more general fashion to underpin his account of the relations between intentionality and rationality.

Elster, along with other rational choice theorists, treats maximizing behaviour as the paradigm case of rationality. This adds a specifically utilitarian dimension to the analysis of intentionality that is not strictly entailed in Davidson's account. Nevertheless, discussion of Davidson's arguments provides a useful introduction to rational choice theory's rather more limited model of behaviour.[4]

To say that reasons explain behaviour is to say more than that they provide an understandable motivation for acting in that way. Good reasons may be merely post-hoc rationalizations or excuses for actions caused in some other way. For reasons to explain behaviour they must also cause the behaviour for which they are reasons. 'A man might have good reasons for killing his father, and yet the reasons not be his reasons in doing it (think of Oedipus)' (Davidson, 1980: 232). The reasons must also cause the behaviour in what Davidson calls 'the right way'. What the right way is remains unclear in Davidson's discussion, but what it is not is illustrated by examples. Think of Oedipus again.

> . . . for suppose, contrary to the legend, that Oedipus, for some dark oedipal reason, was hurrying along the road, intent on killing his father, and, finding a surly old man blocking his way, killed him so he could (as he thought) get on with the main job. Then not only did Oedipus want to kill his father, and actually kill him, but his desire caused him to kill his father. Yet we could not say that in killing the old man he intentionally killed his father. . . . (Davidson, 1980: 232)

Here the intention contributes to the cause but does not directly explain the behaviour. The connection between the intention and the killing of the old man is indirect. The intention does have an effect, but it is only one of a number of elements that combine to provide Oedipus with his reason for killing the old man. 'The right way' seems to involve an immediacy in the relation between intention and action that is missing in Davidson's tale. We shall make further use of this example.

Where does rationality fit in this account of intentional behaviour? For present purposes, Davidson's argument can be described as extending the principle of charity from the analysis of verbal behaviour to the analysis of behaviour generally. In the case of verbal behaviour 'charity' requires that

> . . . the basic strategy must be to assume that by and large a speaker we do not yet understand is consistent and correct in his beliefs – according to our own standards, of course. (ibid.: 238)[5]

What people mean by what they say cannot be understood in the absence of some account of what they believe. Similarly, in the case of choice behaviour, we cannot infer beliefs (or desires) from observation of people's choices without also inferring something about their desires (or beliefs). Beliefs, desires and intentions are so interconnected in intentional behaviour that we cannot analyse one in isolation from the others – and we cannot interpret their interconnections without assuming rationality:

> . . . if we are intelligibly to attribute attitudes and beliefs, or usefully to describe motions as behaviour, then we are committed to finding, in the pattern of behaviour, belief and desire, a large degree of rationality and consistency. (ibid.: 237).

In effect, Davidson presents us with a distinctive version of the hermeneutic account of the process of understanding the behaviour of others. It presupposes a model of behaviour as resulting, for the most part, from intentions which are themselves the product of a portfolio of beliefs and desires. The portfolio's content may change from time to time, but at any given moment it is to be regarded as relatively stable. This portfolio, together with the situation of action, provides the actor with the starting-point for rational deliberation about possible courses of action. The beliefs and desires that we attribute to actors are all, at least potentially, contents of consciousness. This means, in particular, that the desires specified in this model of the actor can always be recognized as such by the actor concerned: they are not unconscious forces. On that account of behaviour, intentional analysis requires that we work back to actors' beliefs and desires by interpreting their behaviour, including their verbal behaviour. The process of interpretation here requires us to presume a fair degree of rationality and consistency, since it stands to reason that we could not otherwise hope to work back from some pattern of behaviour to infer the beliefs and desires that have produced it.

The particular beliefs and desires that we discover and the 'large degree of rationality and consistency' which we must attribute to actors are all artefacts of the portfolio model of behaviour. Similarly for Davidson's description of our attempts at translation. The requirement that we must assume consistency 'according to our own standards' if we are to grasp a speaker's meaning which we do not yet understand is itself an artefact of Davidson's model of verbal behaviour. We may leave aside the question of how far Davidson's account illuminates the practice of anthropological fieldwork – although Evans-Pritchard's classic *Witchcraft Oracles and Magic Among the Azande* (1976), and the uses that have subsequently been made of it, suggest the need for a different story.[6] What matters for present purposes is to notice how the requirement that we presume a large degree of rationality is built in to the model of behaviour as resulting from a more or less stable portfolio of beliefs and desires.

Rational choice theory

There are serious problems with the portfolio model of behaviour which I consider below and in the following chapter. For the moment, notice that rational choice theory takes up that model with the addition of a further utilitarian constraint. In its simplest form, this involves the assumption of a hierarchy of preference among the desires in the portfolio that is both transitive and complete. The order is transitive if, for any three desires A, B and C where A is preferred to B and B is preferred to C, then A is preferred to C. It is complete if, for any two desires, one is preferred to the other or they are preferred equally. Maximizing behaviour requires that it is normally possible to define one or more outcomes that are most satisfactory in a given situation. Where such an outcome can be identified, then behaviour can be understood as an algebraic consequence of the actor's preference structure and the situation of action.

Of course, this basic utilitarian model gives a relatively unsophisticated account of human behaviour. It also allows considerable scope for further refinement and for algebraic complication – and numerous possibilities have been explored in the literature. For example, the well attested fact that preferences change suggests the need to suppose more than one order of preferences, so that superficial changes may be seen as reflecting a more basic stability. Or again, altruistic behaviour may be incorporated on the assumption of interacting orders of preferences.

Elster proposes that we should take maximising behaviour as the paradigm case, and use that as a baseline for the analysis of other possibilities. In his view, intentional behaviour is not invariably rational since the actor occasionally has contradictory desires. In this case, sub-intentional causality determines 'which of the contradictory desires will get the upper hand in a given situation' (1978: 158). For Elster then, as for Weber, intentional behaviour in its purest form is essentially rational. Non-rational behaviour is either not intentional at all, or else it involves a significant intrusion of non-intentional causality.

A rather different set of complications are generated by the related notions of global maximization and deferred gratification. The latter involves a relation to the future.

> Consciousness, indeed, may be defined as a medium of representation, an inner screen on which the physically absent can have a presence and make a difference for action in the present (Elster, 1983a: 71)

This picture theory of consciousness may be left in the obscurity to which it properly belongs. What matters here is that reference to future possibilities brings with it the recognition that preferences may change in response to external constraints and sometimes as a result of choice, and that future constraints may be open to manipulation. This allows Elster to raise questions of personal autonomy and responsibility for oneself.

Now, although Davidson's arguments entail a general presumption in favour of rationality, they do not necessarily support Elster's utilitarian version of intentional analysis. First, there is nothing in the argument that we are committed to finding a large degree of consistency and rationality in actors' behaviour that requires us also to find them employing, for the most part, some version of the utilitarian calculus.

Second, Davidson does not advocate the presumption of rationality and consistency in the paradigmatic form advocated by Elster. Davidson's argument is that we have to assume that speakers are 'by and large' consistent, not that they are consistent *tout court*. On that account, the assumption of 'a large degree of rationality and consistency' (Davidson, 1980: 237) is necessary if we are to be able to identify instances of inconsistency and irrational behaviour. There is nothing here to suggest that cases of irrationality and inconsistency are unimportant from the viewpoint either of the actors concerned or of the wider social consequences of their actions. Indeed, there are good reasons for supposing the reverse – that behaviour standing out against a presumed background of rationality and consistency would cause particular problems both for the actor concerned and for others.

In fact, there are points at which Elster's own arguments accord an important role to irrationality. For example, we have noted that both counterfinality and what Elster calls parametric rationality involve action on the basis of irrational assumptions about the behaviour of others. It is not clear why such behaviour should be regarded as rational, but there is also a further difficulty to be noted here. The paradigmatic character of the assumption of rationality requires that we consider explanation in non-rational terms only when rational explanation proves impossible. The difficulty in this case arises from a tension between explanation in rational terms and in terms of reasons that cause the behaviour in question. The former may give good reasons for the behaviour but does not necessarily mean that they caused it in what Davidson would describe as 'the right way'. In other words, we should be wary of identifying apparently rational grounds for the behaviour in question with motivations that were effective in the mental set of the actor. The paradigmatic assumption of rationality would have us override that caution.

Finally, we have seen that Elster effectively treats irrationality as unintelligible – as resulting from the operation of sub-intentional causality. In the event of contradictory desires, sub-intentional processes determine which comes out on top – and only then does intentionality come into its own. This is unsatisfactory on Davidson's account of mental events (which Elster appears to support) because sub-intentional processes are always at work and there is no reason to treat irrational behaviour as distinctive in this respect. Elster's insistence on sub-intentional causality here can only mean that, in his view, no 'corresponding' intentional processes are involved in those aspects of behaviour that depart from rationality. In effect, Elster maps Davidson's careful distinction between two conceptual registers for the analysis of behaviour (in terms of intentionality on the one hand and a – largely hypothetical – physiological account of brain states on the other) on to a distinction between two kinds of behaviour.

Now, it is one thing to insist on the presumption of a general rationality as a condition for the identification of cases of irrational behaviour, and quite another to argue as if these latter must themselves be regarded as unintelligible – as if they could exhibit no specific pattern, or even 'logic', of their own. Behaviour is certainly affected by unintelligible causal processes but that is no reason to identify non-rational with unintelligible. Think again of (Davidson's) Oedipus, impelled by some 'dark oedipal reason', and going right over the top in killing some old man who gets in his way. We would have to stretch the principle of charity to its limits and beyond in order to interpret the behaviour of that Oedipus (or indeed of the more familiar one) as rational. Yet, we would hardly call it incomprehensible.

Or consider Elster's comments on the idea of a rational plan.

> We must be able to make sense of a person on the whole if we are to be able to say that some of his plans do not make sense. A rational plan must fulfil two criteria. First, the end state in terms of which it is defined must be a logically coherent one . . . . [second] there must be a possible world in which one finds both the plan and its fulfillment (1983b: 11)

Here, if a plan does not make sense, its irrationality is specified by reference to particular criteria for the assessment of plans, not by reference to the intervention of sub-intentional causality. Acting on a plan that appears to make sense, but on closer inspection proves not to, may not be the most rational thing to do, but it is not unintelligible.

The portfolio model of intentional behaviour

I have argued that rational choice theories involve a portfolio model of intentional behaviour, and suggested that there are serious problems with that model itself. The nature of those problems can be seen most clearly if we return briefly to Davidson's account of intentional explanation. There is no suggestion here that Davidson is committed to some rational choice analysis of human action. Indeed, we have seen that his account entails neither the utilitarian superstructures of rational choice theory nor Elster's problematic demarcation between rational and irrational. The suggestion is rather that rational choice accounts depend on something like Davidson's portfolio model, together with some further restrictive assumptions.

The 'large degree of rationality and consistency' that Davidson's account requires us to attribute to actors is an artefact of his portfolio model of behaviour. So too is the difficulty Davidson encounters in specifying, other than by negative example, what is involved in saying that reasons must cause behaviour 'in the right way'. Davidson's account of intentional behaviour suggests a directness in the connection between actors' desires and their behaviour that leaves little space for those discursive processes of evaluation, calculation or reflection which often play an important part in actors' choices between possible courses of action. More precisely, given the assumption of rationality, those processes can be, and are, discounted as transparent intermediaries between beliefs and desires on the one hand and the behaviours they are said to cause on the other. The connection is transparent because it takes the form of a rational deduction leading from premises (the set of beliefs and desires relating to the situation of action) to their conclusion (the behaviour that takes place in that situation). It is a mode of connection exhibited by actors simply by virtue of their rationality. Oedipus' desire to kill his father caused him to kill his father 'in the right way' if, and only if, the connection between the desire and the behaviour did indeed take that form. If the connection was more circuitous, then the desire may have contributed to causing the behaviour, as in Davidson's tale, but it is not a sufficient reason for the intentional explanation of what took place.

The difficulty for the portfolio model is as follows. If, on the one hand, the process of thought involved in making a decision about a course of action is indeed transparent then it can hardly be invoked to explain how a reason causes behaviour in the right, rather than some other way. If, on the other hand, the process of thought is explicitly introduced as a constitutive element in the model then it can no longer be regarded as transparent. Once some definite process of thought is admitted into our account of an actor's decision, then that process must be regarded as a possible object of investigation. Questions may then be raised both with regard to the discursive and other means of assessment deployed by actors, and with regard to the way an actor deploys those means in some particular case. This point undermines any simple dichotomy between rational and irrational behaviour. Actors may deploy what we regard as rational means of assessing the situation and deciding on a course of action, and they may deploy those means correctly or incorrectly. On the other hand they may deploy what we regard as irrational means (the *I Ching*, cost–benefit analysis, Evans-Pritchard's poison oracle) , and they may deploy those means correctly or incorrectly.

However, there are more important points to note here. The first is that questions of the rationality, or otherwise, of behaviour can no longer assume the importance they are accorded in rational choice and much other literature. We have seen that Davidson's principle of charity requires us to suppose a large measure of rationality and consistency 'according to our own standards, of course' (Davidson, 1980: 238) in the intentional analysis of behaviour. But that requirement itself follows from the assumed transparency of connection between beliefs and desires on the one hand and behaviour on the other. I have argued on the contrary that intentional understanding requires us to assume that actors deploy some definite means of assessing the situation and deciding on a course of action. Once the means of assessment deployed by some actor or actors have been identified then, of course, it is possible to identify cases in which they are deployed incorrectly. The intentional analysis of behaviour requires us to identify the means of assessment deployed by actors but requires no judgement as to their rationality. Questions of rationality may well be raised for other purposes (for example, in the course of normative arguments about the relative merits of decision-making procedures) but they are not required for intentional analysis.

The second point to note is that to question the transparency of the connection between beliefs and desires and actors' behaviour is also to undermine the idea that actors must be characterized in terms of a more or less stable portfolio of beliefs and desires. I argued this point in Chapter 3 for the related question of the role of interests in the analysis of behaviour. Briefly, interests, desires or beliefs can enter into some intentional process only if they provide reasons for action that could be formulated by the actor in question. This means that the interests, beliefs or desires that do play a part in an actor's behaviour are themselves dependent on the availability to that actor of the conceptual means of formulating them. If actors' reasons for action depend on conceptual and other conditions that are not inherent features of the actors themselves, then social life is clearly not reducible to the constitutive behaviour of actors.

Third, the character of interests, beliefs and desires as involving reasons that may be formulated renders them open to challenge through discursive means, through reconsideration by the actor in question and through discussion, persuasion and propaganda involving others. Such challenges may be more or less effective, but the fact that they are sometimes successful means that actors' desires cannot be regarded as given elements of their consciousnesses until something drastic and unexpected comes along to change them. There may perhaps be a case for arguing that those beliefs and desires that are the most resistant to challenge should also be regarded as the most basic. But beliefs and desires which are clearly not basic in that sense are perfectly capable of causing behaviour in what Davidson would call the 'right way'.

These points go along with the portfolio model in taking beliefs and desires as legitimate starting-points in intentional analysis. They undermine it by suggesting that at least some important elements of an actor's portfolio may be subject to change through discursive processes involving the actor alone or in interaction with other actors.

However, the model should also be challenged from another direction. Intentional explanation supposes that actors deploy some definite means of assessing situations and deciding on courses of action. I have presented the issue so far as if the actor possesses certain beliefs and desires which are brought in to some definite process of assessment leading to a decision about behaviour. The problem here is that there may well be cases where the attribution of beliefs and desires to the actor, rather than to the course of action, may itself be misleading. Consider Evans-Pritchard's account of his own behaviour during his fieldwork amongst the Azande. He remained firmly convinced of the falsity of Zande beliefs regarding witchcraft and the poison-oracle. Nevertheless he reports himself as reacting 'to misfortunes in the idiom of witchcraft', something he regarded as a 'lapse into unreason' (Evans-Pritchard, 1976: 45). Or again:

> I always kept a supply of poison for the use of my household and neighbours and we regulated our affairs in accordance with the oracle's decisions. I may remark that I found this as satisfactory a way of running my home and affairs as any other I know of. (ibid.: 126)

But it would be misleading to explain his behaviour as resulting from his belief in witchcraft.

The example of Evans-Pritchard is a striking illustration of a more general phenomenon. There is a perfectly good sense in which we might want to say that certain beliefs are presupposed by particular modes of assessment of situations and of reaching decisions and acting on them, but it need not follow that those beliefs would be agreed to, or even recognized, by actors who employ those modes of assessment and of acting. A similar point may be made about desire, in the sense of an actual or potential content of consciousness. Certain desires may be presupposed by some form of behaviour without necessarily being held by those engaged in that behaviour – at least, not in advance of the behaviour itself. Examples can be found in those cases of crowd behaviour which, after the event, are a mystery to many participants.

Weber's account of rational–legal domination suggests, from a very different perspective, that behaviour of this kind is a pervasive feature of more advanced modern societies. This point is not to deny that the beliefs and desires of individual actors are ever an appropriate starting-point for intentional analysis. The patterning of behaviour that commences with individuals' beliefs and desires and moves out from them obviously plays an important part in social life, at least in our culture. The point rather is to insist that intentional behaviour, involving calculation and deliberation, does not always take that form.

Notes
1. See Hardin, 1982 for another version.
2. Including a collection edited by Elster and Hyland. Sen's concluding response is particular helpful.
3. Davidson, 1980, 1984.
4. I have discussed Davidson's arguments at greater length in Hindess, 1988b.
5. See the Introduction and 'Radical interpretation' in Davidson, 1984. There are useful discussions of the principle of charity and its variants in MacDonald and Pettit, 1981 and Doval and Harris, 1986.
6. Cf. Hirst and Woolley, 1983, ch. 15; also Hindess, 1988b.

8 Rationality or styles of reasoning

Some of the most influential usages of the term 'rationality' in the contemporary social sciences are those that refer to certain kinds of maximizing behaviour. Models of maximizing behaviour, which are widely used in economics, and rational choice analysis, can be understood as proposing to extend the use of such models to other areas of human behaviour. In Chapter 2 I quoted Anthony Downs, one of the early exponents of the rational choice analysis of politics, as suggesting that the model of individual maximizing behaviour applies to economic agents

> . . . because they are agents. In short, they are human, and the realities of human nature must be accounted for in any economic analysis. Ipso facto, the same type of reasoning must be applied to every institution run by men. (Downs, 1957: 283)

In such a view, the greater part of social life may be explained as the outcome of individual actors' rational choices. This, and related explanatory usages of the notion of individual rationality, is the concern of this chapter.

Supporters of rational choice analysis have claimed that it is rigorous, capable of great technical sophistication, and able to generate powerful explanations across a range of situations, all on the basis of a few, relatively simple theoretical assumptions.[1] It also appears to take more seriously than its sociological opponents the point that actors do indeed make choices and act on them – that is, that they are not mere pawns in some overarching social structure. Rational choice analysis does not maintain of course that action is always rational. Its claim rather is that the assumption of rationality is a powerful heuristic device. It is a useful simplification and it provides us with means of identifying the role of non-rational elements in human behaviour.

The rigour and technical sophistication of much rational choice analysis seems to me undeniable. Nevertheless, I suggest that those positive features are bought at an excessive theoretical cost. In particular, the use of assumptions about actors and their rationality that are highly questionable and not at all simple has the effect of closing off important areas of intellectual inquiry concerning both the forms of thought employed by actors and the social conditions on which they depend.

There are several well known lines of critical discussion of the assumptions of rational choice analysis. Perhaps the most widely canvassed, by sympathetic critics like Sen[2] and Elster and by others who are less sympathetic, are those that argue for a more complex view of actors' rationality than is normally provided in rational choice models. I have already suggested that the model of actor employed in rational choice analysis is a special case of something more general. This more general model underlies much of the critical literature. It treats actors as human individuals whose actions follow from their beliefs, desires and other states of mind. Imagine that actors each carry with them their own distinctive portfolio of beliefs and desires. (The image is that of an artist or illustrator, not an investment manager.) Given a situation of action, an actor selects from its portfolio those elements that seem to be relevant, and uses them to decide on a course of action. This is what I have called the portfolio model of the actor, and versions of it are widely used in philosophy and the social sciences. Rational choice analysis modifies the portfolio model in assuming that the actor's desires are such that an optimal outcome can be defined in most situations – and also in several other respects which need not concern us here. The first part of this chapter is a critical discussion of the portfolio model.

Rational choice analysis is widely regarded as less than unsatisfactory and yet assumptions of actors' rationality remain significant both in the academic social sciences and more generally in the social, political and economic life of modern societies. The second part of this chapter reflects on that state of affairs.

My discussion of the portfolio model in this chapter operates at two rather different levels. First, the uneasy status just noted of the assumption of actors' rationality is but one instance of a general phenomenon. Many concepts and forms of argument are theoretically problematic and yet play significant parts in social life and in academic discussions of it. Chapter 5, 'Class analysis as social theory', discussed the problematic status of class analysis as a form of social theory, and this chapter started life as a parallel exercise. Other well known examples of significant, but problematic, concepts are power, interests, rights, and democracy. These concepts and forms of analysis are consequential, in the sense that they play a significant part in the life of modern societies and in our investigations of it. They are all too easily undermined by theoretical work. Discussion of rational choice analysis in these terms, then, also raises more general questions about the place of concepts and forms of argument in social life and about those features of modern societies that allow assumptions of actors' rationality to play such an important role.

Second, the results of questioning the presumption of actors' rationality may suggest ways of approaching those more general questions. In particular, they suggest that there is no uniform way in which concepts and forms of argument appear as elements of social life. There is no reason to suppose, for example, that problems with class analysis will have the same kinds of ramifications as problems with forms of analysis based on the assumption of actors' rationality. The more important point to notice here, though, is that these diverse forms of analysis will themselves be embedded in social life in a variety of different ways. The full extent of the social ramifications of problems with the portfolio model, with class analysis, or with notions of power or democracy, are by no means easy to establish. In particular, it would be a mistake to imagine that the social significance of any form of social analysis can be captured in any simple formula – for example, as basically an ideological reflection of some established interest or as a function of its validity or coherence. I will return to this point later.

What's wrong with the assumption of rationality?
I suggested above that the rigour and technical sophistication of rational choice analysis have been bought at an excessive theoretical cost, involving highly questionable assumptions concerning actors and their rationality. Several of these assumptions were discussed in Chapters 2 and 7. For present purposes it will suffice to indicate what is at stake first by reference to general concepts of actor, and second in terms of the limitations of Simon's well known concept of bounded rationality.

Where rational choice analysis modifies the portfolio model of the actor I propose a more general model in which the actor is conceived simply as a locus of decision and action. Actors do things as a result of their decisions. We call those things actions, and actors' decisions play an important part in their explanation. Actors may also do things that are not the result of any decision, and they must be explained in other ways. Now, the portfolio model assumes far more than is required for the general model sketched here. First, it assumes that actors are human individuals, and, as I have argued elsewhere, there are important actors in the modern world other than human individuals. Second, and more important for the present discussion, it treats action as a function of belief and desire. On that view, the explanation of some particular action or actions requires an interpretation of the behaviour of the relevant actors in order to construct an account of their beliefs and desires. Davidson and others[3] have argued that the process of constructing an account of actors' beliefs and desires requires us to presume a substantial degree of rationality and consistency in their behaviour.

The trouble with the account of human action as resulting from belief and desire is that it says nothing about those processes of deliberation that sometimes play an important part in actors' decisions. More precisely, by treating them as transparent intermediaries between belief and desire on the one hand and the action that results on the other, it effectively takes for granted the rationality of those processes. I argue, on the contrary, that once the possibility of deliberation is admitted as an element in actors' decisions then the techniques and forms of thought employed in actors' deliberations must themselves be regarded as objects of investigation.

Societies differ in the range and variety of conceptual and other tools which their members are able to use in their deliberations. Where literacy is widespread there will also be specialized techniques of storing, retrieving and working with written materials, and various distinctive uses of written materials in relation to other activities (the experimental sciences, business management, government bureaucracies, and so on). Specialized styles of literary work may develop in which the products of earlier work provide both tools and materials to work on. Non-literate societies will have their own techniques for storing, retrieving and working with ideas and information. Some of these may be widely used, and others may be specialized and restricted.

In any society there will be many tools whose use is normally taken for granted and which provide the basis for a variety of others that may (or may not) be acquired later on. Most will be acquired relatively early in life, either in the course of interaction with other people or through more deliberate training. Many specialized tools build on or elaborate the use of others, which have to be acquired first. Most intellectual skills, and much of what counts as intelligence, involve interrelated skills of this kind. Those who miss out on some of the more commonplace tools may be severely disadvantaged when it comes to the use or acquistion of more specialized tools.

The result of actors' deliberations and many of the concerns and objectives that motivate them will depend on the conceptual and other tools which they are in a position to employ. The problem with the portfolio model is that, by taking rationality for granted, it treats actors' deliberations as if they too were transparently rational and therefore of little explanatory significance. Rational choice analysis does the same, with a more restricted notion of rationality. Against those positions I argue that there are important areas of investigation concerning the tools employed by actors in their deliberations, their diverse connections with other tools, and the ways in which they depend on various kinds of social conditions.

Bounded rationality

Now, one version of the idea that we should investigate the procedures employed by actors rather than take for granted their substantive rationality is already well established in the literature. It underlies a venerable critique of the rationality assumptions of neoclassical economics, some of the most influential versions of which are conveniently set out in the contributions of Arrow, Simon, Kahneman and Tversky and others to a recent issue of *The Journal of Business*.[4] For present purposes it will suffice to consider what they have in common – namely the claim that the requirements of substantive rationality make too great a demand on the cognitive and computational capacities of human individuals. Actors' rationality is therefore limited, and they use a variety of devices (satisficing, framing, or whatever) for making decisions within their limitations. Simon presents the issue as follows:

If we accept the proposition that both the knowledge and the computational power of the decision maker are severely limited, then we must distinguish between the real world and the actor's perception of it and reasoning about it. That is to say, we must construct a theory (and test it empirically) of the processes of decision. Our theory must include not only the reasoning processes but also the processes that generate the actor's subjective representation of the decision problem. (*Journal of Business*, 1986: 211)

The discrepancy between the real world and actor's perceptions of it implies that those perceptions are not wholly determined by the actor's real-world situation. Limited computational power implies that the actor's reasoning will often depart from the canons of substantive rationality. It follows that similarly situated actors may well differ in their perceptions and in the reasoning processes they employ.

That conclusion is entirely acceptable, but there are problems with the argument leading up to it. Simon locates the source of variation in actors' rationality squarely in the finitude of the actors themselves. Their rationality is bounded by their finitude. Arrow (ibid.: 387f) refers, in addition, to various external limitations on the knowledge available to actors in the absence of equilibrium, perfect competition and completeness of markets. In both cases, the human condition is presented in terms of an implicit contrast with idealized actors whose knowledge and computational power are not so limited. In *The Road to Serfdom* and many subsequent publications Hayek uses a similar idealization to argue for the impossibility of central planning.[5] The implication is that the perceptions of these idealized actors, unlike those of real human actors would properly reflect their situations. Their reasoning processes would be entirely rational, again unlike those of human actors, and therefore predictable. On this view, then, real-world actors' perceptions and reasoning processes are essentially imperfect, and they differ only in the consequences of their imperfections.

It would be difficult to deny that humans have imperfect knowledge and limited computational abilities, but we should be wary of the claim that imperfection is the primary source of variation in their reasoning processes. As a critique of the rational choice approach, the force of that claim is somewhat limited by the response it all too obviously invites – and indeed receives in Lucas' contribution to the same volume. Insofar as actors share a common, albeit imperfect, rationality the combined effects of learning, competition and other situational constraints can be expected to limit, in the long run, the significance of variation in the thinking of similarly situated actors. The argument from imperfection may complicate the rational choice approach but it does little serious damage.

Styles of reasoning

Fortunately, there are more substantial arguments concerning differences in styles of reasoning. The idea that there are significantly different ways of thinking is frequently advanced in terms of some notion of distinct paradigms or rationalities.[6] The suggestion is that there are distinct conceptual schemes or paradigms which are in some sense incommensurable. Different schemes produce different perceptions of reality, with the result that there will be problems of translation between one scheme and another and little point in debating their relative merits. Several contributors to the special issue of *The Journal of Business* referred to above make use of that imagery – although, as the existence of the volume shows, the parties in debate have little difficulty in believing that they understand much of what the others have to say.

In 'The very idea of a conceptual scheme'[7] Davidson has attacked the idea of incommensurability as involving a dualism of scheme and reality. Different paradigms or schemes do not present different interpretations of the same perceptions, but different perceptions of reality – and that is why the claims of one cannot be translated into the other. Davidson argues that the conceptual relativism involved in that idea of distinct conceptual schemes with only limited translation between them cannot be sustained. But there is another relativism concerning styles of reasoning that does not fall under Davidson's critique. Hacking elaborates his notion of styles of reasoning in relation to the history of the sciences, and I propose to adapt it for more wide-ranging purposes.

Briefly, Hacking distinguishes between 'those boring domains of "observations" that we share with all people as people' (Hacking, 1982: 61) and domains in which 'being true or false is a property of sentences only because we reason about those sentences in certain ways' (ibid.: 64). That distinction, although less secure than Hacking appears to suppose, will serve for the present argument.

The history of the sciences provides a wealth of illustrations of domains of the second kind. To take just one example, Hacking cites the doctrines of resemblance and similitude in renaissance medicine, and in particular, the view 'that mercury salve might be good for syphilis because mercury is signed by the planet Mercury which signs the marketplace, where syphilis is contracted' (ibid.: 60). The point here is not that this last was regarded as true within the hermetic tradition of medicine, but rather that it was regarded as something whose truth could be investigated. The problem encountered with such doctrines is not that they are incommensurable with modern science, but rather that they advance propositions and defend them in ways we find entirely alien.

Styles of reasoning, then, differ according to what may be candidates for truth or falsity and how they may be investigated. They do not confront reality in the way that conceptual schemes or paradigms are described as doing. They do not present us with radically different *perceptions* of the world or collections of untranslatable sentences held to be true. What they do offer are different ways of proposing, investigating and arguing about propositions. Hacking is concerned with claims to knowledge and the different ways in which they may be proposed or defended. His differences are differences between cultures.

I propose to generalize Hacking's approach by noting that proposing and defending claims to knowledge are not the only actions that may depend on the use of specialized techniques or ways of thinking. In the Preface to the 1872 edition of *The Communist Manifesto* Marx and Engels remark that: 'One thing especially was proved by the Commune, viz., that the working class cannot simply lay hold of the ready-made state machinery and wield it for its own purposes.' Disputes over the interpretation of that statement played an important part in socialist debates in the early part of this century, and its echoes can still be heard in some quarters. The point to notice here is that Marx's and Engels' lesson, and debates around its practical implications, make sense only in terms of a style of political analysis in which classes are regarded as collective actors, and politics is seen as an arena of conflict between them.

There are other styles of political argument and analysis with significant practical implications in which classes are not regarded as political actors at all. Most of us will be familiar with the range from what remains of European social democracy to the neo-liberalism of the New Right, and there are many other examples. In these styles of analysis some of what is recognized by class analysis as candidates for truth or falsehood would have no sense, but there would be little difficulty in attaching a clear meaning to other of its candidates. These various styles of political analysis differ in part in the premises from which they start, the forms of argument which they employ and the ways in which issues may be identified as important. Where Hacking's styles of reasoning differ mainly in their candidates for truth and falsehood and the manner in which they are debated, these styles of political analysis have other concerns. Consequently, they differ also over the identification of possible courses of action and the considerations involved in choosing between them.

The actions of parties, factions and other political activists partly depend on processes of deliberation employing specialized forms of argument and analytical techniques, means of identifying obstacles and potential allies, and ways of circumventing or coming to terms with them, and so on. The point is easily generalized: there are numerous examples of activities which depend on the representation of particular areas of social life (politics, economic activity, the health of the population, or whatever) as fields of instrumental action. Both the identification of possible courses of action and decisions between them involve forms of analysis which are specializsed in the sense that they represent some part of the world as a field of action and effects in order to allow a calculation of objectives and what has to be done to achieve them.

Rationality and deliberation

To say that actors may employ specialized techniques in their deliberations is to say that action does not always follow directly from belief and desire, but rather from belief, desire and whatever specialized techniques actors employ in their deliberations. I have suggested that these specialized techniques should themelves be regarded as possible objects of investigation. That suggestion threatens to undermine the portfolio model in several respects.

First, the portfolio model implies that the presumption of an overall rationality is necessary if we are properly to treat action as resulting from the beliefs and desires of the actor. In effect, we have to work back from what the actor does, including speech, to construct a picture of the beliefs and desires that give rise to those actions - and we can do that only if we assume some overall consistency in the relations between belief, desire and action:

> . . . the basic strategy must be to assume that a speaker we do not yet understand is consistent and correct in his beliefs - according to our own standards, of course. (Davidson, 1980: 238)

This is Davidson's 'principle of charity' and there are other versions of the same general idea.[8] Once we have identified the actor's beliefs and desires on the assumption that actors are 'by and large' rational and consistent, then we may be in a position to identify particular instances of behaviour that are not rational. This insistence on the presumption of rationality is built in to the structure of the portfolio model and follows directly from the assumption that action is a straightforward function of belief and desire. Remove the assumption of rationality and action then becomes unfathomable. On this view action will be non-rational when the actor's overall rationality is not correctly employed.

Once it is recognized that deliberation may be involved, the issue of what relations obtain between belief, desire and action takes a different form. Questions must be raised both with regard to the identification of the conceptual means employed in actors' deliberations and with regard to how they are employed in any given case. Actors may employ what an observer regards as rational means of assessing their situation and deciding on a course of action. They may employ what the same observer regards as irrational or inappropriate techniques – say, the *I Ching*, cost–benefit analysis, or Evans-Pritchard's poison-oracle.[9] Once the actor's or actors' deliberative techniques employed have been identified then it may, of course, be possible to identify instances in which they have not been employed correctly. There will be other cases in which no unambiguous meaning can be attached to the distinction between correct and incorrect usage, and these give rise to all kinds of interesting possibilities. (The debates within Marxist socialism, one of the more self-consciously rationalistic forms of political analysis, over the class analysis of parliamentary democracy provide an object lesson here.) Intentional analysis of behaviour requires the identification of any specialized techniques employed in actors' deliberations. It does not require that we pass judgement on the rationality or otherwise of those techniques.

Furthermore, the possibility of deliberation involving the use of specialized techniques undermines the requirement that we assume an holistic rationality. Davidson's principle of charity requires us to assume that there is a large measure of consistency and rationality in an actor's behaviour 'according to our own standards, of course' (Davidson, 1980: 238). In effect, he argues that the assumption that action results from belief and desire commits us to a hermeneutic process of understanding others' behaviour. The construction of our picture of actors' beliefs and desires from observation of their behaviour in various contexts requires us to presume a fair degree of rationality and consistency across the board. The assumption that action results from belief and desire in turn requires us to make the further assumption of an holistic rationality. It therefore stands to reason that we could not hope to interpret actors, beliefs and desires from their behaviour without the principle of charity or something very like it.

If specialized techniques may be involved in actors' decisions then there is no reason to suppose that the relations between action, belief and desire will be of the same general character across the range of their behaviour. In the examples given above, the specialized ways of thinking and decision-making techniques relate to particular, limited areas of social life and not to others. The political analysis of Marxist socialism recognizes part of the world as a sphere of possible action and effects, and on that basis is able to identify possible courses of action and ways of debating the choice between them. Other forms of political analysis see matters rather differently. The *I Ching* and oracles may not be specialized in quite the same way since they are not restricted in their sphere of possible application to any delimited area of social life, but, if they are used at all, they are used only for a limited range of important decisions.

I have already suggested that the problem for the analysis of action is to identify the specialized techniques employed in actors' deliberations – not to pass judgement on their rationality. The point to notice here is a rather different one. Since many of the specialized ways of thinking available to actors relate to limited areas of social life, there is no reason to suppose that they will be consistent with each other or that the actor employing them will be particularly concerned if they are not. The academic social scientist may have learned to apply the norms of non-sexist behaviour at work, but behave very differently at home and yet not be aware of any inconsistency. Actors may think differently about different spheres of activity, and there is no need to assume either that their thinking within any one of these spheres is particularly rational or that it takes place within an overall rationality and consistency.

Where do these arguments leave us?
I suggested in my introduction that to dispute the assumption rationality is also to raise questions concerning the techniques and forms of thought employed by, or available to, actors, and also questions of the social conditions on which they depend. One set of

questions, to which I return briefly below, concerns the survival and social significance of particular forms of thought. Another concerns the conditions affecting their availability to, or employment by, particular actors. The cultural and educational diversity of most societies ensures that there will be considerable variation in the forms of thought employed by, or available to, actors.

We may begin by disposing of the idea that such differences in actors' forms of thought can be accounted for simply as a reflection of some aspect of their social location – for example, membership of a class, ethnic group or gender category. The derivation of ideas from social location is usually done in terms of interests (or norms and values) which then operate as transmissions between social structure and actors' decisions. The difficulty with such an argument is that the mechanism connecting social location to the motivations of actors remains thoroughly obscure. I argued in Chapter 3 that interests (or norms and values) have consequences only insofar as they provide actors with reasons for action. In other words, they have to be formulated or at least be within the range of what could be formulated by those who act on them – which is to say that the existence of interests as effective elements of actors' motivations depends on the forms of thought available to those actors. There is therefore a significant element of circularity in any suggestion that actors' forms of thought reflect their interests.

My point here is not, of course, that there are no connections between the techniques and forms of thought available to actors and their social location. In any society there will be reasonably clear cultural differences (that is differences in forms of thought employed by actors) which relate to features of its social structure. The point is simply that these patterns should not be seen as reflecting any general mechanism in which one kind of thing – namely, actors' forms of thought – are determined by another kind of thing – namely, social structure. There are many different ways in which the forms of thought employed by, or available to, actors may be related to their social location (some examples follow later), but what the connections are in any given case will have to be a matter for investigation.

To say that there is no general mechanism of determination of actors' forms of thought by their social structural location is to say that the relations between them will depend on features of both. Perhaps the most obvious connection is that the occupation of a social position involves engaging in a range of associated activities. It therefore involves the techniques and forms of thought required to perform those activities. The point is particularly clear in the case of professions and other more or less skilled occupations requiring specialized training, but it applies far more generally – in fact, to anything that depends on socialization. This is an important respect in which features of the forms of thought employed by actors can be read off from their social position, but it would be thoroughly misleading to talk as if the one were determined by the other.

A rather different kind of connection follows from the fact that many techniques and forms of thought are preconditions for the acquisition of others. I argued above that some specialized techniques build on, or elaborate, other techniques which have to be acquired first. Even where that is not the case, access to training may be restricted to those who can demonstrate their possession of certain skills. Or again, actors' current beliefs, concerns and pre-occupations condition what specialized techniques and forms of thought seem worthwhile acquiring or investigating further. For example, all employees in a manufacturing enterprise may be affected by its investment strategy (if there is one), but they would not all be affected in the same way and they are not equally well placed to influence that strategy. Senior managers and wage-labourers are therefore likely to have very different attitudes towards the acquisition of the accountancy and other skills involved in formulating and evaluating long-term financial strategies. To take a different example, barristers and other professionals may find it difficult to locate themselves in terms of a class-based socialist discourse. In these ways the social distribution of some techniques and forms of thought has consequences for the social distribution of others.

What can we say of the conditions affecting the survival and social significance of particular forms of thought? If there is no general mechanism of determination of actors' forms of thought by their social structural location, then there is little to be said in general about the conditions affecting their survival or social impact. There are numerous different ways in which specific forms of thought employed by actors may be related to other forms of thought and to features of their social location. Many of them will be clear to anyone familiar with the society in question. It would be necessary to trace those relations for the form of thought in question in order to account for its survival or social impact.

However, there is one form of thought whose survival and social significance should be considered in this concluding section. I noted above that there are academics and political activists who analyse politics, at least in part, in terms of some notion of class struggle. There are others who do so in terms of rational individual actors. In the academic social sciences and in much of economic and political life, tales of rational economic man and his more or less close relations are far more influential than tales of classes and the struggles between them. Systematic argument certainly plays its part in some of these tales, but it would be a rationalist illusion to imagine that the influence or survival of either of these doctrines depends primarily on their objectivity or coherence. I discussed the explanatory pretensions of class analysis in Chapter 5, but what of the model of rational economic man and related conceptions of the actor? How could these inadequate conceptualizations nevertheless play such an important part in the modern world?

Note first that the significance of the presumption of rationality is not a matter of 'realism', in the sense of approximating to an accurate description of how people behave. Models of rational economic man and his descendants may have emerged in developing Western capitalist societies, but they do not have their origins in careful observation of human behaviour and they will not disappear merely because they can be shown to be inadequate. In my discussion of class analysis I suggested that any reasonably complex body of social thought can be expected to provide resources for dealing with recalcitrant observations and counterarguments. The doctrines associated with the portfolio model are no exception.

I have already noted how the structure of the portfolio model itself generates the view that understanding others' behaviour requires us to suppose, often despite appearances, that they are by and large rational and consistent. This is the basis for Davidson's 'principle of charity' and Grandy's (1973) 'principle of humanity'. (Notice how the terminology here reveals the ethical undertones of much of the debate about the rationality of others.) The same view appears in a rather different form in Winch's argument that, while another culture might not seem rational in *our* terms, it must nevertheless be considered as rational in its own:

> . . . there must be features of its members' use of language analogous to those features of our use of language which are connected with our use of the word 'rational' (Winch, 1970: 99)

Rational choice analysis has further resources of its own. Perhaps the most striking is the methodological position that models should be judged by their predictions, not by the realism or otherwise of their assumptions. Downs (1957) and Becker (1976) both refer us to Friedman's forceful statement of that view in 'The Methodology of Positive Economics' (1953). The methodological claim is not that the model of rational action is a realistic portrayal of actors' decision-making, but rather that it generates successful predictions.

Bernard Williams has argued that 'nothing can explain an agents (intentional) actions except something that motivates him so to act' (Williams, 1979: 22). On this view what has to be investigated is what Williams calls 'the subjective motivational set' of the actor or actors in question. The 'economic approach' of Downs or Becker takes a different view. Instead of enquiring into the subjective motivational set of the actors concerned it asks us to investigate what would motivate hypothetical rational actors to perform the actions we wish to explain. As the editors of the special issue of *The Journal of Business* noted above put it 'economists revel in showing how apparently anomalous behaviour is in fact consistent with the maintained hypothesis' (*Journal of Business*, 1986: 190). One result of this procedure is to preserve the assumption of rationality from empirical refutation.

The second point to notice is that the assumption of rationality tells us little about what actors can be expected to choose in the absence of further assumptions concerning the character of their preferences, the shape and dimensions of the utility function, and so on. It is for this reason that Simon regards the conclusions reached by Becker and others as crucially dependent on 'auxiliary' hypotheses. In fact Simon goes further, taking his examples from Becker's *A Treatise on the Family*.

> Almost all the action, all the ability to reach nontrivial conclusions, comes from the factual assumptions and very little from the assumptions of optimization. (*Journal of Business*, 1986: 212)

There is a related problem in the attempts by Elster, Przeworski and other rational choice Marxists to show that analysis of structural features of social life is consistent with a thorough-going methodological individualism. The problem here can be simply stated: the assumption of actors' rationality tells us that there will be a certain consistency in their behaviour but tells us nothing about the substance of their motivations. Explanation of structural features of social life as resulting from the rational actions of large numbers of individuals therefore requires some further assumptions concerning the content of those motivations. The usual procedure is to assume that actors' concerns reflect their membership of one of the social categories employed by the model in question. In their rehabilitations of Marxism, for example, both Elster and Przeworski derive actors' concerns and perceptions from their class locations. Structural determinism is (rightly) rejected and then brought back in to account for actors' motivations.

Third, and more sophisticated than Friedman's simplistic positivism, is Hardin's suggestion that 'the assumption of narrowly rational motivations yields predictions that are the most useful benchmark by which to assess the extent and the impact of other motivations' (Hardin, 1982: 11). The argument here is reminiscent of Weber's case, in the opening sections of *Economy and Society* (1978), for the use of rational ideal types – namely, that observed deviations measure the impact of non-rational factors in human action.

Of course, the assumption of rationality yields predictions. The question is: why should those predictions be taken as a benchmark for further enquiry? To see what is at issue here consider Hardin's own illustration. The assumption of narrowly rational motivations 'helps us to understand why half of eligible Americans do not vote, but it does little to help us understand the other half' (ibid.). The explanation tells us what narrowly rational actors would do were they to join that large number of Americans who do not vote, but it tells us nothing about what motivates the non-voters themselves. It takes no account of the forms of thought they employ, nor of the manner in which the question of whether to vote or not arises, if it arises at all, nor of the considerations that are taken into account when it does.

In other spheres of social activity it is clear that the test of falsifiability is not a significant element in the life of the doctrine of rational individual action – any more than it is in class analysis. In the case of the presumption of rationality, I suggested in Chapter 6 that what is at stake is not just a matter of popular belief in particular economic or political theories it is also a matter of concepts of the person that play an important part in the social life of modern societies – for example, in the forms of criminal and civil law, in our conceptions of contract and the wage–labour relationship, and in many of our assumptions about the organization and content of education. Concepts of the person as rational actor are major components of the social life of modern societies rather than accurate reflections of what goes on within them.

While realism is not necessarily to be expected of these tales of rational economic man and his descendants, they must nevertheless provide those who use them with some purchase on the situations in which they are supposed to apply. They must provide means of assessing those situations, deciding on objectives to pursue within them, and means of identifying potential obstacles and deciding what to do about them. What they must also do, of course, is provide means of coming to terms with the all-too-common experience of practical and explanatory failure. Any reasonable complex body of contemporary social thought provides resources appropriate to these purposes, and that associated with the presumption of rationality is no exception.

In the case of rational economic man and his descendants, it must be possible to represent the relevant aspects of human behaviour in terms of the actions of such persons, and to have some means of accounting for actions that fail to conform – for example, through concepts of mental disability, illness, and incapacity, affectual and other non-rational sources of motivation, and so on. The proposal that we treat models of rational action as paradigmatic, introducing affectual and other non-rational elements only when strictly necessary to account for deviations allows social scientists to analyse large areas of social life in these terms. So, at a rather different level, do the normalizing discourses of psychiatry, penology, and the like.

What is required then for talk of rational economic man and his relations to be implicated in significant areas of social life is that participants should not be confronted with too many apparent departures from the norm, and that there be ways of accounting for whatever departures cannot be ignored. For the rest, models of rational action are implicated in significant areas of social life to the extent that the relevant actors make use of such models in their own assessments and decisions. To say that, of course, is not to say that other significant elements might not also be involved, or that the models are descriptively adequate to the actors' own behaviour.

Notes

1. Olson, 1965, 1982 provides perhaps the most forceful version of this claim. See Hardin, 1982, for a more measured account.
2. Especially 'Rational fools' and other papers in Sen, 1982.
3. Davidson, 1980, 1984; Macdonald and Pettit, 1981; Doval and Harris, 1986.
4. *The Journal of Business.* (no.4, part 2, 1986).
5. I have discussed Hayek's arguments in *Freedom, Equality and the Market*, 1986.
6. Kuhn, 1970; Feyerabend, 1975, 1978.
7. In Davidson, 1984.
8. See Grandy, 1973 and the discussion in Macdonald and Pettit, 1981.
9. Evans-Pritchard, 1976.

9 Liberal individualism and corporate actors

I suggested in my introduction that the critique of the portfolio model of the actor and associated positions developed in these chapters poses problems for some of the most common ways of conceptualizing political concerns, objectives and commitments. The class analysis of politics usually involves a conception of interests as objectively given in the structure of social relations, sometimes combined with a notion of classes as actors. I outlined some of the problems with this style of political analysis in Chapter 5, 'Class analysis as social theory'. There are other styles of analysis that make use of individualistic versions of the portfolio model of the actor, some of which have been discussed in the last three chapters. This final chapter considers a view that has considerable influence in modern social thought – namely, that human individuals can, and should be, the ultimate point of reference for decisions about social conditions and objectives.

This fundamental principle of liberal political thought is usually taken to involve, first, the claim that there is no strictly *social* good distinct from the ends and purposes of human individuals and, second, a commitment to liberty, understood in the negative sense as the absence of constraint. The view that, in the last resort, there are only individual goods takes many forms. Nozick's account of why individuals may not be violated for the social good, which I quoted in the Introduction is a particularly clear example. Related individualisms appear in many discussions of democracy and in those versions of public choice theory that attempt to construe social choices in terms of an imaginary aggregative mechanism operating over the views of human individuals. The second element, the commitment to a negative conception of liberty, requires that individuals should be free to pursue their own ends in their own way provided that they do not conflict with the freedom of others to do the same. This is usually taken to imply that the state should secure a structure of rights that will minimize coercion and thereafter leave indviduals to do as they will within that structure. Liberty in this sense is identified with an absence rather than any positive capacity of individuals to achieve their potential, pursue their objectives, or whatever.[1] Liberals are invariably concerned with the defence of liberty but they may also have other objectives such as the provisions of welfare, the pursuit of social justice, or the defence of property about which they differ.

In 'Two kinds of person' (Chapter 4), I argued against individualistic social theory, and claimed that there are important actors in the modern world other than human individuals. This argument makes possible a conception of social concerns and objectives not reducible to those of human individuals. I return to this point in the final sections of this chapter, but first it is necessary to consider a different, and long-standing, criticism of the liberal commitment to negative liberty in the name of a more positive conception founded on some particular conception of human nature. The suggestion is, that liberal political thought is mistaken in its account of human individuals and the social world they inhabit. If there are important respects in which the ends and purposes of human beings, and even their very personalities, depend on conditions that transcend the level of the individuals concerned, then there is no particular merit in the claim that social choices should be grounded in their decisions.

I begin by commenting on the limitations of that line of argument. The most influential contemporary version is perhaps the 'communitarian' argument, variously advanced by MacIntyre, Sandel and Taylor,[2] that human individuals are not the constitutive subjects of social life. The suggestion is that the liberal idea of negative freedom involves a misleading substantive conception of the person as an autonomous chooser of ends. In an essay on the idea of negative liberty, Taylor maintains that, if human nature has an essence, then it is not unreasonable to suppose that its full realization may be possible only 'within a certain form of society' (Taylor, 1979: 193). The implication is that our interests would best be served by the establishment and maintenance of that form of society whether we are aware of the fact or not. Under other conditions human capacities are stunted and their energies are frequently misdirected. On that view, the liberal claim that individuals are best left to pursue their own ends in their own way is mistaken.

If only things were so simple. There are several problems with this communitarian critique of liberalism. First, it is far from clear that a negative understanding of liberty need depend on any particular substantive conception of the human individual.[3] Liberal political thought certainly involves a normative individualism but it need not be individualistic in other respects. In Chapter 4, I referred for example, to Coleman's work which combines an argument that there are important actors in the modern world other than human individuals with a normative commitment to the human individual. A more important example in the present context is the work of John Rawls to which I shall shortly return.

Second, the communitarian critique aims to establish political conclusions by means of an argument about human nature. I have already noted for later discussion that there is a difficulty with the assumption that human individuals are the only significant actors in social life. For the moment consider a consequence of analysing human individuals in terms of the abstract concept of actor outlined in earlier chapters. Human individuals are actors, but that is to say very little about their characteristic concerns and objectives, or about the conceptual devices, habits of thought, and the practical activities to which they resort in dealing with them. I have argued that consideration of the conceptual and other conditions which make it possible for actors to reach and formulate decisions of the kind they do in some particular society indicates a variety of ways in which their choices are not reducible to the constitutive activities of the actors themselves.

So far, perhaps, so good for the communitarian position. The claim that humans are actors and that their capacities as actors depend on a variety of conditions external to any one individual certainly suggests that the concerns and objectives of human individuals and their personalities are inescapably bound up with the communities in which they live. However we shall see in a moment that these points need not be particularly damaging to the liberal position. If anything, their implications are precisely contrary to those which the communitarians would have us draw. What we know about human societies suggests that human nature is compatible with a considerable variety of social arrangements. This is not to say, of course, that human nature is infinitely plastic. We can agree with Taylor that there may be many 'forms of society' in which humans are unlikely to flourish – for example, if they were made to live like ants or orang-utangs – but that tells us nothing of value about the kinds of political arrangements at stake in the idea that people should be left as far as possible to pursue their own ends in their own way. Whatever can reasonably be said about human nature is likely to have little bearing on the distinctive types of concerns, pleasures, habits of thought, moral and political ideas and the like to be found in any particular society.

Now, there are certainly versions of liberal political thought that involve a limited conception of human nature. Nozick's *Anarchy, State and Utopia* (1974) is an influential recent example. But it is far from clear that the liberal commitment to negative liberty and the associated political arrangements need depend on any particular substantive conception of human nature. In *A Theory of Justice* (1971), Rawls develops an account of the principles of justice in terms of an imaginary social contract. The contract is one that would be agreed to by reasonable men meeting under conditions which ensured that they had no knowledge of the positions they would be likely to occupy in society. They are assumed to be familiar with whatever knowledge the social sciences have to offer and to be well-informed about the structure of society. Rawls suggests that consideration of their own interests would lead such reasonable and well-informed men to agree on the principles of justice he wishes to establish.

As Rawls does not tell us what knowledge he believes the social sciences might have to offer, it would not therefore be unreasonable to suggest that his account of the principles on which reasonable men would agree depends on a particular substantive view of human nature. To that extent, his arguments are open to the communitarian attack. However, in his more recent writings, Rawls claims to provide a different foundation for his account of justice. It is now said to be based, not on some substantive conception of human nature, but rather on ideas that are embedded in the major institutions of liberal democratic societies. There are certainly problems with this argument but, as we shall see, they have little to do with his view of human nature. The more serious difficulties lie in his account of the societies in which those ideas are said to be embedded.

'A fair system of social cooperation'?
In several papers published since *A Theory of Justice*, Rawls has described his account of justice as fairness as being political rather than metaphysical.[4] It aims to develop a conception of justice appropriate to societies governed by constitutional democratic

regimes. Since these are, on the whole, culturally plural societies Rawls maintains that:

> . . . as a practical political matter no general moral conception can provide a publicly recognized basis for a conception of justice in a modern democratic state. (Rawls, 1985: 225)

A workable conception of justice must not therefore depend on philosophical and religious doctrines that are controversial in such societies. Accordingly he aims to present not so much

> . . . a conception of justice that is true but one that can serve as a basis of informed and willing political agreement between citizens viewed as free and equal persons' (ibid.: 230)

The point then is not to base the idea of justice in some substantive account of the essential character of human agency, but rather to locate the foundations for such an idea in

> . . . basic intuitive ideas that are embedded in the political institutions of a constitutional regime and the public traditions of their interpretation. (ibid.: 225)

Rawls' account of the role of these 'ideas' is reminiscent of Parsons' account of central values. Both recognize that there is considerable cultural diversity in modern democratic societies, yet both nevertheless regard their basic institutions as organized around certain ideas or central values. In Rawls' argument these ideas are the foundation of his account of justice. Two of the most important of these ideas are that of society as a system of cooperation between free and equal persons and that of the person as 'citizen, that is, a fully cooperating member of society over a complete life' (ibid.: 233). The idea of the person as an autonomous chooser of ends is indeed fundamental to Rawl's enterprise. However, he does not claim that it provides an adequate description of human individuals and their social existence, rather that 'in the public political culture of a constitutional democratic regime citizens conceive of themselves as free in [the appropriate] respects' (ibid.: 244).

The communitarian argument that human individuals are not autonomous captains of their fate would do little damage to this version of Rawl's position. The problems lie elsewhere. Perhaps the most obvious is that the presence and practical significance of the liberal idea of the person in our culture do not suffice to establish its normative priority. The liberal idea of the person suggests that all persons (or at least all citizens) have certain minimal rights by virtue of their status as members of the relevant political community and that those rights should be accorded equal respect. There are also elements in our culture which suggest otherwise – for example, that the rights and wishes of the rich and powerful are considerably more important than the rights of the rest of us. Other elements foster an egalitarianism far more radical than most liberals would wish to countenance. There is nothing in Rawl's account of the liberal idea of the person that can require any one of us to accord it priority over these others. Or, again, members of the political community might well also belong to other communities, as Aborigines, Palestinians, or Croatians, whose claims they regard as significant. Why should the claims of the political community to which they belong as citizens be given priority over the claims of these others?

In fact, on Rawls' account of the practical political aims of his argument, its failure to establish normative priority may not be too significant. He starts from the assumption that a variety of conflicting conceptions of the good are affirmed by citizens. What matters for the unity of such a society is that the willingness of its citizens to live together in peace should have a secure foundation. Rawls takes this to mean that they do so not primarily for pragmatic reasons but rather because they share what he describes as an overlapping consensus in which the same conception of justice is affirmed by adherents of different world-views.

> Social unity and the allegiance of citizens to their common institutions are not founded on their all affirming the same conception of the good, but on their publicly accepting a political conception of justice to regulate the basic structure of society. (ibid.: 249)

The assumption is that the foundations of this conception of justice are already embedded in the main institutions of the societies with which Rawls' argument is concerned. In those societies there is no reason for conflicts over normative priority of the kind noted above to arise.

This point suggests a more serious problem for Rawls' argument, concerning his account of the society in which his practical political aims are to be realized and, in particular, how far the ideas of society as system of cooperation and of the person as citizen within it do in fact serve in modern liberal democracies 'as a basis of informed and willing political agreement between citizens' (ibid.: 230). I have just noted that there are other elements in our political culture which have rather different practical implications. Rawls assumes that we live in societies where the normative priority of the liberal position does not have to be established because, did we but know it, we already agree on its basic principles. Here again, the parallel with Parsons is clear. Both assume that the relative stability of contemporary liberal democracies reflects a significant underlying consensus rather than a *modus vivendi* accepted by different groups for a variety of pragmatic reasons. Whether we (or Rawls) do indeed live in such societies is certainly open to question, but I will not pursue that issue here.

However, there are other aspects of Rawls' account of liberal democratic societies that should be questioned. These societies are said to have a basic structure of political, social and economic institutions which 'fit together into one unified system of social cooperation' (ibid.: 225). His account of justice as fairness is intended to apply in just such societies. It starts from the ideas of person as citizen and of 'society as a fair system of cooperation between free and equal person' (ibid.: 231). Cooperation itself involves a number of elements of which the most important are: first, it is not just a matter of activity coordinated by some central authority, but is guided by rules and procedures regarded as properly regulating their conduct by those concerned: second, it involves fair terms of cooperation: and third, it 'requires an idea of each participant's rational advantage or good' (ibid.: 232). These ideas are said to be embedded in the political institutions of modern constitutional democracies. Together they provide

> . . . a publicly recognized point of view from which all citizens can examine before one another whether or not their political and social institutions are just (ibid.: 229)

There are at least two points to note here. First, it is doubtful whether the idea of society as a system of cooperation properly captures what is embedded in the economic institutions of liberal democratic societies. Consider the institution of property. One person's ownership of an object involves restrictions on its use by others. The existence of property, in other words, presupposes a regime of coercion.[5] In fact, it may well involve two rather different regimes of coercion. In liberal democratic societies the existence of freedom of contract in employment implies that neither party to a contract is coerced by the state to enter into that particular contract. It does not rule out coercive relationships within the employment relations it makes possible. Property and employment certainly involve cooperation, but they also involve significant elements of coercion.

Second, even if we were to accept that the conception of society as a fair system of social cooperation between citizens and related ideas were embedded in the main institutions of a contemporary liberal democracies, it does not follow that those societies are properly characterized in such terms. Rawls assumes that the one implies the other. To the extent that the account of liberal democratic societies as fair systems of social cooperation between citizens is misleading so too will be Rawls' account of the practical significance of those ideas.

To see what is at stake here consider Weber's very different account of the role of such ideas in modern democratic societies. Weber does not deny that these ideas are embedded in democratic societies but he is far from describing those societies as systems of social cooperation in Rawls' sense. Rather than describing such societies these ideas are presented by Weber as serving to legitimate a distinctively modern form of rule in capitalist societies, one which combines a bureaucratic state and significant elements of charismatic domination. Agreement by citizens may be willing but no serious student of political behaviour would analyse government in electoral democracies as embodying the informed agreement of its citizens. Ideas of popular sovereignty and the considerably weaker idea of the mandate are certainly invoked in democratic societies, and not only when elections are imminent. They play a significant part in political life, but they do not properly describe it. In fact, according to Weber, the part they *do* play in political life requires precisely that they do not describe it.

We need not accept Weber's account of the system of domination characteristic of modern democratic societies in all its details, but we should note that his argument exemplifies an important cautionary thesis concerning the role of ideas in social life. Ideas concerning the workings of particular social institutions are frequently embedded in the social institutions themselves and function as essential lubricants in their day-to-day activities, but it does not follow that those ideas properly describe the institutions in which they operate. I made a similar point in earlier chapters regarding the class analysis of politics and the idea of rational action.

So, even if we were to accept that the *idea* of society as a fair system of cooperation amongst citizens and its associated characteristics are embedded in the principal institutions of liberal democratic societies, we would not then have to accept Rawls' account of those societies as if they were in fact fair systems of cooperation amongst citizens. It follows that the practical political consequences of those ideas are not necessarily the ones that Rawls envisages.

We must also consider at least two further possibilities in addition to the point about property noted above. One is simply Weber's point that, in addition to providing a practical foundation for cooperative activity between its citizens in some aspects of their social life, those ideas might also serve to legitimate their domination. The other is that the citizens might not be the only significant actors in society.

Finally, if Rawls' account of liberal democratic society is misleading in a sense that is important for his argument, there is another context in which it is seriously incomplete. The idea of equal basic rights and liberties is formal and abstract. It tells us nothing about what life would be like, except that we would all be equally free to do whatever it was that we wanted to do. Unfortunately, what we might want to do will depend significantly on the character of the society in which we live and the conditions we found ourselves occupying within it. If there were significant changes in social conditions we would have different concerns and objectives but we may not be any more or less free. Many liberals would argue for social ends in addition to the protection of individual liberty. In *A Theory of Justice*, Rawls used the subterfuge of an imaginary social contract to introduce ends other than individual liberty, but the resulting picture of a just society nevertheless remains remarkably empty.

There are two related issues to note here. One concerns relations between 'justice as fairness' and other social concerns we might have. Gutmann raises the issue in her defence of Rawls against the communitarian attack. Imagine

> . . . a society in which no one does more or less than respect everyone else's liberal rights. People do not form ties of love and friendship (or they do so only in so far as necessary to developing the kind of character that respects liberal rights). They do not join neighbourhood associa-

tions, political parties, trades unions, civic groups, synagogues, or churches. This might be a perfectly liberal, arguably even a just society, but it is certainly not the best society to which we can aspire. (Gutmann, 1985: 320)

In Gutmann's view, the point indicates the need to supplement liberal values not to undermine them. But this returns us to the problem of normative priority: why is it a matter of supplementing liberal values rather than replacing them with others? The problem in this case is that there are matters of concern to citizens relating to the quality of social life that cannot be derived from Rawls' conception of justice. It is compatible to take a rather different example with a society in which disputes are normally settled by public brawls between consenting adults and with a society in which they are normally settled without violence. The question of how disputes are normally settled illustrates the general point that there are invariably important features of the individuals' social conditions which lie outside the control of the individuals concerned. If public authorities were to regulate these matters by requiring us all, say, to have at least ten friends, to join not less then five associations, to have third-party motor insurance whenever motor vehicles are used on public highways, or to abstain from settling disputes by violence, even when both parties are willing to fight, that might well be thought to limit the freedom of citizens. Why should the demands of justice, as Rawls describes it, be given priority over these other matters?

The second issue is simply stated. If these matters of the quality of the social environment in which we conduct our lives are not determined by public authorities, then they will be determined in other ways – sometimes, for example, by the blind action of a plurality of actors through the market and sometimes through the influence of a small number of powerful private agencies. The picture of society as a fair system of cooperation between its citizens suggests that there are no significant private agencies apart from citizens themselves and the associations they choose to form. Otherwise it is indifferent between these possibilities.

Liberty and republican virtue
I have noted that the picture of society presented by exponents of negative liberty tells us nothing about the substantive character of social life other than that it should sustain liberty and justice. The most common response by their critics has been to seek further

substance in some particular concept of human nature and an argument about the form of society in which it can be expected to flourish.[6] Berlin, Rawls and their supporters maintain, correctly in my view, that there is no prospect of agreement on these matters. They argue, furthermore, that it is a dangerous mistake to link the defence of liberty with any particular conception of civic virtue. If these positions were the only alternatives then it would be difficult to resist the appeal of what Skinner has called their 'gothic' vision of liberty.[7]

However, there is another approach to the discussion of liberty which goes considerably further in its account of the substantive character of social life, while not invoking a concept of human nature. Skinner has forcefully advanced this 'republican' view of liberty in his discussion of the contemporary relevance of Machiavelli, and closely related accounts are presented in the recent work of Pettit and in what might be called the new socialist republicanism.[8] It starts from the assumption that we each have an interest in the freedom to pursue our chosen ends, but it also involves something more than the usual doctrine of negative liberty. The presence of negative liberties is certainly important, but we should also be assured 'of having them in a suitable measure . . . where it is also common knowledge that this conditions is fulfilled' (Pettit, 1988: 23). How far such an assurance can be provided will depend on the politics and institutional framework of the society in question. The republican view therefore construes liberty 'as the condition of citizenship in a suitable legal order' (ibid.).

We must therefore consider what might threaten the legal order of such a republic and what can be done to defend it. Threats may be external or internal. If the republic is not self-governing it can hardly assure its citizens that an appropraite legal order will be maintained. Against external threats, Machiavelli argues that the best defence is a citizens' army and he goes on to consider the personal qualities required for it to be most effective. The most serious internal threats involve subversion of republican institutions. In Machiavelli's account they arise from the *ambizione* of the leading citizens and their attempts to bribe or coerce the people into serving their ends. In the long run this can be prevented only if the polity remains in the hands of the citizens as a whole. There must be laws to keep the *grandi* in check and differences in income and wealth should be prevented from becoming too extreme. In particular, no significant number of citizens should be effectively disenfranchised by their poverty or lack of education. The polity must be organized so that each of its citizens is able to play a part in determining the actions of the republic. This implies that the citizens must be willing and able to serve in public office and to pursue a life of public service. The latter in turn requires definite personal qualities on the part of the citizens.

The precise details of Machiavelli's argument need not concern us. The general style of this account has the considerable advantage over many liberal positions and their communitarian critics in that it does at least address the question of the political conditions in which liberty is most likely to be maintained. It suggests that liberty depends on the ability and willingness of citizens to perform a variety of civic duties and therefore on their cultivation of the appropriate personal qualities or virtues. The question of what is required for those conditions to be assured is a question not so much of 'the sort of value that freedom is taken to be, but rather [of] the sort of institutions that are thought to be most desirable under a dispensation of freedom' (Pettit, 1988: 24). I referred above to Gutmann's picture of an imaginary society in which personal ties were kept to a minimum and nobody joined political parties and voluntary associations. Such a society may be, as she suggests, 'a perfectly liberal, arguably even a just society', but it can offer no assurance that either liberty or justice will be maintained.

This republican argument is certainly attractive. It establishes connections between the maintenance of liberty, the institutional character of social life and the personal qualities of citizens in a way that presupposes little about its citizens except that each has an interest in the maintenance of liberty. It is easy to see how the argument can be adapted in contemporary liberal democracies to provide cases for a universally high level of general education, academic freedom and freedom of information, redistributive policies to eliminate the extremes of wealth and poverty, provision for public access to the media and restrictions on the extent and concentration of private ownership, and so on.

Unfortunately, the contemporary relevance of this republican line of argument is less clear than these relatively straightforward extensions might suggest. The most obvious objection to Machiavelli's position is the one raised by Montesquieu's argument that a republic could exist only in a small community with a relatively homogeneous population. Republican government was based on the active consent of the population and therefore presupposed a moral consensus and a broad similarity of interests within the population. Government of large and diverse populations, on the other hand, depended on a unitary authority imposed from the top downwards.

Whatever the merits of Montesquieu's particular arguments, there are a number of respects in which the size and diversity of the community bears on the republican position. One concerns a commonplace of the contemporary literature on collective action. Citizens may find all kinds of reasons to vote, for example, but few will do so on the basis of a rational assessment of the difference their individual vote might make to the outcome. Similarly, in a large and diverse community it is far from clear that the cultivation of civic virtues and active participation in public affairs by any one individual would make an identifiable contribution to the maintenance of liberty.

Furthermore, the assumption that since 'we all have various goals we are minded to pursue, it will obviously be in our interests to live in whatever form of community best assures us the freedom to pursue them' (Skinner, 1984: 206) conflates two rather different states of affairs. One allows me to pursue the goals I in fact have while the other leaves me free to pursue whatever goals I might wish to pursue consistent with a similar freedom for others.

Perhaps in a small and suitably homogeneous community there would be no clear distinction between these states of affairs. What citizens in fact wanted to do would also be the kind of thing they might wish to be free to be able to do. In such a society freedom and the ability to do what one in fact wanted to do might seem to coincide. In general, however, the two are quite distinct. This suggests that what is likely to matter to citizens is not so much freedom *per se* but rather a variety of specific freedoms[9] – and that only under very particular conditions would they regard them as equivalent. The specific freedoms that were thought to be important would, of course, vary from one society to another, according to the social situation of individuals within any one society, and over time. The first state of affairs does not entail the second, and may indeed conflict with it. On Machiavelli's account, the maintenance of the second state of affairs involves considerable personal costs. It is not clear why we should assume that citizens would each prefer that state of liberty and its accompanying personal costs to a state in which they were less free but better able to do what they in fact wanted to do. The argument that we should all cultivate civic virtues may suggest an attractive kind of society, but it cannot be based on an appeal to individual self-interest.

Like Rawls' later account of justice, this republican argument may not depend on any particular substantive concept of human nature, but it does presuppose a very particular kind of community. In this case, it is a community in which the major problems are external defence and ensuring that the rich are kept under control. It would be difficult to maintain that liberal democratic societies were communities of that kind, or that they had successfully resolved those problems – after all, the rich are still with us and so, of course, is the outside world. Nevertheless, there are other significant features of these societies to be considered. One concerns the considerable development of the state in most modern societies, and the other concerns the role private corporate agencies in modern capitalist societies. Both issues were signalled in my discussion of Rawls and they bring us to the final set of arguments in this chapter.

Corporate actors
Both Rawls' liberalism and the republican position outlined by Skinner are individualistic in the sense that they take human individuals to be the only effective political actors. If the claim that human individuals are not entirely captains of their fate does no great damage to these positions, a more serious set of problems arise from the growing importance in the modern world of actors other than human individuals – that is, of state agencies, capitalist enterprises, political parties, unions, churches, and many others. There were, of course, corporate actors in the world before the emergence of modern capitalism but there has been a remarkable growth in both their numbers and their significance since the emergence of the joint-stock company form of organization in the mid-nineteenth century, and especially since the early years of this century.[10]

Although most of these new corporate actors have been capitalist enterprises, there has been a growth of private, non-commercial organizations as well. The number and variety of state agencies has also expanded enormously over the last century. These developments pose two rather different difficulties for liberal political thought and they suggest a clear sense in which there may be social concerns and objectives. The first difficulty, posed by private corporate actors, is that while they are an increasingly influential part of our liberal democratic societies – and indeed of societies that are not remotely either liberal or democratic – they are not human individuals. The concerns and objectives of many such actors therefore have a somewhat problematic status in terms either of liberal political theory or the republican position considered above.

I suggested in Chapter 4, 'Two kinds of person', that the most common way of evading the difficulties corporate actors pose for social theory is simply to deny their ontological status as actors and to suggest that, while we may of course refer to the actions of the state or of IBM, those actions are ultimately reducible to the actions of human individuals. This device allows us to admit that corporate actors may indeed be influential while insisting that their concerns and objectives can all be boiled down to a complex mixture of those of human individuals. If, as Rawls suggests, we regard liberal democratic society as a fair system of cooperation between its citizens, then corporations and other social actors would have to be understood as representing some complex set of cooperative relations between human individuals. From this point of view, problems posed by the power of interest groups and large corporations are really just a matter of the power of some groups of individuals over others.

There are usually two aspects to the claim that corporate actors were reducible to human individuals, as if the latter were the only real actors. One concerns a view of human subjectivity as an essential component of action and the other is the claim that human individuals are the only actors whose actions do not always depend on the actions of others. I have argued throughout this book that, while there are certainly differences between human individuals and other actors, there is nothing in the character of those differences to justify such reductionist claims. In practice, they rarely amount to more than an assertion of reductionism in principle, a gesture towards a programme of work that has yet to be followed through. They do not tell us how the actions of, say, IBM or the Roman Catholic Church could be usefully resolved into the actions of the relevant individuals. Reductionism in principle is little more than an evasion of the difficulty corporate actors pose for modern social thought. It offers no worthwhile guidance in practice. Even if there were a clear sense in which the actions of corporate actors could, in principle, be reduced to the actions of human individuals, we should still have to reckon with the concerns and objectives of corporate actors and their actions in pursuit of them.

The reductionist manoeuvre offers no practical resolution of the difficulty corporate actors pose for liberal political thought. If the interests of human individuals are the only interests legitimately involved in determining the policies and personnel of government then there is a strictly limited place for the political activity of corporate actors. In effect, parliament and many government agencies are recognized as legitimate corporate actors, and so perhaps are political parties and interest groups, but the status of others is more problematic. We return to the point that the political activity of many private corporate actors is presumptively illegitimate. It is partly for this reason that many discussions of corporatist arrangements between government, business and organized labour describe them as undermining democratic institutions. And, again, in an otherwise valuable discussion of the significance of corporate actors in the modern world, Coleman argues that we need to correct the balance of rights and responsibilities between corporate actors and human individuals in the interests of the latter.

The difficulty with this response is that many corporate actors in addition to political parties and interest groups are now influential figures in liberal democratic (and other) societies whether their citizens like it or not. It is impossible to imagine a complex modern society in which corporate actors of various kinds did not play a major role. In the liberal democracies there will be powerful private corporate actors for the forseeable future, and there is therefore little to be gained by treating their political activity as if it could in principle be eradicated or reduced to the activities of human individuals. Capitalist enterprises, unions, churches and other corporate actors all have an interest in the policies of government. With the partial exception of political parties and interest groups, corporate actors are normally excluded from formal channels of political participation, but it would be naive to expect that to remove their influence. At best, it is simply to favour those best placed to make their wishes felt in other ways.

An approach to the analysis of modern societies that recognizes only human individuals as effective actors must be regarded as seriously incomplete. An approach that recognizes other actors as irreducible but treats their political action as illegitimate is little better. A large part of what is often regarded as the improper influence of corporate actors over the actions of government and state agencies relates to a problem of public control over these agencies. I return to that problem in a moment. For the rest, the problem is to bring their political activities within the realm of public control and to establish conditions in which it could be regarded as legitimate. Legislation requiring the establishment of internal mechanisms of self-regulation has been proposed as a means of regulating some forms of corporate crime,[11] but the idea of compulsory self-regulation clearly has more general application. After all, it is already required of citizens.

State agencies and the public good
The second difficulty posed by corporate actors concerns state agencies. The growth of the state in the modern period has undermined whatever plausibility there may have been in the image of the polity as a system of cooperation between citizens. I have already noted that, while ideas of the person as citizen and of popular sovereignty play a part in the political life of liberal democracies, they are far from being descriptively adequate. Electoral democracy means little more than that a number of significant public appointments and public decisions are made as a result of majority voting following relatively open public debate. The conditions of public debate allow individuals and groups critical of government policy to develop alternatives and to campaign for wider political support. The prospect of elections provides conditions in which governments may be rendered vulnerable to public criticism and to more or less organized public opposition.

In liberal democracies a complex system of state agencies have their rule legitimized by ideas of popular sovereignty, and they are subject to various mechanisms of public control which ensure some limited degree of government responsiveness to minority interests. These controls may be more or less effective in some cases, but they clearly do not amount to a system in which government is merely the institutional frame for 'a fair system of cooperation' (Rawls, 1985: 234) between citizens. Even where national and local governments are themselves vulnerable to public criticism and the threat of elections, the public sector agencies for which they are formally responsible are considerably more remote. In this respect, the libertarian attack on big government does address, however inadequately, a real and important issue. If, as Nozick insists, there is no social entity but only human individuals hiding behind it, then the lack of responsiveness of public service agencies is hardly surprising. They may well pretend to serve social or public ends but in fact, since only human individuals have ends, that pretence must be understood as a cover for the ends of others – for example, of politicians and public servants. On this view, the way to deal with the problem is not to attempt reform of the bureaucracies but rather to abandon the pretence that there are social ends to be served by government over and above what is required for the defence of liberty.

Not all liberals would be entirely happy with that conclusion, of course, and many would argue that there may be important ends other than the protection of individual liberty. In *A Theory of Justice*, (1971) for example, Rawls introduces other ends by means of a long detour through the imaginary social contract of a kind that would be agreed to by reasonable and otherwise well-informed men meeting under conditions in which they had no knowledge of their likely positions in society. The conditions under which the imaginary contract is to be drawn up are contrived so that the reasonable men in question would be led by consideration of their own interests to agree on the principles Rawls wishes to establish. Rawls' argumentative strategy here is radically distinct from that of Skinner's Machiavelli, but there is an important respect in which they are very similar. In both cases, ends other than liberty are slipped into an otherwise individualistic social theory through a device that claims to relate those ends to the interests of individuals.

We therefore have at least three reasons for insisting on the significance for political thought of decisions by public authorities. One is that there are social entities with concerns and objectives of their own, not reducible to those of human individuals. Public corporate actors provide an important sense in which there may be public concerns and objectives, not reducible to those of human individuals. There is therefore no reason to pretend that all public goods could, in principle, be derived from the wishes of human individuals, either by imaginary contract or by the aggregative character of election.

Second, as I suggested earlier, if matters are not decided by public authorities it does not always follow that they will be *decided* by other actors. Individual choices are always made under definite social conditions, and many of those conditions cannot be within the control of the individuals concerned. If those conditions are not established by public choice they will be established in some other way, but they will not necessarily be established by decision, still less by the individuals affected. The performance of state agencies may well leave much to be desired but that should not be seen as demonstrating the imaginary character of public goods, and it is certainly no reason to abandon the idea of choice by public agencies.

Finally, we can no more dispense with public corporate actors in complex modern societies than we can with private ones. Here too, it should be possible to modify their internal structures and the manner in which they operate. The problem we face is to reconstruct the agencies of public choice, not abandon the idea of decision by public authorities in favour of an illusory alternative in which individuals decide for themselves.

Notes

1. The best known contemporary defense of this 'negative' view of liberty is Berlin's 'Two concepts of liberty' (in Berlin, 1969). For a variety of criticisms see the works of MacIntyre, Sandel and Taylor referred to below, and, from a rather different perspective, my 'Liberty and Equality' in Hindess (ed.) 1989.
2. MacIntyre, 1981; Sandel, 1982; Taylor, 1979, 1985.
3. See the discussions of Rawls and the communitarian critique in Gutmann, 1985 and Mulhall, 1987.
4. Rawls, 1980, 1985, 1987. For purposes of the present argument I shall concentrate on Rawls, 1985.
5. See Cohen, 1979 for a forceful statement of this argument.
6. Baldwin, 1984.
7. See the first part of Skinner, 1983.
8. Pettit, 1988 (page references are to the manuscript); Skinner, 1983, 1984. For the new socialist republicanism see Barber, 1984, Cohen and Rogers, 1983, Keane, 1988.
9. A similar conclusion is reached, for rather different reasons, by Dworkin, 1981 and Wootton, 1945.
10. Graphically illustrated in the first chapter of Coleman, 1982.
11. Braithwaite, 1982; Braithwaite and Fisse, 1985.

References

Abrams, M., Rose, R. and Hinden, R. (1960), *Must Labour Lose?*, Harmondsworth: Penguin.

Althusser, L. (1971), 'Ideology and the ideological state apparatuses' in *Lenin and Philosophy and other essays*, London: New Left Books.

Anderson, P. (1976), 'The antinomies of Antonio Gramsci', *New Left Review*, no. 100.

Arrow, K. (1963), *Social Choice and Individual Values*, New Haven: Yale University Press.

Bachrach, P. and Baratz, M. S. (1962), 'The two faces of power', *American Political Science Review*, no. 56.

Bachrach, P. and Baratz, M. S., (1963), 'Decisions and non-decisions', *American Political Science Review*, no. 57.

Baldwin, T. (1984), 'MacCullum and the two Concepts of freedom', *Ratio*, no. 26.

Barber, B. (1984), *Strong Democracy*, Berkeley, University of California Press.

Barry, B. (1965), *Political Argument*, London: Routledge and Kegan Paul.

Barry, B. (1978), *Sociologists, Economists and Democracy*, (2nd edition), University of Chicago Press.

Barry, B. and Hardin, R. (eds.) (1982), *Rational Man and Irrational Society*, Beverly Hills: Sage.

Becker, G. S. (1976), *The Economic Approach to Human Behaviour*, Chicago: University of Chicago Press.

Benton, T. (1981), '"Objective" interests and the sociology of power', *Sociology*, no. 15.

Berle, A. A. and Means G. C. (1968). *The Modern Corporation and Private Property*, New York: Harcourt, Brace and World.

Berlin, I. (1969), 'Two concepts of liberty' in *Four Essays on Liberty*, Oxford: Oxford University Press.

Bernstein, E. (1961), *Evolutionary Socialism*, New York: Schocken.

Braithwaite, J. (1982), 'Enforced self-regulation: a new strategy for corporate crime control', *Michigan Law Review*, no. 80.

Braithwaite, J. and Fisse, B. (1985), 'Varieties of responsibility and organizational crime', *Law and Policy*, no.7.

Campbell, A., Converse, P. E., Miller, W.E. and Stokes, D. (1960), *The American Voter*, New York: Wiley.

Carling, A. (1986), 'Rational choice Marxism', *New Left Review*, no. 161.

Cohen, G. A. (1979), 'Capitalism, freedom and the proletariat' in A.Ryan (ed.) *The Idea of Freedom*.

Cohen, J. and Rogers, J. (1983), *On Democracy*, New York, Penguin.

Clegg, S., Boreham P., and Dow, G. (1986), *Class, Politics and the Economy*, London, Routledge and Kegan Paul.

Coleman, J. S. (1973), *Power and the Structure of Society*, Pennsylvania: University of Pennsylvania Press.

Coleman, J. S. (1979), Rational Action in Macrosociological analysis, in R. Harrison (ed.), *Rational Action*, Cambridge: Cambridge University Press.

Coleman, J. S. (1982), *The Asymmetric Society*, Syracuse: Syracuse University Press.

Connolly, W. E. (1983), *The Terms of Political Discourse*, Oxford: Martin Robertson.

Cousins, M. and Hussain, A., (1984), *Michael Foucault*, London: Macmillan.

Cripps, F. *et al.* (1981), *Manifesto*, London: Pan Books.

Crosland, C. A. R. (1956), *The Future of Socialism*, London: Cape.

Crosland, C. A. R. (1960), *Can Labour Win?*, Fabian Tract, 324.

Cutler, A. J., Hindess, B., Hirst, P. Q. and Hussain, A. (1977, 1978), Mary's Capital and Capitalism Today (2 vols.), London, Routledge and Kegan Paul.

Dahl, R. A., (1958), 'A critique of the ruling élite model'. *American Political Science Review*, no. 21.

Dahl, R. A., (1961), *Who Governs?*, New Haven: Yale University Press.

Davidson, D. (1980), *Essays on Actions and Events*, Oxford: Clarendon Press.

Davidson, D. (1984), *Inquiries into Truth and Interpretation*, Oxford: Clarendon Press.

Doval, L. and Harris, R. (1986), *Empiricism, Explanation and Rationality*, London: Routledge and Kegan Paul.

Downs, A. (1957), *An Economic Theory of Democracy*, New York: Harper.

Dworkin R. (1981), 'What is equality?', *Philosophy and Public Affairs* nos. 10 and 11.

Elster, J. (1978), *Logic and Society*, Chichester and New York: Wiley.

Elster, J. (1979), *Ulysses and the Sirens*, Cambridge: Cambridge University Press.

Elster, J. (1983a), *Explaining Technical Change*, Cambridge: Cambridge University Press.

Elster, J.(1983b), *Sour Grapes*, Cambridge: Cambridge University Press.

Elster, J. (1985), *Making Sense of Marx*, Cambridge: Cambridge University Press.

Evans-Pritchard, E. E. (1976), *Witchcraft, Oracles and Magic Among the Azande*, (abridged edition), Oxford: Clarendon Press.

Feverabend, P. (1975), *Against Method*, London: New Left Books.

Feverabend, P. (1978), *Science in a Free Society*, London: New Left Books.

Fine, B. *et al.* (1984), *Class Politics: An Answer to its Critics*, London: Leftover Pamphlets.

Foucault, M. (1970), *The Order of Things*, London: Tavistock.

Foucault, M. (1973), *The Birth of the Clinic*, London: Tavistock.

Foucault, M. (1977), *Discipline & Punish*, London, Allen Lane.

Foucault, M. (1979), *This History of Sexuality, vol. 1,* London: Allen Lane.

Foucault M. (1980), *Power/Knowledge*, Brighton: Harvester Press.

Friedman, M. (1953), 'The methodology of positive economics' in *Essays in Positive Economics*, Chicago: University of Chicago Press.

Friedman, M. and R. (1980), *Free to Choose*, Harmondsworth: Penguin.

Giddens, A. (1973), *The Class Structure of the Advanced Societies*, London: Hutchinson.

Giddens, A. (1976), *New Rules of Sociological Method*, London, Hutchinson.

Giddens, A. (1984), *The Constitution of Society*, Oxford: Polity.

Goldthorpe, J. H. (1980), *Social Mobility and Class Strcuture in Modern Britain*, Oxford: Clarendon Press.

Goldthorpe, J. H. (ed.) (1984), *Order and Conflict in Contemporary Capitalism,* Oxford: Oxford University Press.

Goldthorpe, J. H., Lockwood, D., Beckhofer, F. and Platt , J. (1968), *The Affluent Worker,* Cambridge: Cambridge University Press.

Grandy, R. (1973), 'Reference, meaning and belief', *Journal of Philosophy*, no. 70.

Gutmann, A. (1985), 'Communitarian critics of liberalism', *Philosophy and Public Affairs*, no. 14.

Habermas, J. (1971), *Knowledge and Human Interests*, Boston: Beacon Press.

Habermas, J. (1979), 'Aspects of the rationality of action' in T. F. Gereats (ed.), *Rationality Today*, Ottawa: University of Ottawa Press.

Hacking, I. (1982), 'Language, truth and reason' in M. Hollis and S. Lukes (eds.), *Rationality and Relativism*.

Hadden, T. (1977), *Company Law and Capitalism*, London: Weidenfeld and Nicolson.

Hardin, R. (1982), *Collective Action*, Baltimore: Johns Hopkins University Press.

Hayek, F. (1944), *The Road to Serfdom*, London, Routledge and Kegan Paul.

Heath, A. (1976), *Rational Choice and Social Exchange*, Cambridge: Cambridge University Press.

Hindess, B. (1976), 'On three-dimensional power', *Political Studies*, vol. 24.

Hindess, B. (1978), 'Humanism and teleology in sociological theory': in B. Hindess (ed.), *Sociological Theories of the Economy*, London: Macmillan.

Hindess, B. (1982), 'Power, interests, and the outcomes of struggles', *Sociology*, vol. 16, no. 4.

Hindess, B. (1983), *Parliamentary Democracy and Socialist Politics*, London: Routledge and Kegan Paul.

Hindess, B. (1984), Rational choice theory & the analysis of political action, *Economy & Society*, 13.

Hindess, B. (1986), *Freedom, Equality and the Market*, London: Tavistock.

Hindess, B. (1987), *Politics and Class Analysis*, Oxford: Blackwell.

Hindess, B. (1988a), 'Class analysis as social theory' in P. Lassmann (ed.), *Politics and Social Theory*, London, BSA

Hindess, B., (1988b), *Choice and Rationality in Social Theory*, London, Unwin Hyman.

Hirschman, A. O. (1977), *The Passions and the Interests*, Princeton: Princeton University Press.

Hirschman, A. O. (1982), *Shifting Involvements: Private Interests and Public Action*, Oxford: Martin Robertson.

Hirst, P. Q. (1979), *On Law and Ideology*, London: Macmillan.

Hirst, P. Q. and Woolley, P. (1983), *Social Relations and Human Attributes*, London: Tavistock.

Hobsbawm, E. (1983), 'Labour's lost millions', *Marxism Today*, September.

Hobsbawm, E. (1984), 'Labour: rump or rebirth', *Marxism Today*, March.

Hobsbawm, E. (1985), 'The retreat into extremism', *Marxism Today*, April.

Hollis, M. (1979a), 'Rational man and social science in R. Harrison (ed.), *Rational Action*, Cambridge: Cambridge University Press.

Hollis, M. (1979b), 'The epistemological unity of mankind' in S. C. Brown (ed.), *Philosophical Disputes in the Social Sciences*, Brighton: Harvester.

Hollis, M. (1981), 'Economic man and original sin', *Political Studies*, no. 29.

Hollis, M. (1983), 'Rational preferences', *The Philosophical Forum*, no. 14.

Hollis, M. and Lukes, S. (eds.) (1982), *Rationality and Relativism*, Oxford: Blackwell.

Journal of Business (59, 4, pt.2) (1986), papers by Arrow, Hogarth and Reder, Lucas, and Simon.

Keane, J. (1988), *Democracy and Civil Society*, London, Verso.

Kuhn, T. (1970), *The Structure of Scientific Revolutions*, Chicago: Chicago University Press.

Lash, S. and Urry, J. (1984), 'The new Marxism of collective action', *Sociology*, no. 18.

Lenin, V. I. (1961), 'What is to be done?' *Collected Works*, vol. 5, London: Lawrence and Wishart.

Lenin, V. I. (1964), 'The discussion of self-determination summed up'. *Collected Works,* vol. 22, London: Lawrence and Wishart.

Levi, I. (1982), 'Conflict and social agency', *The Journal of Philosophy*, no. 79.

Lipset, S. M. (1963), *Political Man*, London: Heinemann.

Lukes, S. (1976), *Power: A Radical View*, London: Macmillan.

Lustgarten, L. S. (1983), 'Liberty in a culturally plural society' in A. Phillips-Griffith (ed.), *Of Liberty*, Cambridge: Cambridge University Press.

Macdonald, G. and Pettit, P. (1981), *Semantics and Social Science*, London: Routledge and Kegan Paul.

MacIntyre, A. (1981), *After Virtue*, London: Duckworth.

Margolis, H. (1982), *Selfishness, Altruism and Rationality*, Cambridge: Cambridge University Press.

Marx, K. and Engels, F. (1968), 'The Communist Manifesto' in *Selected Works*, London: Lawrence and Wishart.

Miliband, R. (1969), *The State in Capitalist Society*, London, Weiderfeld and Nicolson.

Minson, J. (1985), *Genealogies of Morals*, London: Macmillan.

Mulhall, S. (1987), 'The theoretical foundations of liberalism', *Archives européenes de sociologie*, vol. 28.

Nelson, R. and Winter, S. G. (1982), *An Evolutionary Theory of Economic Change*, Cambridge, Mass.: Harvard University Press.

Nicholls, D. (1975), *The Pluralist State,,* London: Macmillan.

Nozick, R. (1974), *Anarchy, State and Utopia*, Oxford: Blackwell.

Olson, M. (1965), *The Logic of Collective Action*, Cambridge, Mass.: Harvard University Press.

Olson, M. (1982) *The Rise and Decline of Nations*, New Haven: Yale University Press.

Panitch, L. (1976), *Social Democracy and Industrial Militancy,* Cambridge: Cambridge University Press.

Parsons, T. (1969), 'On the concept of political power' in *Politics and Social Structure*, New York: Free Press.

Pettit, P. (1988), 'The Freedom of the city: a republican ideal' in A. Hamlin and P. Pettit (eds.), *The Good Polity*, Oxford: Blackwell.

Polsby, N. (1959), 'The sociology of community power', *Social Forces*: no. 37.

Przeworski, A. (1982), 'The ethical materialism of John Roemer', *Politics and Society*, no. 11.

Przeworski, A. (1985), *Capitalism and Social Democracy*, Cambridge: Cambridge University Press.

Przeworski, A. and Sprague, J. (1986), *Paper Stones*, Chicago: Chicago University Press.

Rawls, J. (1971), *A Theory of Justice*, Oxford: Oxford University Press.

Rawls, J. (1980), 'Kantian constructivism in moral theory: the Dewey Lectures', *The Journal of Philosophy* no. 77.

Rawls, J. (1985), 'Justice as fairness: political not metaphysical', *Philosophy and Public Affairs*, no. 14.

Rawls, J. (1987), 'The idea of overlapping consensus', *Oxford Journal of Legal Studies*, no. 7.

Reeve, A. and Ware, A. (1984), 'Interests in political theory', *British Journal of Political Science*, no. 13.

Roemer, J. (ed.) (1986), *Analytical Marxism*, Cambridge: Cambridge University Press.

Rose, R. and McAllister, I. (1986), *Voters Begin to Choose*, London: Sage.

Roth, G. and Schlucter, W. (1979), *Max Weber's Vision of History*, Berkeley:

University of California Press.

Ryan, A. (ed.) (1979), *The Idea of Freedom*, Oxford: Oxford University Press.

Sandel, M. (1982), *Liberalism and the Limits of Justice*, Cambridge: Cambridge University Press.

Savage, S. (1981), *The Social Theories of Talcott Parsons*, London: Macmillan.

Schlucter, W. (1981), *The Rise of Western Rationalism: Max Weber's Developmental History*, Berkeley: University of California Press.

Scott, J., (1979), *Corporations, Classes and Capitalism*, London: Hutchinson.

Sen, A. (1977a), 'Rational fools: a critique of the behavioural foundations of economic theory', *Philosophy and Public Affairs*, no. 6.

Sen, A. (1977b), 'Social choice theory: a re-examination', *Econometrica*, no. 45.

Sen, A. (1982), *Choice, Welfare and Measurement*, Oxford: Blackwell.

Skinner, Q. (1969), 'Meaning and understanding in the history of ideas', *History and Theory*, no. 8.

Skinner, Q. (1983), 'Machiavelli on the maintenance of liberty', *Politics*, no. 18.

Skinner, Q. (1984), 'The idea of negative liberty' in R. Rorty, J. B. Schneewind and Q. Skinner (eds.), *Philosophy in History*, Cambridge: Cambridge University Press.

Taylor, C. (1979), 'What's wrong with negative liberty?' in A. Ryan (ed.), *The Idea of Freedom*.

Taylor, C. (1985), *Philosophy and the Human Sciences: Philosophical Papers*, vol. 2, Cambridge: Cambridge University Press.

Taylor, M. (1982), *Community, Anarchy and Liberty*, Cambridge: Cambridge University Press.

Thompson, G. (1986), *Economic Calculation and Policy Formation*, London: Routledge and Kegan Paul.

Tilly, C. (1978), *From Mobilization to Revolution*, Reading, Mass.: Addison-Wesley.

Tomlinson, J. (1981), 'The "Economics of Politics" and public expenditure', *Economy and Society*, no. 10.

Tomlinson, J. (1982), *The Unequal Struggle*, London: Methuen.

Toye, J. F. J. (1976), 'Economic theories of politics and public finance', *British Journal of Political Science*, no. 6.

Turner, S. P. and Factor, R. S. (1984), 'Weber, the Germans and "Anglo-Saxon convention": liberalism as technique and form of life', in R. M. Glassman and V. Nurvar (eds.), *Max Weber's Political Sociology*, Westport, Conn.: Greenwood Press.

Weber, M. (1930), *The Protestant Ethic and the Spirit of Capitalism*, London: Allen and Unwin.

Weber, M. (1946), *From Max Weber: Essays In Sociology*, London: Routledge and Kegan Paul.

Weber, M. (1949), *Methodology of the Social Sciences*, New York: Free Press.

Weber, M. (1975), 'Marginal utility theory and "the fundamental laws of psychophysics"', *Social Science Quarterly*, no. 56.

Weber, M. (1978), *Economy and Society*, Berkeley: University of California Press.

Wickham, G. (1983), 'Power and power analysis: beyond Foucault', *Economy and Society*, no. 12.

Willer, D. (1987), *Theory and the Experimental Investigation of Social Structures*, New York: Gordon and Breach.

Willer, D. and Anderson, B. (1981), *Networks, Exchange and Coercion*, New York: Elsevier.

Williams, R. (1976), *Keywords*, London: Fontana.

Williams, B. (1979), 'Internal and external reasons' in R. Harrison (ed.), *Rational Action*, Cambridge: Cambridge University Press.

Williams, J., Williams, K. and Thomas, D. (1983), *Why are the British Bad at Manufacturing?*, London: Routledge and Kegan Paul.

Winch, P. (1970), 'Understanding a primitive society' in B. R. Wilson (ed.), *Rationality*, Oxford: Blackwell.

Winter, S. G. (1964), 'Economic "natural selection" and the theory of the firm', *Yale Economic Essays*, no. 4.

Winter, S. G. (1971), 'Satisficing selection and the innovating remnant', *Quarterly Journal of Economics*, no. 85.

Wood, E. M. (1986), *The Retreat from Class*, London: Verso.

Wootton, B. (1945), *Freedom under Planning*, London: Allen and Unwin.

Wright, E. O. (1978), *Class, Crisis and the State*, London: New Left Books.

Wright, E. O. (1985), *Classes*, London: Verso.

Wrong, D. (1976), 'The oversocialized conception of man in sociology' in *Skeptical Sociology*, New York: Columbia University Press.

Wrong, D. (1979), *Power*, Oxford: Blackwell.

Index

action
  actors as loci of   2, 3–4, 7, 57,
    63, 64, 71, 88–90, 107, 126,
    132, 169
  constraints on   148–9, 160
  means of 8, 28, 29, 31, 33, 34–6,
    40, 41, 80, 81–2, 83, 118
  preferences and 148–9, 160
  reasons for 8–13
    see also beliefs; deliberations;
    desires; interests; rational
    choice theory; rationality
  sites of 15–17
  social structure and 14–17, 21,
    51, 60, 70, 71, 78–84, 107–8
  Weber's concept of 123–4, 143
actors
  concept of 3–8, 78, 88–90,
    134–7, 187
  human individuals as 2–3, 4, 8,
    49, 53, 57, 64, 71, 86–102
    passim, 133, 168, 185–203
    passim
  interaction between, in
    intentional analysis 153–6
  as loci of decisions and action 2,
    3–4, 7–8, 29, 30, 57–8, 59–60,
    63, 64, 71, 88–90, 107, 126,
    132, 169
  purposive-parametric actors 155
  rationality of 44, 47, 49, 53–4,
    56–7, 63, 90, 116, 120, 122–40
    passim, 134–7, 168, 169,
    171–2, 180, 182–3
  social actors 4–8, 22, 30, 53,
    57–8, 64, 75, 86–102 passim,
    132–4, 186, 187, 193, 198–203
    see also capitalist enterprises;
    class analysis; government

  agencies; political parties;
    social systems; trades unions
  Weber's model of 122–9, 132,
    135, 137, 139–40
agents
  defined 29
Althusser, L. 2, 132
Anarchy, State and Utopia
    (Nozick) 188
Anderson, P. 27
arenas of struggle
  articulation of 30–33, 35
  defined 28–9
    see also capitalist enterprises
Arrow, K. 58, 171, 172
articulation
  of arenas of struggle 30–33, 35
assessment
  forms of 73–7, 79–81, 83, 84,
    118, 120, 133–4, 137, 154, 163,
    165
associations, membership of
  pluralism and 100
Asymmetric Society, The
    (Coleman) 5, 93, 98
atomism, social
  in rational choice theory 49,
    50–1

Barry, B. 49
Becker, G. S. 48, 60, 181
beliefs
  as reasons for action 157–9,
    162–6, 168, 170, 175–7
Benton, T. 26, 29, 34–5
Berle, A. A. 86
Berlin, I. 195
Bernstein, E. 106, 119, 120
Birth of the Clinic, The (Foucault)
    16